ABSOLUT

ABSOLUT

Biography of a Bottle

CARL HAMILTON

TEXERE

NEW YORK • LONDON

This book is printed on acid-free paper.

Translators: Scott Clarke, Steven Leto.

Published by TEXERE LLC.

Published simultaneously in the United Kingdom

Original edition of this work in Swedish was published by
Norstedts Förlag, Stockholm.

Library of Congress Cataloging-in-Publication Data is available upon request.

ISBN: 1-58799-002-4

Printed in the United States of America

10 9 8 7 6 5 4 3 2 1

CONTENTS

PREFACE

In the summer of 2000, the TBWA advertising agency marked the twentieth anniversary of Absolut Vodka by putting out a stunning brochure.

The cover shows a picture of the now classic Absolut Vodka bottle, under spotlights, uncapped, and ready to be photographed. The title on the cover page is in tiny white letters and reads: "In celebration of Absolut Vodka's 20 years in America, we invited 20 people to share with us their favorite Absolut ad. Happy anniversary!"

Inside are the twenty celebrities photographed by *Vanity Fair's* Annie Leibowitz. Here is Absolut Pop Culture and Absolut Highbrow side by side: Jerry Lewis with a glass stuck in his mouth and a cutout of the bottle on his tuxedo; Spike Lee crowded in by cameras, with an Absolut ad on the monitor; and a seductive Queen Latifah in her limousine with her mink stole and her ad, across from a sober Philip Johnson presiding over his own reflection. Salman Rushdie is featured in a sly reference to his own fatwa, clutching a burning Absolut ad.

Also pictured are Gore Vidal, Philippe Starck, and Julian Schnabel; Philip Glass at his piano with pencils and eraser on his Absolut ad, as if he had composed it himself. Even Susan Sontag at her desk, familiar white stripes in her hair, elbow on a writing pad, reading glasses on a clean white sheet, with a single thumbprint: ABSOLUTE EVIDENCE.

American TBWA and the Swedish Wine and Spirits

Corporation (V&S Vin & Spirit AB) had a lot to celebrate. After twenty years they had topped anyone's wildest expecations. Not only had they made Absolut Vodka the best-selling import vodka in the United States, but they had succeeded in the impossible. They had turned the bottle into a celebrity.

And then they got rid of it. In the celebratory brochure, the product is missing. There are no bottles.

How did a bottle that twenty years ago started out so transparent that it was dismissed as completely unmarketable become so visible in American culture that you can remove it from its own ads, and it is still there?

Absolut vodka comes from Sweden—the least likely place in the world for the birth of one of America's top-selling liquor brands. Even today, the state-run Swedish Wine and Spirits Corporation—the old liquor Monopoly—is banned from advertising its products at home. There is probably no country in Europe with stricter laws against the sale of alcohol than Sweden. Yet twenty years ago, against all odds, the Swedes succeeded in pulling off an impossible trick: conquering the huge U.S. liquor market with a new vodka and a campaign that brought about a revolution in American advertising.

It has taken six years for this book to reach American readers. I started researching and writing the Absolut book ten years ago when I was lecturing in business ethics at the Stockholm School of Economics. At that time, very little was known about the success of "Absolut Country of Sweden Vodka" in the Country of Sweden. For reasons of official alcohol policy, the Monopoly had kept a tight lid on its incredible American success. In the spring of 1990 my Swedish publisher asked me if I'd be interested in writing a complete account of Absolut Vodka and promised unlimited access.

Once I started interviewing everyone involved, I knew I had a great story on my hands. I also had some great characters, from the gray suits at the Monopoly in Stockholm to the creative admen on Madison Avenue, from old Lasse the bottlemaker in his overalls all the way to the hip Andy Warhol crowd at the golden height of Studio 54.

The more people I talked to, the more I was struck by the absurdity of the whole Absolut story. I realized that telling it truthfully called for something more than the usual bland business school case study. I had to capture what one major player involved called the "cheerful unreality" of the whole process.

The real problem with writing a historical case study is piecing together the hard facts and at the same time capturing the vague essence of people's actions: their confusions, idiosyncracies, vanities, and big dreams—as well as the spirit of the times.

This story turned out to be an account of the little guys, those unknown Americans and Swedes, who came up with the original ideas for the campaign and saved the project from being dropped on many occasions. They deserve some recognition.

I've put together the events described in this book from extensive interviews, documents, and background research. All of the major players, and some of the minor, have been given the chance to comment on the text. When piecing together a story based on many different accounts, you find that recollections are as varied as interests and motives.

Officials at the Swedish Liquor Monopoly tried many times to halt publication of the book. They even got me fired over it.

Of course, the Monopoly men were entitled to their own version of their success, yet the inside story had to come out—and it finally did.

Now, five years later, I find it fitting that as this book is finally being published, the Wine and Spirits Corporation is using the

Absolut billions to try and take over the liquor division of Seagram and become one of the major global players.

Twenty years ago, at the beginning, there were no ads, only one word and one player, Gunnar Broman, with his suitcase full of plastic bottles . . . .

Carl Hamilton
AUGUST 2000

I DEDICATE THIS BOOK TO

MY FORMER STUDENTS

ABSOLUT

CHAPTER 1

THREE SWEDES

American admen want to buy Gunnar Broman's agency in Stockholm. Broman wants them to sell a nonexistent vodka.

It was early 1978 when Gunnar Broman finally brought the bottles to New York.

Sixth Avenue opened up like a fjord in front of the three Swedes as they turned the corner at 49th Street, hauling their heavy baggage behind them. The plump and jovial Gunnar Broman, head of the Carlsson and Broman advertising agency in Stockholm, went first, waving his hands, explaining what everyone should say, and not say, at the coming meeting.

With his assistant Hans Brindfors, of course, this instruction was quite unnecessary. The moment they'd arrived in the big city, Brindfors had just got quiet. Broman's right-hand man had always been a man of few and very carefully chosen words. Now, it seemed, he had nothing left to say. Broman thought he should encourage Hans Brindfors to share his views and develop his visions. Brindfors was, after all, in charge of the bottles. But, no. A little shake of the goatee, and that was it.

Peter Ekelund gaped up at the small patch of sky above them, hemmed in by the midtown skyscrapers. At that time Ekelund was just big and walleyed. A blond, lumbering twenty-four-year-old, walleyed like an owl. Some of his colleagues at the Liquor Monopoly didn't particularly like Ekelund and said that he reminded them of a Picasso. (Early cubist period.)

If you had evaluated the situation at the time, completely sober, you might have said that Broman had landed in New York with one assistant who didn't talk and another who looked like he couldn't focus—literally. Each eye doing its own thing in space.

There was a lot to take in. Wherever they looked, they saw products celebrated like stars, the sly tag lines praising, pushing, promising: Coca-Cola (things go better), Tab (for beautiful people), Virginia Slims (you've come a long way, baby).

They were just in from Sweden, a country where twenty years ago advertising was regulated to such a degree that visitors found the place oddly lifeless. People got home and said it was so clean . . . so organized . . . so tidy . . . so, so. . . . What they meant was—there was very little advertising. No billboards. Only the odd poster at the bus stop. There was lots of information, of course. But very few ads. And on radio and television, no commercials at all.

Liquor ads were illegal, except on matchboxes, where the available space was so prudently measured out by concerned bureaucrats that the adman's playing field could fit under Gunnar Broman's right thumbnail.

At 50th Street the three men stopped for a second to catch their breath. Well, here they were. Back home, they were nobodies really, they were just "in the advertising business," pretty low down on the food chain in the aftermath of the Sixties.

But here was an entire city run by ad people.

Here they were in the Capital of Con, with their bottles . . . that were not bottles at all.

The vodka bottles in their bags were solid lumps of plastic. They looked like the wooden clubs people used way out in the Swedish backwoods to kill piglets, a highly illegal practice. The bottle workshop, in a basement down on the Southside of Stockholm, ought to have been illegal, too. Broman's people had been forced to negotiate a difficult path in and out, clambering over half-empty paintcans and around the paint splashes all over the floor. They left desperate for fresh air, fleeing the fumes escaping from glue, paint, ammonia, and the various body odors of Old Lasse, the boss of the place, who sat hunched over his molds. The smell alone was enough to make anyone doubt the whole project. Old Lasse, prying loose one Frankensteinian bottle after another, mumbled to himself: "Perfect . . . perfect . . . ."

Everyone at home had been so happy about Gunnar Broman's good fortune. Advertising giant N. W. Ayer in New York wanted to buy up his agency. Planeloads of American lawyers came to shiver in Stockholm, the icy capital of Sweden. Arriving at the office in the morning, Broman would find legal drafts thicker than the city's phone books stacked on his desk, demanding his attention.

The lawyers flew in to interview Broman's copywriters, go through his files, and contact his clients. Gunnar Broman was a lucky man, they said. He was going to be rich. Stinking, filthy rich. Broman was being bought out by Americans.

There was no need for him to even come to New York. At fifty, the lucky guy could retire. He might just as well head straight for the golf course.

But the only thing the lucky guy himself had wanted to talk about was the vodka. The Swedish vodka.

Back at the airport, the United States customs officer had informed Gunnar Broman that there was no way they would ever let him bring one single drop of his "Swedish vodka" into the U. S. unless he could certify right then and there that he had an American importer.

But the only way for Broman to get an importer was to get the liquor into the country. So here was a problem.

The American lawyers were eager to help Broman straighten this little thing out, but where was the vodka?

Had anyone, any of the Americans—or, anyone at Broman's agency—actually seen the stuff? Had they held the bottle in their hands? Had they tasted it? Had anyone tasted it?

Well, no.

Because there was no vodka. There were no bottles. There was nothing.

The elevator lifted Broman and his two companions up to the meeting with N.W. Ayer. They were all silent now.

Broman's plan was outrageous. He was going to pull off the vodka illusion in the Advertising Capital of the World, on the best in the business. He had promised Lars Lindmark, who ran the Swedish State Liquor Monopoly, that he could do it. He had given him his word as an advertising professional. He had claimed that the most experienced people in America didn't know what it took, but that he, Gunnar Broman, the hick from Sweden—Sweden, where they pushed booze on matchbox covers—he knew. Broman knew. He knew that advertising meant "the turning of the mind."

The reason for Brindfors' silence was not only a lack of words. Thrust up into the sky by pure Otis force, he felt that what Broman was up to was so preposterous, it was just too much.

Broman was going to con the con men.

•

When Broman got off the elevator on the 41st floor of Burlington House, he stepped into the creative sanctum of N.W. Ayer, the first advertising agency in the history of humankind. This was not a threshold you crossed lightly—or at all—unless you were bringing some precious offering with you, unless you could present "a good idea." This was the kingdom of Jerry Siano.

Secretaries in suits scurried in and out of offices all down the hallway. A steely-eyed woman at the reception desk effectively ignored the three shuffling Swedes. Stylish British shoes creaked across the floor—you could *see* them creaking and *see* their leathery smell.

The walls were covered with celebrities, all flavors of ice cream cones, shoes, jet planes, jewelry.

A pair of sharp little eyes set between sizable sideburns and a droopy mustache, like something from a Sergeant Pepper cutout kit, approached Broman. This was Jerry Siano, the new wizard of Madison Avenue, chief creative executive of N.W. Ayer. The two men took each other in, shook hands, smiled, mentioned common acquaintances. Broman had once known another Jerry, presiding not very far from here. Jerry Gury, a fine old rascal, truly one of the best—and possibly one of the worst—at the Ted Bates agency down that same street, down at number 666. What an address! The Beast's own number right on Sixth Avenue.

And Gury's business card had read: Creative Director of the World.

Siano gave Broman's shoulder a friendly little squeeze and said how happy everyone at Ayer would be to meet him. Jerry Siano had invited colleagues, some of America's best account managers, copywriters, and art directors, to rise up to his floor and hear out the Swedish guy.

"Well, this is our friend Gunnar Broman from Sweden," Siano announced, as the two men entered the conference room.

Broman burst into hearty laughter. No one laughed like Gunnar Broman. He laughed with joy. He laughed his way through the creative process.

"I come to you from the land of the thirsty," Broman solemly declared.

And then laughed. And the Americans laughed, too.

It always started with the laugh. Broman laughed, and soon everybody was laughing together. The laughter meant they were starting to pick up the message.

Everyone at the headquarters of the Swedish Liquor Monopoly in Stockholm had been growing increasingly worried as the launch of the nonexistent vodka became increasingly real. Where were the Americans? Broman had promised them Americans. "Wasn't it time," people at the Monopoly began to ask, "to get our American partner on board?" The Liquor Monopoly's leaders had decided early on that it was only in New York, that glittering citadel of persuasion, that people knew how to sell a product in the United States. "After all, the whole idea is that we are going to do this thing in, well, America." And every day, it was the same story: Still—No—Americans.

But Broman wasn't ready to go to the U.S. quite yet. Through the nine-month Swedish winter he paced back and forth at his agency, carefully studying the strange bottles that were brought up to him from Old Lasse's basement by his wheezing and coughing assistants.

Broman had started to build his platforms.

Besides the walleyed Peter Ekelund, who was just a managerial assistant at the Liquor Monopoly, fresh out of school, consultant Curt

Nycander, who was soon to be named vice president in charge of sales, had been involved in drawing up the plans to market a Swedish vodka in the new world. Sitting around a table in the Monopoly's castle-like headquarters, these were the men Lars Lindmark, powerful head of the Liquor Monopoly, had chosen. This was the human brew he had prepared behind the back of his own board of directors.

With serious eyes fixed on Broman, Nycander explained in his grave voice, with that terrible patience that could drive an adman crazy, the importance of conveying to the Americans the world heavyweight status of the Swedish Liquor Monopoly. "They must be made to realize who we are," intoned Nycander. "We are the world's largest importer of distilled and fermented beverages." So, by consensus it was agreed upon by Curt Nycander that Broman would give the Americans an exhaustive account of the Monopoly's unparalleled standing in the global market.

Nycander's idea was for Broman to carefully put in place the general framework of "the export project." Organizing the backing of the American advertising agency N. W. Ayer would be the Swedes' first step into the great American market. Deemed to be in the long-term interest of the Monopoly, an export venture, however small and symbolic, might also help balance the country's huge volume of imports. Thus it would improve the Swedish current account. Thus it was in Sweden's national interest. And Curt Nycander couldn't stress enough that they had nothing to be ashamed of when it came to the quality of their products. The Monopoly had had enormous success over the years without having to resort to . . . to advertising.

Impressive, Broman thought to himself, when you hold a complete monopoly.

"We've done tests," Nycander assured him, "tests that conclusively show that Swedish products stand up extremely well against foreign competition. We've done tests . . . ."

But all Gunnar Broman said to Jerry Siano and eleven of the most experienced admen in western civilization, assembled on the 41st floor of Burlington House, was:

Gentlemen, I represent an organization that last year produced one hundred and forty-seven million liters of pure human happiness.

That was it.

Broman was wearing a plaid shirt and a cardigan, chinos and brown loafers. Reading glasses hung on a cord around his neck. He could have just strolled in after a Sunday afternoon spent weeding the garden. Broman never wore a tie. Whenever he went to one of the upscale Manhattan restaurants, his American hosts had to fill the void around his neck with a few silken words of explanation to the maitre d'. Gunnar Broman was a well-known advertising man from Sweden. Why would such a person wear a tie?

Broman had thrown away the tie when he quit the Ted Bates agency back in the sixties. That was what everyone dreamed of doing in those days. Hey—let's get creative. Let's start our own hotshop. Let's change. And let's drop the goddamned tie.

There were a dozen Americans in the conference room at Burlington House. They all wore ties.

Broman poured praise on all Sweden's classic alcoholic beverages. Sweet, sticky punsch. Mmm . . . . Served on a silver tray, cold as liquid ice burning your tongue. Hot, spicy winter Glogg. Candy liqueurs. And, of course, aquavit, the traditional Swedish schnapps. Broman praised aquavit in all its incarnations: Skåne. O. P. Anderson. The Colonel Aquavit. The Mansion Aquavit. Östgöta Wheat. Broman sighed, transported by the vision of a tall, icy Garbo of a schnapps, taking form, hovering right there in front of the guys.

But, he went on, aquavit was in reality nothing but vodka, just purified alcohol. It had just gone through a simple spicing or sweetening process. You always worked from the pure alcohol—

"What we call Renat," Peter Ekelund explained, always keen to help.

"Purified alcohol? Is he talking about grain alcohol?" one slumping listener asked of another.

There were those, Broman went on, foreigners mostly, who felt that Swedish vodka lacked character. A regrettable point of view, as it was quite incorrect, and also completely beside the point, but unfortunately not everyone could see the whole picture. The pure alcohol was the basis for making a good aquavit. That was the platform. You couldn't make a good aquavit without it. Impossible.

But, Broman underscored, if your parents-in-law (for example) were to serve you the pure stuff, just that and nothing else, that would strike you as odd. But then again, if you happened to be an alcoholic, well then, pure regular alcohol was just the thing for you.

Myron Poloner had come up to the meeting from the fortieth floor where CEO Lou Hagopian's office was located. Myron had caught wind of a supposedly important meeting on Jerry's floor. When Broman mentioned the vodka, well, Myron Poloner nodded and said, sure, that sounded interesting, the market being huge, you know. But he couldn't get what this Swedish thing was all about. Swedish vodka—what was that? Vodka was Russian, right? Even the American vodka, Smirnoff, was Russian. So how could this guy Broman be pushing Swedish vodka when it didn't exist?

Well, vodka had existed in Sweden since 1467, Broman explained. (He was serious now that history had entered the picture.) A royal privilege to distill liquor had been bestowed upon Cort the

Bottlepuller. That was a historic, and a scientific, fact. A historian in Stockholm had confirmed this for Broman. Swedes had been drinking vodka for a long, long time. The historian had also mentioned that pure alcohol was first used to produce gunpowder. Later people realized that they could put the stuff in their mouths and swallow.

"It took us five hundred years to bring this Swedish vodka to America," Broman proclaimed. "Now the time is right. Now it's here."

Brindfors and Ekelund opened the leather bags.

The people at the Liquor Monopoly had warned Broman many times that there had been previous attempts to export its products. Efforts that had all ended in failure.

But Broman felt this time would be different. The Monopoly even had an in-house American researcher, Dr. Stanley Noval, who had done studies, all pointing to the same trend: consumption of brown liquor was falling fast, while white liquor was on the rise. Every time Broman talked to Doctor Stanley, the American told the story of the three great waves of liquor that had swept across the American continent. First, the brandy wave that came with the English. Then the whiskey and rum with the slavetraders and the pirates. And then, the vodka wave with—well, with whom, actually? Probably with the big-city businessman and his liberated lady friend.

We are now at the crest of the third wave, Dr. Stanley declared, a decisive statement for Broman's whole outlook. He felt he was in tune with the spirit of his time. Whiskey—on its way out, and there were hard numbers to prove it. Rum—out. Brandy—most certainly out. Now people want to get bombed on the clear stuff.

Broman got a bottle of pure alcohol from a Stockholm state

store, just to see what it was like. It was repulsive. Like licking a piece of frozen metal. "I am right in the eye of the trend," Broman thought.

"What we are trying to achieve with this project, our target . . . ," visionary Peter Ekelund told the group of American admen, "what we are in fact reaching for here . . . ."

"We want to create the Chivas Regal of vodkas," said Broman.

Ekelund enthusiastically explained that there were lots of people who actually believed what it said on the Chivas label, that the whiskey had been brewed out on some damp Scottish moor since the late eighteenth century. Wrong.

"Chivas is twenty years old," Ekelund revealed.

"So I've heard," Siano said.

"Interesting," said Myron Poloner.

"Isn't it?" Ekelund smiled.

The big conference room on the forty-first floor was equipped with the most advanced audiovisual support 1978 could offer: a 35-millimeter projector and a 16-millimeter projector, plus seventeen slide projectors. At the front, movie screens of various sizes could be lowered. You could regulate the lighting, the heat, the ventilation, the entire arsenal of technical equipment. Except for Broman, everyone sat in black leather swivel chairs, thinking from side to side as they listened.

Broman started to work his way through his "platforms." Every marketing line needed a platform, and Broman had five: Country of Sweden Vodka, The Blonde Swede, Royal Court Vodka, Damn Swede Vodka, and pure vodka.

But Broman had a bonus idea: they should also market a black vodka. This was not part of the Monopoly's plan. In fact, it was contrary to Broman's own thinking. It might have been that he just loved the name. Black vodka. "But it's not a vodka," Ekelund objected. It was an aquavit made from black currants, and everyone knew Americans didn't drink aquavit. Ekelund had in fact discovered a tiny religious sect in the Chicago area whose members imbibed a black-currant liquor while performing their time-honored rites. Every time Broman got carried away with the black vodka, Ekelund coolly reminded him of the Chicago connection.

The first platform Broman put up on the screen was the Country of Sweden Vodka.

All the drafts he would present that day were simple sketches made with ordinary felt-tip pens. This set his agency apart from most others, where draft ads were often pasted together from glossy magazine cutouts, seducing the client with a finished image. Broman strongly believed that if any campaign was to be effective, the client must understand the concept behind the campaign.

The Country of Sweden bottle displayed on the screen was a plain symmetrical bottle, but it looked as if it was wrapped in silk paper and it had a print on it.

Broman and Brindfors had borrowed the idea of printing a motif on silk wrapping paper from the packaging of a Danish orange juice. Broman thought you could take this idea much further. This is serious business now, he had said to Brindfors. We have to go all the way.

Broman wanted the spirit of Sweden printed on the silken wrapper.

What the Americans saw was a Sound-of-Music landscape, covering the whole wrapper. A lake, blue water, green grass with green hills rolling away into the distance. Nestled in the hills was a little red hut. And not a human being in sight.

"This is a classic Swedish scene," explained Ekelund.

A lonely little hut, or a tool shed, with a couple of farm animals walking around on somebody's farm.

One listener piped up, throwing out an idea:

"Can we add some action—a horse and carriage, going on a picnic, a family maybe?"

"It's a vodka bottle," Siano said.

"Oh yeah, sorry. It's nice."

"This is the essence of the Swedish countryside," repeated Peter Ekelund.

"All empty like that?"

The Americans studied the image of Broman's home country. It really did look bleak. It looked like it needed to be filled with something. It needed a development plan. It needed a golf course.

But, generally speaking, they were positive.

"Well, I like the wrapping paper thing," said one of the art directors.

"The paper is nice," Siano agreed. "Creative."

"No one has done that before, as far as I know," somebody else added. "A silk wrapping paper. That's new."

Broman decided not to mention the Danish O.J.

"Just a minute! There's something about that paper," one of the copywriters said.

Too feminine, he thought, as if it had been folded around a bottle of perfume. He liked it, sure. He just couldn't connect it to a vodka.

Broman moved to the next picture. The wrapped bottle was pictured on an enormous billboard. On the billboard were the lake, the hills, the spirit of Sweden. There was a nice little trick here. The part of the scene that was hidden behind the bottle could be seen on the wrapping. The Americans thought it looked pretty good.

"That's good," one of Siano's boys said.

"The bottle and the billboard. Yeah, I guess that is pretty good."

The billboard said: *It's only natural.*

"I'm always looking for simple, basic concepts," Broman said. "I don't want to see ads with wiseguys in turtlenecks smiling at each other in front of a big open fireplace with cocktails in their hands. You know, show them a lifestyle and stick your logo in the corner. I can't stand that. I mean, Jesus, I'm not selling turtlenecks, am I?"

The ads for Country of Sweden Vodka were supposed to show that the product came from Sweden, nothing more. Sweden, to Broman, really wasn't a country. It was just another platform.

Peter Ekelund pulled the bottle out of the bag. On the paper wrapped around the bottle the landscape was clear to see. The green hills. The hut.

"It looks crumpled," someone muttered.

Now everyone was looking a little troubled. What was wrong with the wrapping?

It occurred to one of the Americans that this packaging would be a smash with the city's outdoor drinkers—brown paper bag included.

"Definitely looks crumpled," Siano said, and nodded towards the screen.

"You have to solve the paper thing," one of them said.

"It is supposed to be silk paper," Peter Ekelund reminded them cheerfully.

"Sure," Siano said. "It has to be. The paper has to be so soft that it hugs the bottle. That's what's so creative. Silk paper."

They all smiled at the bottle with the shiny wrapping, relieved now that the paper thing had been settled.

•

One funny thing was that when Broman was first contacted by the Liquor Monopoly, he had just moved his agency to an apartment near the king's castle in central Stockholm. The place was once owned by another king, the Liquor King—L. O. Smith. Smith had controlled a large part of the European liquor trade at the end of the nineteenth century.

Broman's staff looked around in awe. The rooms were spacious, grand and stately, with high ceilings and somber wood panelling. Broman had had everything painted white. Everything.

There was just one item that was spared the white—the Liquor King's safe. People said it was filled with old bonds, securities, and even the King's own liquor recipes, worth a fortune. But the giant iron thing was locked and none of the keys left in the apartment could help. Sometimes Broman's staff would put their ears against it and knock to determine whether it was empty or not. Sometimes, when clients came, the admen would start the pitch with the safe, taking nothing and making it something.

They'd say: There's a fortune hidden in here.

"And now: the Viking!" Broman bellowed, pulling up the next slide.

A wild man, with flowing blond locks and a beard, sword swinging from his side, was standing between two female partygoers wearing cocktail dresses. They held martini glasses in their hands, and one stood charmed by an olive stuck on the end of a toothpick.

The problem with the Country of Sweden platform was, Broman explained, that it lacked punch. It was weak. Sweden was OK, and the silk paper was OK, sure, but the whole thing was just too soft. Vodka, after all, was a strong drink. The strongest, in fact. There was even a brutality to vodka, Broman said. Not just anyone could handle vodka. It took a Viking.

An American stirred.

"Where's that hat they had? That horn hat?"

"We have to see the hair," Peter Ekelund explained. "You know, *Blonde* Swede."

The blond Viking steered his longship with one manly hand on the tiller and the other pointing toward unknown continents. The caption read: *The Blonde Swede*. The wind was blowing hard around Mr. V. Down in the corner was a little round bottle with no neck. It looked strange.

"That's what I call a real man," Broman commented.

"And," he proudly declared, "the Vikings discovered America. Scientifically proven fact."

The next slide snapped up. The real man had been invited to a party. Lustful women were pawing him and eyeing him hungrily as they downed their drinks. There were two other men at the party. They were pretending not to notice Mr. V's big success with the ladies. Instead they solemnly studied the contents of their drinks.

Someone commented that they weren't wearing turtlenecks.

The Americans watched as the blond Viking steered his ship through an urban landscape. He turned up at the Acme. He pulled over on the side of the highway. He landed in a parking lot.

"Beware! The Blonde Swede!"

"We can work with this one," an American decided.

And added:

"It has legs. It could run for a long time."

The blond Peter Ekelund thrust forward two Viking bottles. But the Viking on the bottle looked different from the one in the slides. The label was like a mediocre eighteenth-century painting in stark, garish colors.

"That's something else," Siano protested. "That's not a premium brand."

"Well, OK. Right," Broman conceded. "But you see, I want to take every line as far as it can go, push it to its limit. That's how I work."

"I see," Jerry said. "All right, Gunnar, I like the bottle. It's creative. But the artwork just doesn't have the sophistication we're looking for here. I see no prestige at all in that Viking."

"OK," Broman, descendant of Vikings, said. "Let's move on. I'll show you how I'm approaching this. We need to stick to a coherent platform. I find a platform, I stick to it. You can never make me leave my platforms."

Another bottle appeared on the screen.

"This is the Royal Court Vodka," Broman announced. The bottle is handcrafted in an old glassworks in southern Sweden.

"The part we call *Småland,*" Ekelund helped.

He looked around the room for any remote sign of a tourist's recognition. In vain.

"Småland," he continued, "is known for its deep forests and . . . ."

"Anyway," Broman interrupted, "the bottle is handcrafted by a real glassmaker, so no two bottles will look exactly alike. See, Jerry, this is exclusive."

The new bottle on the screen was not round but shaped almost like a flask, with asymmetrical edges, as if wax had run down the side. The glass was smooth and frosted. The cap was a cork with a metal ring. There was no label. The brand name was printed directly on the frosted glass. Two royal-looking lions were rampant and roaring, tails swung proudly over their heads as they presented a crest. On the crest was a royal crown. Below the lions the bottle said *Royal Court Vodka* in an elegant script. There were four lines of tiny copy under the brand name, but the Americans couldn't make out what they said. Ekelund carefully held the bottle, with a contented smile.

"That's it," Jerry said. "Something like that. Exactly. I like the brand name printed right on the glass instead of an ordinary label. Gives a sense of purity. Purity and tradition. Yeah, I like this. It's very creative. The crest, the lions, the crown. Pretty."

Several of the Americans nodded, agreeing that the lions and the crest, especially the crest, looked really nice.

"Mm, interesting," said Myron.

"But, you see," Broman tried to say. "The crest—"

"Oh, but it's gorgeous, Gunnar," one of the art directors said.

"The crest is, as a matter of fact, a very conventional theme," Broman explained. "So we decided to add a bit of humor to liven it up."

"Humor?" Jerry asked.

The next sketch showed a room with a view. Beyond the room's balcony the Americans could see a bay lined with palm trees. On the far horizon was a sailboat . A royal crown and a royal robe hung from a hook on the wall. The Royal Court Vodka bottle and a glass stood waiting on a table. Below the picture they read: *The king is back.*

"The king is, simply, back," Broman laughed.

In the next picture the king's robe was thrown across a giant four-poster bed. On one of the bedposts perched the crown, and on a bedside table stood the bottle. The bed, however, was made and empty. The copy read: *The king is back.*

"The king is back!" Ekelund exclaimed.

One of Broman's artists had found the crest for Royal Court Vodka, along with the crown and the lions, in a dictionary of heraldic symbols and then pieced it together like a royal jigsaw puzzle. Almost as an afterthought, someone at Broman's agency got the idea that they might want to check the new ultra-royal crest with the National Heraldic Governor before Broman left for the U.S. The Heraldic Governor, it turned out, did not care for Broman's coat of arms one bit. There were rules, he explained gravely, firm rules that regulated the way a crown can look on a crest. The crest itself could not be drawn just any old way, whatever advertising people might think. And if you did not follow the rules, you could be sued in court. Not even a royal court. Well, that's how it worked it Sweden.

On a more personal level, Broman had grown weary of crests. A few years back a Swedish brewer had asked him to create an advertising campaign for what seemed to be an unsellable beer. The brewer had probably expected Broman to design a couple of punchy ads and leave it at that. But Broman did not work that way. He changed everything. Broman took the product and put it on a platform. He changed the name and gave the bottles and cans a whole new look. He brought in a crest, two old schooners charging off to sea with billowing sails and waves crashing. Then he plastered heraldic symbols all over the ships, all over the whole can. He went through most of the heraldic symbols in existence in this process. Sweden had never seen anything like it.

At that time all the advertising agencies in the country were trying to make their products look as new as possible. But Broman had made this beer age a hundred years. When the new old beer was launched, it struck a nerve. The country was hit by a beer epidemic. Everyone wanted to get eighteenth century with Gunnar Broman. On Friday nights teenagers would be found face down in the gutter, clasping empty beer cans covered with heraldic symbols. Finally, the best-selling beer was debated in Parliament, where it was, of course, banned.

"Here you get a real sense of tradition," one of Siano's copywriters said.

Suddenly the Americans saw that Broman had turned Sweden into a platform. They weren't really sure where Sweden was, but it seemed like they had a king, and that could work.

"This could be the angle," one American said. "The king thing."

The next bottle was a pocket flask made of clear glass. Sketched right on the glass in quick brush strokes was a man running away into the bottle, arms flailing wildly. His shirt was flapping behind him, and his huge felt hat had blown off his head. It was clear that the guy had been doing some drinking. In contrast to the offhand style of the sketch, the vodka's surprising name appeared on the bottle in elegant print: *Damn Swede.* Under the sketch were six lines of dummy text written by hand in graceful, gentle loops. It read:

No matter what we say
or show in our advertising efforts,
or what others have said
in praise of Seville, it is only in the driving
that you will fully understand
what kind of car it is.

Ted Regan, an Ayer veteran, couldn't help but smile. *Damn Swede.* What a scream. These guys certainly had a sense of humor to come up with such a, such a . . . well, "platform," because it was so utterly, completely impossible. And still, Regan felt a strange enthusiasm not only for the running man, but for the whole project.

Myron Poloner was thinking, "Damn Swede—damn silly! You can't swear in advertising." Besides, he could see it now, the way it would go: Dumb Swede.

"Interesting," Myron chipped in. "Very interesting."

They all looked at the running man on the screen.

"The drawing was done especially for us by Lamm," Peter Ekelund said.

The Americans felt they should acknowledge Lamm's contribution, but who was he? Lamm, *Lamm?*

Sensing their puzzlement, Ekelund explained:

"A well-known Swedish intellectual, actually."

Before Broman had decided whether pure alcohol could be marketed as a vodka, he had thought of creating a whole new category for it. "Damn Swede" was what he had come up with. People all over the world would learn to say "Damn Swede" when they needed a quick shot. Broman wanted to give Sweden its own Wild West—a place of refuge up north, up in outlaw country. He had imagined sepia-colored photographs of the Wild North.

"Gunnar is crazy about the 'Damn Swede,'" Peter Ekelund revealed. "He's got hundreds of 'Damn Swede' slogans on his walls."

"'Give me enough snuff, liquor, and Swedes,'" Broman cited from memory, "'and I will build a railroad to hell.'"

"That should go on the bottle," remarked an American.

Ekelund piped up:

"You see, the guy is a . . . What do you call it? Not a tramp . . . He builds the railroad. He is . . . you know, a damn Swede."

Broman laughed. Peter Ekelund laughed. Jerry Siano laughed. All the Americans laughed. From Brindfors, more silence.

Everyone was laughing along nicely. Only when Broman started fishing black bottles from his suitcase did the merriment subside.

"Black? Is that black?" one of Siano's account managers asked. "Can a vodka be black? Vodka is supposed to be clear, right?"

"Gunnar, is this a political thing?"

Broman stooped over his suitcase.

"Let me show you something."

Bottle after bottle appeared from the trunk. All black, one after the other. A magician's black rabbits.

Back home, two of Broman's assistants had set up the bottles in the bathroom and sprayed them black. Beside the vault, the bathtub was the only place in the office that wasn't white.

"Yeah, this is great," Broman said. "This is plain vodka in black bottles. But it's got something extra. We've *added* black currant."

He paused to study the black bottle, and suddenly sighed: "In fact there isn't anything in this bottle. It isn't even a bottle. I've been having problems getting the stuff past customs and into the country."

"You know, Gunnar," Ted Regan said, "the Swedish concept is just fine. Don't worry about that. It conveys a sense of . . . purity and naturalness. Sweden seems like a place you could conceivably go to on vacation. But now with the black, black, what's that all about?"

"Gunnar just has a thing for the black vodka," Peter Ekelund smiled.

"We can get back to this later," Broman said, and watched sadly as a Royal Black Vodka and a Blonde (but now Black) Swede went back into the bag.

"We should come back to that."

He clicked for the next slide. Two bare bottles popped up on the screen.

"Uh, oh! What happened there?"

The Americans stared at the bottle. It had no label, no decorations, and no neck. On the glass was written in silver: *Absolute Pure Vodka*. Below that they saw:

DR. BÖGER PHOTOSATZ

CELLO-TAKMEG

CHARTPAK

"What the hell is this?" an American exclaimed.

"Oh, yes," said Broman. "Pure vodka."

"It looks like one of those medical bottles. Like for blood plasma or something. A plasma bottle."

"Interesting," whispered Myron Poloner.

But someone there was a by-the-book guy: "In the United States you cannot call a product Absolute Pure Vodka," he said. "Absolute Pure Vodka cannot be the brand name of anything. You see, Gunnar, my Lincoln is the perfect car. That doesn't mean we can rename it The Perfect Car. It just isn't done. Here I am driving along in Perfect Car. No way."

"It's a generic expression," someone clarified.

"Well, the bottle is creative," Siano said. "But it's cold. You'll have to add some warmth, some life to it. The American customer wants to feel that there is heart to a product. Something he can feel close to as an individual."

"Gunnar, you can't find two Americans who're the same. It has to be personal."

"We're individualists. That's the basis for this country. And that's why . . . a bottle like that . . . just doesn't speak to us."

"That bottle, it's like East Berlin. It is un-American."

"A brand has to smile, Gunnar. It has to laugh. You know that."

"Well, you still can't use a name like that," By-the-Book repeated. "You can't call a toothpaste 'Best Possible Toothpaste.' Absolute Pure Vodka is not a name. It's a description, a judgment. Judgments in advertising? I don't think so."

"They'll never get it registered," By-the-Book added to his colleagues. "Maybe they can get a thing like that registered in Sweden. I don't know the laws over there. But not in the state of New York. No way."

"Ed is absolutely right."

"You know, Jerry," another member of the jury interjected, shaking his head. "To me this looks like a bottle of antifreeze."

"Listen," someone else jumped in, "the problem is . . . this bottle completely lacks form. It has no design, no label, not even a name. It is actually nothing."

"But Tom," Broman objected.

"Tony."

"Tony," Broman said. "Don't you see?"

Tony turned to his boss. "Jerry, I still think it looks like a plasma bottle. You can't sell a thing like that. Well, you might be able to sell it to doctors."

They all laughed. All of them, that is, except Broman.

• • •

In the early seventies, Broman and his agency partner, Per Blomstrand, had agreed to create ads for the Swedish Agricultural Producers Cooperative. The task was to market porridge. Not any particular type or brand of porridge, just porridge in general. Porridge as a way of life, porridge as a Principle. The directive that came down was Increase Consumption of Porridge. It was exactly the sort of assignment Broman loved. The subject matter: boring. The public: uninterested. The product: unbearable. Their contact at the Agricultural Producers Cooperative was a humorless woman who insisted that the campaign emphasize the nutritional value of porridge. Bran, oats, and rye. So very good for working those intestinal canals. "Well," Broman said to Blomstrand when they left, "I don't think so. We're not going to get involved with intestines. "There are people," he went on, who have had a pretty hard time, and who actually rely on porridge, not for nutritional value, but for a living." Broman intended to tell those people that porridge was OK. So he had a T-shirt printed up that said, "Eat more porridge." "That's what the Agricultural Producers Cooperative wanted, wasn't it?" he asked. People should eat more porridge, right? Well, that's what they got.

He put the Swedish flag on the T-shirt. Then he put the shirt on a busty Swedish girl in braids. The first week after the campaign was launched, the Agricultural Producers Cooperative received eight thousand orders. But not for porridge. People wanted Broman's T-shirt. When Sweden's most popular jazz band toured the country that summer, the musicians all wore the porridge shirt. Television anchors took off their jackets and ties and put on the porridge shirt with the flag. Finally, people were actually throwing away their ties. It became a kind of catch phrase: to cheer someone up, you gave them a friendly slap on the back and said, "Eat more porridge!"

It was a classic Gunnar Broman campaign. "It must be simple," he said. "It must be so simple that it's ridiculous." When the campaign was over, the Cooperative had sold 650,000 T-shirts. One of Broman's staff bragged that half the population of Sweden was walking around advertising to the other half.

What was funny about the porridge campaign was that it broke all the rules in the advertising book. Several years earlier, Broman had heard all about the rules from the mouth of Rosser Reeves, a legend in advertising and a talking addict. It was over lunch in London. Reeves explained how he had invented a concept of persuasion he called the unique selling proposition, which was now used all over the world. According to Reeves' proposition, the adman should find out what was special about, say, a certain diaper (like its state-of-the-art volume, or its rate of absorbency), isolate that, and hammer home the message until the consumer finally got it.

Reeves's lunchtime lecture in London stopped abruptly. It suddenly became more important for him to launch a violent assault on his steak. Stabbing away and sputtering that it was completely inedible, he barked for the waiter, but was met with chilly English disdain. Reeves bawled out that he'd be damned if he didn't get either a sharper knife or an edible steak. The waiter ignored him. Reeves stabbed again, this time with the fork, and with one flip of the wrist sent the tough T-bone across the room. It hit the disdainful waiter between the eyes and the poor fellow fell backwards through the revolving door. "Damn arrogant Brit!" Reeves muttered. Broman was impressed. The scene could have been one of the action-packed commercials that Reeves produced. Even a bad steak could be a star.

There was no unique selling proposition in the porridge pitch. "Eat more porridge" was simply a great slogan—so simple it was ridiculous. So how had Broman won over the consumers? He could have gone for a bowl heaped with glorious steaming porridge. Rosser Reeves probably would have trotted out old Atlas, muscles pumped up by years of eating premium oat porridge, pounding the proposition into some poor devil who would dutifully shovel the stuff. But Broman picked the most impossible of all images back in the seventies, the national flag, at precisely the time when such symbols had fallen from favor. The king had been stripped of his power, young people were citizens of the world, and even the middle class had stopped flying the flag. As all this was going on, Broman put the flag on the chests of half a million

Swedes. His staff said, "You can't use the flag. It's pathetic. It won't reach anyone." But Gunnar Broman just grinned, and said, "Do it wrong, guys. Do it wrong."

A couple of years later Broman took a vacation in Kenya. One day, walking on an endless white beach with the Indian Ocean booming alongside him, Broman saw a local man coming toward him wearing a faded T-shirt with the slogan "Eat more porridge" and the Swedish flag.

• • •

Another Ayer executive pointed to the plasma bottle and said: "You know, on the shelf, even if you put it up front, you'd see a Smirnoff label magnified right through it. And that name, Absolute Pure Vodka. It won't work."

"Smirnoff, yeah. You can't get around it. That's vodka," Al sighed. "With a brand like that . . . ."

"'*Smirnoff leaves you breathless.*'"

"Unforgettable."

"A classic."

"Wrote their own rules."

"Let's put the crest on it, for God's sake. We've got the lions and the crown, and that crest. Why can't you use the crest and do a real label?"

It was all so obvious.

But Gunnar Broman was skimming through his slides, looking for something important, while Siano's men kept up the barrage of sound advice. Broman found a picture with all the well-known, best-selling brands: Bacardi, Smirnoff, Four Roses, J&B, the whole party crowd.

"Well?" he asked. "What do you see?"

No one saw anything.

"When all the others are screaming," Broman said, "then you must . . . ?"

In true adman fashion, he waited for them to fill in the blank.

". . . you must . . . ?"

Everyone had probably all but forgotten about silent Hans Brindfors by this time. Brindfors had an uncanny capacity to become part of the furniture. His lips had been sealed during Broman's entire presentation. But now he stirred. He knew the answer. Everyone looked questioningly at Broman.

"Come on, Hans," Broman said. "Tell them."

Brindfors sighed. Oh, the heavy burden of being a communicator who can't communicate.

"When all . . .," he began. "When all the others . . . ," he began again.

"Yes? What?"

"When they . . . shout . . . scream . . . ," he struggled.

And then he uttered something very important, but unfortunately no one heard it.

Broman laughed. "Listen to Hans. It's so simple. Ridiculously simple."

He looked around the room at Jerry and the Americans. It was then Peter Ekelund felt something. Vibrations on the train track.

Siano spun around. "You know what I'm thinking? I'm thinking *the absolute Bloody Mary.*"

"Like . . . yeah?"

"Jerry?" Broman said.

"The absolute Martini. The absolute Russian."

The American was picking up speed. Broman was out of it now.

"Absolutely pure," Jerry Siano said, foot on the accelerator. "Absolutely clear. The absolute date. An absolute party. Absolutely . . . absolutely . . . ."

"It's one hell of a theme," the copywriter who thought it looked like a plasma bottle said.

"Absolutely . . . *anything!*"

"That's exactly what we've been looking for, Jerry!"

"Absolutely anything!"

"It's got the smile, it's got the heart! It's even got legs!"

"Absolutely anything!"

"It's so fucking creative!"

"Absolutely anything!"

All of them were shouting, coming up with different variations on the theme in one grand collective orgasm of creative joy.

"You're *absolutely* right, Gunnar," Jerry Siano declared as he rose. "This is explosive stuff. And I love it. We just have to redo the bottle and change the name, and it will be perfect."

"Interesting," Myron said, very quietly.

"Whisper," Brindfors thought. "Whisper."

CHAPTER 2:

MODEL MAN

Lars Lindmark thinks Sweden's fusty state-owned Wine and Spirits Monopoly should be exporting for profit. But is that really "Lagom?"

Lars Lindmark, who always came on as a real outdoors man, had once driven his car into a snowbank at a ski resort in northern Sweden and got stuck. He phoned his office in Stockholm and howled across the mountains that he was trapped in the snow and so everyone in the office should just carry on without him. "Carry on with what?" they wondered. "Carry on," he answered. "Just carry on with it."

Later, Lindmark became head of the Swedish Wine and Liquor Monopoly and all that alcohol must have gone to his head, because he got the idea that he was God Almighty, and no one, absolutely no one, was allowed to carry on without him. When people congratulated Lindmark on the great job he'd done modernizing the whole Monopoly, "an incredible service to Sweden," he went utterly ballistic. He wasn't fucking finished yet! Not by a long way. He just didn't know what to do next.

Lindmark was given less and less to do. Often, he wouldn't be in his office at all, but away on some business trip. Once, he flew down to Gothenburg after first dispatching his chauffeur, complete with limousine, to meet him at the airport there. What Lindmark was intending to do with a limo in Gothenburg, no one could imagine.

A neutral observer would probably have agreed that the modernization of the Monopoly was complete. The plants were built, the organization was working, and pure alcohol was pouring from every tap. But Lindmark sniffed a conspiracy. Those people who had been trying to screw things up for him for years had merely switched tactics. On the one hand, they were complete meatheads; yet, on the other, so fiendishly cunning that they had let him win only to deprive him of anything more to do!

He threw tantrums. His management style was like a bedroom scene from a French farce, as he stomped in and out of rooms, doors slamming as he hurtled along. He asked his wife if people really expected him to go on like this, managing a smoothly ticking clock until the day he retired. Was that the meaning of life? Well, in that case, he wanted no part of it. He stormed around a little more, opened and closed a few doors, and then the thought hit him: he had to do something . . . something unexpected, something big. And the first idea that came into Lindmark's mind was that he would sell some of that Swedish alcohol to foreigners. Not just the odd bottle of mulled wine here and there, but some honest quantities. Yes. Some honest quantities. *Millions* of liters of liquor. *Seas* of alcohol. Lindmark was going to drown those foreigners in Swedish State liquor.

• • •

Even as a rookie in the public sector at the end of the 1940's, Lars Lindmark had begun to suspect that a large proportion of the State Administration was populated by lunkheads. When he was promoted to budget chief at the Treasury Department in the late fifties, his suspicions matured into convictions. It was as though his colleagues spoke another language. No one understood a word he said. He explained matters calmly and methodically to ministers and secretaries of state, to political analysts and all the rest of the insubstantial figures who wandered through the offices. He told them in plain terms that the budget was stretched to the limit, resources were exhausted, and there *was no money.* But they didn't hear him. They weren't even listening. Yet these were grown men. To look at them, you would assume that they were possessed of the normal faculties of mind and body. But they just didn't get the message. After talking to the ministers, he was left with the impression that every department in the Swedish government was responsible for crippled widowed homeless single mothers with no source of income. He pointed to the figures in black and white. There—that's how much money your department has. Please allocate it in an economically responsible fashion. Oh, no! That didn't apply to *their* department, you see, they were *prioritized.* "Show us the money." That was their mantra.

These were the years when welfare policy reached its zenith. Ignorance was no longer acceptable. Illness was no longer acceptable. Waiting lists were no longer acceptable. Unemployment was definitely not acceptable.

Sometimes, when ministers sat down in Lindmark's office with their suave smiles, clutching their vinyl briefcases between their knees, it made him think of a hot-air balloon. A huge, colorful hot-air balloon floating up on a thermal, taking them all on a long, dreamy journey into the clouds.

"Lars," they said to him. "This is not a budget problem. This is the Great Welfare State."

In the mid-1930s, people all over the globe were radicalized from one day to the next. Fanatics marched up and down with their hammers and sickles and swastikas and jackboots. Communism and fascism were mobilizing for the final showdown, a last battle for all the world's lost souls. As this was going on, Marquis Childs, a journalist from Iowa, was visiting Stockholm. Childs had a revelation. He saw the Swedish people dealing with their conflicts calmly and reasonably. The Swedes even had a word for it. Not only that. They had a word for it that didn't exist in any other language in the world. *Lagom.* Neither too much nor too little. A reasonable compromise. *Lagom.* "Welcome to Lagom Land," they said to Marquis Childs.

When Childs got home, he wrote *Sweden: The Middle Way.* Much to the surprise of the author, the book became an immediate and enormous success. One edition after the other sold out almost before it was off the press. It was quoted and discussed in the major American and European newspapers, and it was a topic of debate at Princeton, Harvard, Oxford, and Cambridge. The editor of the *New York Times* advised Franklin D. Roosevelt to take a walk, and to take it in Sweden, because Roosevelt was too far to the left. Sweden was the Middle Way, the way of compromise and rational cooperation. Roosevelt should become a bit more *lagom.*

Childs' book probably received no more attention anywhere in the world than in Sweden itself. The country's politicians had been under the impression that they were building roads and apartment blocks and schools and hospitals. Now they suddenly realized that they were engaged in an earthshaking project. Without knowing it, they had been constructing a model. The Great Big *Lagom* Model.

After the war, when the old world lay in ruins, bombed to smithereens, delegations of social scientists and politicians descended on Stockholm. They all wanted to see this earnest beauty, surrounded by water, jutting proudly out into the Baltic Sea. They were all in the hunt for a model.

The visitors wanted to see Childs's miracle with their own eyes. They wanted to see a modern society where the State cooperated with the Capitalists, where union bosses and management agreed on reasonable, equitable solutions. After all the wars, all the revolutions, everyone wanted to be a little bit more Swedish.

Everyone was desperate to see if they could find a working solution that was a little more—*lagom.*

At the Treasury Department, gaggles of Japanese, Americans, and Germans turned up. They studied the figures and the tables and the diagrams, and they couldn't believe their eyes. The Swedes, who had lived in holes in the ground not a century before, had become rich. Per capita, Sweden was the third richest country in the world. And what were they doing with the money? Health care for all. The best schools in the world. Old people's homes and kindergartens. And it was all free. *Free.* New, well-planned residential estates with modern facilities were springing up around the cities, designed by bold young architects who were eager to create state-of-the-art apartments but with rents ordinary folks could afford. This was change. This was transformation. This was *lagom.*

Lagom? It made Lars Lindmark extremely surly. The system was absolutely insatiable.

No one seemed to give a damn about how much it cost.

When television gripped Sweden in the early 1960s and the Prime Minister could speak directly to his citizens, the first thing he did was to spread his arms wide, as though he'd just landed a prize pike, and cry, "WE HAVE THE RESOURCES!"

The only dissenters were a few retired admirals and semidead professors from the old guard of the right wing rattling their dentures in protest. They mumbled a few syllables about the virtue of moderation, the lodestar that must shine over the country. They preached THRIFT, but who gave a shit about thrift? The Swedes had been scrimping and saving since Viking times. A thousand goddamn years of thrift!

The wise, sober, reasonable, *lagom* Swedes sat at home, perched on their new three-piece suites, drinking coffee from their shiny, practical, aluminum percolators, and eating ice cream from their brand new refrigerators, as they stared at the prime minister in the black-and-white glow from their smart new televisions, and the entire country was transfixed as the prime minister explained to all who would listen that WE HAVE THE RESOURCES.

The minister of finance, Gunnar Emmanuel Sträng, always looked like he had come down with a case of chronic gastritis. The last time anyone at the department had seen the minister laugh was when the sales tax was introduced in the early fifties.

Ironically, Sträng had decided to turn his back on politics in his youth to cultivate a small family farm. But, through no fault of his own, he was elected union representative, and his career took off. He became a politician, then a member of Parliament, then minister of finance, and eventually a *legendary* minister of finance.

Sträng put Lars Lindmark, future boss of the State Liquor Monopoly, in charge of the budget. Lindmark was the diamond-hard point on which the whole welfare edifice rested. Lindmark kept the books for the *Lagom* Model.

The minister of finance praised the *eminent* way Mr. Lindmark handled the parasitic politicians when they came crawling with their vinyl portfolios—no doubt to pilfer one or two departmental ashtrays on their way out. Sträng liked what he saw. Lindmark was not equipped with the minister's own in-built stoniness, true; he could even be described as cheery on occasion, normally when he'd managed to save a crown or two. However, he could be forgiven such seizures of levity. Lindmark had other redeeming features. Like his famous temper.

One time, Lindmark was asked to come to the State Department for a presentation. "It's more practical if you come over to us," croaked the undersecretary of state on the telephone. More *practical?! They* had some business they wanted to present to *him,* but he was supposed to go running to *them?* Stars, whole constellations, passed before his eyes. For a second, Lindmark thought he would faint. With trembling voice he explained to the undersecretary that the State Department had apparently misunderstood the position the Treasury Department occupied in the pecking order, and His Excellency the secretary of state had better lace up his boots damned fast and get his ass over to Lindmark's office on the other side of Gustav Adolfus Square before there was a regrettable accident.

At about that time, Sträng felt it was time his head of budgets met the country's leading academic business researchers. And it was through the professors at the School of Economics that Lindmark became acquainted with the ingenious concept of program budgeting, which would develop into such a thorough disaster for him.

The professors convinced Lindmark that even a nonprofit-driven operation like the state could show a plus and a minus. In Chicago, the Americans had been practicing program budgeting since 1919. The basic tenet, as Lindmark explained it to Sträng, was that all public operations could be divided into a series of goals, and the goals themselves divided into subgoals. And it was all quantifiable. Every activity could be measured and evaluated by treasury staff as though they were running a real business, as though it were actually a company, like . . . like . . . a family farm.

With hindsight it was easy for anyone to see why the elegant concept of program budgeting would flop like a dead fish the minute is was thrown outside the treasury. No one wanted to touch it with a ten-foot pole. One general director tried to explain it to Lindmark as ungently as he could: "It's all about people here, Lars," he said. "We never talk about efficiency." Then he leaned forwards and whispered.

"You see, efficiency sucks."

That's probably how the rumor got started. Well, it wasn't exactly a rumor. It was worse than that. It was true. Someone had discovered that Lindmark wasn't a member of the Party.

At first, people thought it was a joke, as though Khrushchev had forgotten to pay his annual dues to the Bolsheviks. Lars Lindmark, the strong man at the Treasury Department, the man keeping the books for the Great Big *Lagom* Model, was not even a member of the Social Democratic Party! And then of course, some people in the administration had to insinuate, not without a certain glee, that Lindmark perhaps wasn't a true believer. He did not exude that aura of solidarity.

Sträng moved Lindmark to the National Audit Authority and made him general director. Lindmark's mission was to use the clout of the Authority to enhance efficiency in the public sector. He started by ordering all the other general directors to attend a compulsory one day class on the merits of program budgeting. Sulking like schoolboys in summer school, the barons of the public sector arrived in their big black limousines. Everyone knew that Lindmark had Sträng´s ear; not turning up was a certain way to get their knuckles rapped.

When Lindmark decided to make the day an annual event, his popularity sank to a new low.

Three years later, half of the employees of the National Audit

Authority had either been fired by Lindmark or left of their own free will. At last, he thought. At last we can get moving.

But it was getting late for Lars Lindmark. A brilliant career had gone strangely awry. Dejectedly he flipped through the state budget and noticed how vague and watered down the writings on "raising productivity and efficiency in the public sector" had become.

• • •

There was a dark secret in paradise that the American journalist Marquis Childs could never quite understand. So he buried it deep down in a footnote in his book. All the statistics proclaimed Sweden's superiority in education, health, life expectancy. But unfortunately, the Swedes were not just world champions in well-being. They were also world champions in self-destruction. Childs wrote gloomily of "the deeply buried conflict between the secret forces of good and evil inherent in the Nordic temperament."

The truth was that when the international delegates had gone home, the first thing these *lagom* people went looking for was a bottle of liquor.

True, it was an open, democratic, and just society. There were no secret police spying on the citizens. They had no Propaganda Central. (They hardly had any advertising.) But they sure as taxes had a Spirits Central. In fact, they had the world's most elaborate system of alcohol regulation. Booze was strictly rationed. The citizens of Sweden didn't need a passport, a visa, a green card, or a work permit. All anyone wanted was a Liquor Ration Book.

Here was a society obsessed with booze. And it came only in one form: Renat, a clear liquid with an unsettling smell of nothingness.

The Swedes had marched straight into Paradise on condition that they never look back and touch the clear stuff again.

They simply weren't allowed to mix *lagom* with Renat.

• • •

Sometimes, Lars Lindmark wished he could move to the private sector, become a regular CEO, head a regular private company. But that was impossible. In the business sector he was considered an integral part of the government: Lindmark, the man who kept the books of the welfare state. A politician, and certainly a social democrat.

He didn't belong anywhere. Sometimes Lindmark longed for his own family farm (somewhere small and nice), a place where he could rule absolutely.

He was so tired of it all. And all of this bragging about the historical triumph of their ridiculous "model." Couldn't they see the endless inefficiencies everywhere?

Then suddenly Sträng called and offered him the Swedish State Wine and Liquor Monopoly.

Now he would show them.

CHAPTER 3

INVISIBLE BOTTLES

Myron Poloner, chief fixer at the N. W. Ayer agency, doesn't believe in Swedish vodka, but there's something about that bottle . . . .

Broman laughed, but Myron Poloner smiled. Myron was just one big beam. He had said "interesting" so many times during Gunnar's presentation on the forty-first floor of Burlington House that he almost believed it himself.

"Aha," Myron had said. "A Viking. Very interesting."

Eventually, Gunnar Broman had hauled his magic black bottles up from the trunk and started talking about black vodka. Black Vodka? Myron hoped that idea would flit quickly by and crash-land somewhere out of sight.

Myron Poloner was the youngest advertising man in the conference room, but the most powerful and the most dangerous. Some people did wonder, though, about the source of Myron's clout. Myron couldn't be found on any of N. W. Ayer's organizational charts. Myron wasn't assigned to any particular account. He didn't belong to any of the usual teams. He seemed to have no boss above him and no subjects below him. And no one could say what Myron really did. The only person Myron Poloner obeyed was Ayer's executive director, Lou Hagopian. Myron was Lou's ear.

If you wanted to say something in confidence at Ayer, you

always looked over your shoulder to make sure that Myron Poloner was not there.

But Myron always was.

Lou Hagopian was a powerfully built ex-sales promotion man from General Motors, Detroit, blessed with a fiery will and the biggest nose in New York. Hagopian's father had grown up as a shepherd in the Armenian part of Turkey in the early 1900s and had traveled to the United States as a young man to make money. One day he learned that Turkish soldiers had massacred all the residents of his home village, including his wife, his three sons, his parents, his brothers, and his sisters. A new marriage was arranged through relatives to a young Armenian widow who had escaped to Paris and was trying to emigrate to America. The woman came from a wealthy family that had lost its property in the same Turkish slaughter. Soldiers had drowned her husband and father in the lake in front of their estate. The shepherd and the widow were married up in Pontiac, Michigan.

There Louis Hagopian was born.

Lou Hagopian ran Ayer like a football team. He was a ball of fire, determined to drive them on from a park league to the NFL. Phil Dougherty, legendary advertising columnist of the *New York Times,* had begun to use the expression "Hagopian's Ayer" when he referred to the agency. Hagopian loved to storm in unannounced among the art directors and writers at Ayer and declare, "I'm Lou Hagopian! Hello! What are you working on?"

When Hagopian was appointed CEO and chairman of the board, one of his first moves was to offer young Myron Poloner a newly created position as his personal assistant. At that time Poloner was working in the Market Services Group, a small elite force that operated freely throughout Ayer's operations and could be called in at short notice to work on any account. The Market Services Group did strategic analyses of customers' products, or "positioning," a term coined fifteen years earlier that had become indispensable to the admen.

Poloner's obsession was that all creative work must be rooted in strategic analysis; without planning and positioning, the inventiveness of the creative staff was meaningless. Not surprisingly, conflicts often broke out among the Market Services Group and Ayer's writers and art directors. In spite of this, Poloner often had a long line of Ayer executives waiting outside his office to harness his talent as a problem solver.

When the gigantic—and vital—U.S. Army account was renegotiated and saved, Neal O'Connor, at that time Ayer's executive director, had hired Myron Poloner as an in-house consultant on a six-month contract.

Myron's time cost money. If they wanted to make use of his talent, they would have to pay. Every half hour was billed to one of the agency's accounts.

On Monday he might be in Philadelphia working on the airline account, on Tuesday cars in Chicago, on Wednesday soft drinks in New York.

Hagopian had told Myron Poloner to write his own job description. Myron shouldn't have to sit on any permanent groups or committees. He could have the freedom to do exactly as he pleased. The only condition was that he should report directly to Lou Hagopian. And only to him. And Hagopian had another wish: the Ayer CEO wanted Poloner to put together his own advertising team, a small agency within the agency, consisting of the best writer and the best art director at Ayer. It was to be Hagopian's own little Ministry of Truth that had one and only one task: to sell Ayer internally to its personnel.

Myron accepted the invitation with pleasure.

After just four years at Ayer, Myron Poloner was now the personal assistant and right-hand man to the CEO. He had a special button on his phone that opened directly to Lou's office. At thirty-two Myron was the youngest executive in Ayer's history to be elected vice president.

Lou Hagopian trusted Poloner completely. The CEO of Ayer discussed all his decisions with his young protégé and kept him in the tightest internal loop. In time, the managers at Ayer learned to bring their ideas directly to Poloner since they would eventually be floated there anyway.

Myron Poloner had built up a formidable position. Sometimes, though, he got the feeling that the people at Ayer didn't treat him with the respect that his success should have merited. Emboldened by long hours of overtime, a couple of the boys would pop their heads through his doorway and bellow, "Are you still here, Myron? Isn't it time for you to go home and put Lou to bed? Put on his little Batman pajamas and read him a bedtime story?" The taunting was good-natured, and Myron laughed along with them, but not very reverent, was it? He couldn't help but detect the ridicule in the humor. Everyone agreed that Myron Poloner was smart and talented. He could keep things from piling up on Lou's desk. He was a capable manager. But with knowing looks, the leading creative talents and writers hinted that there was something lacking: a certain decisive quality, a touch, a feel, that certain . . . something.

People said that Myron did not understand what it was that made Ayer an advertising agency and not, say, a soup producer or a car manufacturer; the thing that made Ayer different from its clients. Without it ever being openly said, everyone knew what the real problem was.

Myron wasn't creative.

•

Still, Myron Poloner could tell that something was brewing when the vodka-packing Swedes arrived. Jerry Siano, the chief creative officer at Ayer, and one of the three members of Hagopian's personal Ministry of Truth, had pulled together a dozen of the agency's best art directors and copywriters on short notice. This was highly unusual. And not only that—Neal O'Connor was there, the same O'Connor who had stepped down as CEO two years earlier and was currently serving as chairman of the company's executive committee. Basically, Neal O'Connor concentrated on one thing only: he traveled the world buying up foreign advertising agencies. Word was out that Neal wanted to buy some Swedish agency—Broman's agency. That might have been the reason for this get-together. Oh, and another thing: Ayer didn't have a vodka account. In fact, they didn't have any liquor account at all.

Ever since William Fry had refused to take on the Canada Dry Gin account in 1932, dividing management and risking the agency's survival, Ayer had sorely lacked a liquor account. New kinds of liquor—light rum, vermouth, and vodka—had poured onto the market during the seventies, and Ayer was missing the boat.

The old warhorse, copywriter Ted Regan, was the third person besides Siano and Poloner in Hagopian's little Truth Team. When Siano invited him to the vodka meeting, Regan accepted enthusiastically. Siano had told him that Broman was a person of international standing, a personality in the advertising world. Neal O'Connor had also mentioned Broman's name in glowing terms.

Also attending Broman's vodka presentation at Ayer were: Al Wolfe, executive vice-president account management, recently headhunted from a top position at Wells Rich Green; vice president Tony Spaeth from the Market Services group; Group Art Director Wing Fong, and Senior VP Account Management Dick Golden, plus a handful of their associates.

Broman's pitch brought Siano's praise. The laughing Swede was a brilliant presenter, even though he made his point in a slightly roundabout, European fashion. Broman was not selling any particular solution. He tended to treat the advertisement as though it were a philosophical problem. He spent considerable time reviewing the project's conceptual underpinnings: a Swedish vodka, the Swedish background, the Swedish liquor tradition, and the vodka market. It was charming in a grade school sort of way. Broman had spoken at length about the problems that his suggestions were trying to solve: the historical credibility, the product personality, its uniqueness, and so on. Only then had he presented his ideas, his . . . well, his platforms.

The most striking thing about Broman was the number of angles of attack. An American agency would have presented no more than two or three basic plans, perhaps even just one plan with variations. Broman was a volcano of ideas. The Swede had six or seven platforms, and every time he jumped to a new one, his eagerness seemed to increase a couple of notches. By the time he finished, he was gushing with enthusiasm.

But a vodka from Sweden? To Myron Poloner, it sounded like a bad joke. The world was hardly waiting for a vodka from Sweden. What disturbed Myron was Jerry Siano's reaction to that unbelievably ugly medicine bottle. Jerry actually seemed to like it. Everyone else was generally agreed that the bottle looked like hell when Jerry suddenly went nuts and distracted them by spouting off about how fantastic the term "Absolute" was. And not only that, Jerry had claimed that it was virgin territory, a great blank spot on the map of advertising, that no one except this Gunnar

Broman, this hick from Sweden, had discovered. A grotesque suggestion. The "absolute of vodkas" as Jerry had put it. The absolute martini. The absolute drink. The absolute bottle.

An absolute hangover, was Myron's immediate reaction.

After the meeting, Siano announced that he intended to put together a small informal group that would work directly with the Swedes. It would be a creative group; Siano and Broman both insisted on that. Ted Regan would be the copywriter, and Siano himself would come in as art director. Al Wolfe, who had worked on a Seagram account before coming to Ayer, would also pitch in.

The Swedish vodka, a product that still did not exist, had suddenly attracted a star-studded cast that outshone those of N. W. Ayer's most prestigious multimillion dollar accounts. At that point, Myron Poloner decided that the show needed a directing hand. Himself. He would come in as manager of the group and handle strategic issues. With Myron's move, Lou Hagopian's entire Ministry of Truth was cast in the Swedish vodka epic.

Myron's position was that the beaming Swede needed help in preparing a presentation for potential American importers. The Swedish Liquor Monopoly didn't have an importer in the United States, and there was probably no serious American importer that would touch an unidentified, rumored Swedish vodka. They would ask exactly the same question that Poloner had put to Siano: "Was there any reason at all to think that a Swedish vodka might be successful in the States?" The answer was still no.

So, all the grunt work remained: the market needed to be analyzed, a strategic plan laid out, and the product positioned. That last part was Poloner's job. Myron's understanding was that the positioning had to be as complete as possible before the Swedes started courting American importers. The brand name had to be there. The angle of the advertising should be decided. And, above all else, they must not end up standing in front of the booze mongers, asking them their opinion—that would just confuse them.

It was true that the Swedes had put forward a lot of amusing ideas, Poloner thought, as he reviewed the Swedish liquor show. Let's see . . . Vikings, kings, lions, rolling hills . . . all great stuff, but it was really only Siano and Poloner who could determine how to bring the Swedish product to the American market. It was time for Ayer to take over.

Jerry Siano couldn't get that medicine bottle out of his head. He wasn't sure he had understood what "Absolute" really meant, but he sensed that this could be something so unusual that no one would have seen anything like it since old Henry McKinney had won the world's biggest advertising account for Ayer at the turn of the century by christening the National Biscuit Company's *Uneeda Biscuit*. As far as Siano could see, the Swedes—who still had not produced one drop of liquor—thought they would just breeze into the American market, plant their flag, and claim the territory. Basically all they had to start with was a box of mock-up bottles. It was like a grade-school project.

But Siano was intrigued. He wanted to check out that medicine bottle one more time. He explained to Broman that, in his opinion, this was the line they needed to work with. The other ideas weren't bad, not at all, but there was something about that bottle . . . .

Siano had caught a fleeting glimpse of the hard currency of the advertising world. He had seen something new.

Jerry Siano had joined Ayer just after he turned twenty. He started out doing simple sketches, lettering, coloring, and layout. No one noticed anything exceptional until Wing Fong found him standing alone in a corridor one day and asked him what was up. It emerged that Jerry's boss didn't like Jerry. So Wing Fong took Siano in and discovered that the kid from Pennsylvania was a natural. Jerry Siano was a totally unsophisticated boy who had learned how to draw at the Philadelphia College of Art. He was a football player, not an intellectual. But there was magic in him. It wasn't only his talent in design and layout; quite simply, the kid had the touch.

Wing Fong watched over his pearl for a couple of years and noticed that everything that Jerry waved his wand over was charmed. Jerry was cool, inventive, mobile, exciting. Jerry was creative.

Some time after the pitch, Gunnar Broman and the taciturn Hans Brindfors stepped into Jerry Siano's office. Brindfors set his bulky leather bag of bottles on the glass table. Myron Poloner and Al Wolfe stood in the background while Jerry explained that he would like to take another look at the bottles. There were some details he had been mulling over. Myron talked about how much he had liked Broman's presentation. It had been genuinely interesting, he said. Jerry asked to see that last bottle, the Swedish medicine bottle. Swedish medicine bottle? Brindfors didn't know anything about any medicine bottle. He stuck his hand in the trunk and felt around.

Hans Brindfors had found the bottle on page 117 of the classic work on *American Bottles.* It showed a picture of a fine old American bottle in colored glass, probably blown more than two hundred years ago, when the first traders rode across the untamed country, saddlebags heavy with firewater. He lifted the likely item out of the trunk while Siano watched carefully. As the silent Swede held it up for all to see, the bottle began to slide out of the plastic strip wrapped around it, the one that read, "Absolute Pure Vodka," "DR. BÖGER" and "CHARTPAK." Breaking free of its label, it started to fall. It plummeted like the five-pound chunk of solid plastic it was.

About the time Brindfors spotted the bottle in the pages of *American Bottles,* Gunnar Broman had found it (or, the bottle had found him) as he was rummaging through a thrift store in Stockholm's Old Town. To Broman, it was a medicine bottle, an old Swedish medicine bottle from the beginning of the century. And it was his bottle. He had never heard about any *American Bottles* book.

Broman watched the bottle slide. That chubby little no-neck bottle that had come all the way from a stinking basement in Stockholm up into the conditioned air of a forty-first floor office on Sixth Avenue, NYC, was going down. It was about halfway between Brindfors' outstretched hand and Jerry Siano's glass table when Al Wolfe glimpsed it from across the room. Yes, there it was, that non-bottle, just as he had remembered it from the presentation, the one with the icy Scandinavian design and a kind of horrid Ingmar Bergman chill that suggested it had once contained something much worse than vodka, something dangerous. Maybe poison. Maybe snake oil.

The bottle was about to make impact.

Until now, Brindfors had uttered only a dozen words in public in the U.S., and he intended to keep it that way. He had not crossed the Atlantic to embarrass himself in front of the staff of one of the world's largest advertising agencies. Brindfors had intended to remain in the background and let Broman do the talking. He had been completely clear about his plan. And then, look, he goes and drops the bottle in Jerry Siano's office. So clumsy. Brindfors squeezed his eyelids shut, waiting for Siano's table to shatter into a shower of glass. The bottle hit with a loud smack. But the table held, and the bottle spun around and around as they watched, captivated.

"But—it has no label!" Myron Poloner blurted out.

"Yes, it does," said Brindfors quickly, triumphantly, grateful for a way to divert their attention to the limp little strip of transparent acetate.

"And I've got it!"

• • •

When Peter Ekelund got back to Sweden after the pitch to Ayer, he told everyone at the Liquor Monopoly how the Americans had given them an enthusiastic reception. People had actually stood up and cheered! And Jerry Siano, the creative manager at Ayer, had endorsed "Absolute Pure Vodka." That was the clincher. Now it was just a matter of keeping up the momentum. He didn't say much about the "plasma bottle," the "antifreeze," or the questions about the existence of Swedish vodka—that whole awkward issue was best ignored.

Ekelund and the Monopoly's troubleshooter, Curt Nycander, had made previous trips to the United States to present the vodka project to prospective importers, but with little success. They had been to Seagram, one of the world's largest liquor producers, and had been received with open arms every time they showed up. They had had the pleasure of meeting a large number of Seagram people, since they met with a different executive on every visit. Apart from the vodka, which still did not exist, Nycander had promised Seagram the rights to all Sweden's quality drinks. "We are the Monopoly," Curt proclaimed. "We control everything."

But their wide social network at Seagram had not really led

anywhere. After that, they hired an out-of-work liquor executive, Joe Tomassi, as a consultant. Tomassi suggested that the Swedes come out with a big bottle, the biggest one they could find, slap a red label on it and as many lions, seals, and crests as possible. After all, Sweden was a monarchy. "The bottle has to have *shelf impact,*" explained Tomassi. There was a war raging on the shelves of America's liquor stores—a ruthless, merciless war. Labels that were not aggressive ended up as casualties. The bottle must be crimson, compelling, crushing.

Peter Ekelund was frustrated with the slow pace at which everything chugged along at the Monopoly. It was like trying to get to Boardwalk from Marvin Gardens and getting a Go-to-Jail card. This is not the way things are in the private sector, the fresh-out-of-school Ekelund confided to Lindmark, the Monopoly´s mighty boss.

Ekelund had worked at the Liquor Monopoly during his school breaks, and when he graduated he was offered a permanent job as an assistant. He was faced with the choice of fine-tuning the new plant on the West Coast or working on the even newer export project. The general feeling was that the fully automated liquor factory was a technical marvel, an achievement of cutting-edge engineering, an extraordinary opportunity for a young man starting out on his career. The "export project," on the other hand, was seen as dead in the water. But in Ekelund's wandering eyes, it was a choice between the sleepy little seaside town of Falkenburg and the Big Apple.

When the six-foot seven-inch giant with the cubist gaze first showed up at Gunnar Broman's advertising agency and presented himself as the State Liquor Monopoly's new export man, Broman took it as a sure sign that Lindmark had finally decided to abandon the whole project.

Ekelund must have weighed 220 pounds, and he poured them into Broman's sofa. He interrogated Broman about the agency's work and asked why nothing was happening with the bottles. "It doesn't look like it is going to amount to anything," Broman said. The advertising men didn't have the impression that the Liquor Monopoly was serious about the project, and they needed money down. "How much cash do you need?" asked Ekelund. "Seventy-five thousand dollars," Broman replied. "Okay," said Ekelund. "I'll take care of that."

It was such fun to see Peter Ekelund in action at the Monopoly. He was so young and cocky, laughable, but also slightly alarming. Ekelund made decisions about everything under the sun. The staff would be waiting for a decision to be made in the usual way, somewhere higher up the chain of command, and Peter Ekelund would get wind of it and just make the decision himself. One small problem: did anyone control what he decreed in the name of the State Monopoly?

One day Ekelund ordered new bottling equipment for the Åhus plant. Who in the hell had asked him to do that? A million out the window and Ekelund just smirked and said, "Yeah, well, it was something they needed." And then he cruised into Lindmark's office to let him know. Everyone was certain that Lindmark would rip the guy to shreds. Anyone else would have taken a three-ring binder in the back of the neck, but with Ekelund Lindmark just found it incredibly amusing. Ekelund, the business-school graduate whose daddy headed up a public corporation—so self-assured. For Lindmark, Ekelund's chutzpah was uplifting in an odd sort of way.

In his pitches to American liquor distributors, Ekelund claimed that the Monopoly could sell one hundred and fifty thousand cases of vodka in the United States within three years. Joe Tomassi burst out laughing when he heard that fanciful number. But the Monopoly had done a market survey, Ekelund assured them, scanning the room. A scientific investigation had concluded that the Swedish vodka would sell at least one hundred thousand cases, probably more, probably two hundred thousand cases. Several of the Americans asked to see the report, but it was, most unfortunately, written in Swedish.

Some time later Ekelund invited executives from Brown–Forman, one of the world's largest liquor producers and marketers, to Stockholm. They were to tour the plants, taste the vodka, smile, and shake hands with Lars Lindmark, distinguished head of the State Liquor Monopoly. A big reception was planned, too. Then Brown–Forman sent a telegram saying that something had come up stateside, they couldn't make it, and could the Swedes suggest an alternative date. Ekelund fired back: Gentlemen, you will be made most welcome in Stockholm on the date we agreed. If that doesn't suit you, please don't come at all.

The civil servants at the Liquor Monopoly weren't completely at ease in Ekelund's company. What bothered them was that the kid knew no fear. Maybe because of his powerful dad, maybe something else. But no fear at all. And Peter kept butting into things, like that time he ordered the new bottling equipment as if he was ordering a pizza. Or when he telexed one of the biggest liquor producers in the world and more or less suggested they go fuck themselves. Curt Nycander loved having Peter Ekelund along on the sales pitches.

The toughest thing to take was not Ekelund's telegram, but the fact that the Brown–Forman big-shots actually showed up, and on the appointed day.

The seventy-five grand that Ekelund had promised Broman for the vodka project duly appeared.

• • •

What bothered Jerry Siano about the bottle was that it looked so modern, like it was made in a factory where there were no living creatures. The bottle appeared to have been designed and made by a robot.

Siano felt that it needed heritage. The younger the product, the more important it was to claim a history. That was simple advertising logic. People don't like drinking modern liquor; they aren't prepared to pay for it. The Swedes themselves had pointed that out when they talked about Chivas Regal.

"What this piece of packaging needs," Jerry Siano told Broman, "is a human element. Something written by hand, so that you can tell that people have been around it." And, having got started, Siano added that it also needed something in relief, "You know, a red thing, in wax," a bigger and better logo, and letters in all sizes (preferably large). "And it needs a seal." It should have dates and curlicues and, of course, symbols. And then something about the king of Sweden. Just a little something. A sticker, maybe.

"But apart from that," Siano concluded, "the simplicity—I love it."

Hans Brindfors made a rare attempt to speak. Brindfors was opposed to this creative direction. He, Hans Brindfors, had created a bottle with the classical purity of a Greek statue. Now Siano was trying to turn this Brindforsian masterpiece into a Christmas tree. A plastic, American Christmas tree! Worse still, instead of sticking to purity, clarity, and simplicity, Siano wanted to decorate the tree, one sparkling glass ball after another, and the American was merrily announcing that the more decorations he hung, the more festive it would become. Well, it wasn't festive at all, Brindfors felt. It was just confusing.

Nothing of all this came out. Brindfors had the vision, but he didn't have the words. Just one word emerged: "Silver."

"Silver?" Jerry inquired.

"Silver lettering," Broman interpreted. "There will be silver lettering on the bottle."

"Silver is crazy! You can't see it. Everyone knows that."

"Hans says silver is purity."

A lot of people at Broman's agency had been mistaken about Hans Brindfors. When he first showed up, they thought he seemed a little indolent. In his threadbare coat he reminded them of a shy office clerk from the twenties. Out of kindness, they gave him a table and some pencils. A year later, Hans Brindfors was presiding over one of the largest rooms in the agency, the walls were covered with sketches from an impressive number of projects, and the tables were covered with cans and bottles and boxes, all works in progress. Brindfors worked like a dog. And he could push any number of projects at once.

Broman could not have found a better art director. Brindfors managed to transform any fleeting vision into something tangible. When Broman described his platforms, Brindfors nodded. Everything was noted. Brindfors had another rare talent. In his room there was a large cabinet crammed with magazines. He seemed to be able to remember every picture he had come across, and what's more, could locate it within seconds. Once, after having explained some of his latest ideas, Broman barely managed to get out of the room before his young art director came rushing out. "Did you mean like this, Gunnar?" Brindfors had cut and pasted an ad in a minute flat.

Brindfors acted as a catalyst. He accelerated the creative process without being used up himself.

But now, Hans Brindfors was demonstrating few catalytic qualities. In fact, he was irate. Siano had thought that the Swedes would appreciate his suggestions, but the meeting was degenerating into a heated exchange of ideas. "Little Caesar!" Siano thought, when he heard Broman declaring that he might be laughing, but he would never give up his platform. Never.

And then there was Myron. During one summit session Brindfors told Myron that they had been toying with the idea of running ads in the new experimental magazines that young people were reading. They would avoid *Esquire*, *Playboy*, *Time,* and *Newsweek*, he explained, and advertise the vodka in, for example, *Rolling Stone*. They would look for the "eye of the trend." Poloner cut them off. "That magazine will not exist in two years." Brindfors and Broman felt like two hicks. *Rolling Stone* was doomed to die.

And here they were, almost having booked space in it.

• • •

During one stalemate, Jerry Siano invited Gunnar Broman and Hans Brindfors out to his house in Bucks County, Pennsylvania. On Saturday morning Jerry picked up the Swedes at the train station, and then they filled up the big station wagon with vegetables, meat, cheese, and bread.

Siano's house was beautifully situated in a grove of pine trees. Jerry introduced the Swedes to his wife, Ireene, and they all prepared an Italian pasta lunch that took a couple of hours to make and just as long to eat.

And how those Swedish guys liked to eat! Jerry was impressed by their Viking appetites. It was like they had never seen food before.

Gunnar Broman told Jerry about the time when he was creative director at Ted Bates's agency in Stockholm in the early sixties. He had been responsible for 120 illustrators and copywriters, quite apart from his own accounts, which made up half the agency's turnover. Eventually the American owners offered Broman the position as managing director. That's when he had had enough. He turned his basement into a studio and went down there to write ads. "Never a manager again," said Gunnar Broman.

Jerry Siano couldn't understand why the Swedes didn't want to make a career out of it. And they kept pointing out that he was such a skilled illustrator. Jerry had recently turned his garage into a studio, and it was filled with his own paintings and sketches. As the three admen sat down to work in this improvised headquarters of the vodka campaign, Broman exclaimed: "But you're so damn creative, Jerry! You sure as hell don't need to lower yourself to being a managing director!"

There wasn't a shadow of a doubt in Jerry Siano's mind that "Absolute Pure Vodka" was the angle they had to work with. But he had doubts about the name. It was "Absolute" he liked, or "Absolute Vodka," not "Absolute *Pure* Vodka," because—what had that guy said at the meeting?—that was a description, not a name.

Siano asked Broman what he meant by "Absolute Pure." Either a vodka was pure or it wasn't—right? And if it wasn't pure, then it wasn't a vodka, right? So how can you talk about an "absolutely" pure vodka?

Their idea seemed to be, as far as Siano had understood it, that all the others, Smirnoff (which had practically created the vodka market), Popov, Wolfschmidt, and the other American labels, as well as the imported brands, Stolichnaya, Wyborowa, and Finlandia, had somehow all failed to produce a real vodka.

Well, Broman said, this part was easy. All vodkas are pure, sure, or else they wouldn't be vodkas. But there is also a vodka that is the purest of them all. "Absolute" simply means "the purest of the pure."

And what if the Swedes were sued in court for suggesting that their vodka was pure and the others weren't, Siano wondered. They didn't have any actual proof, did they?

"But how could we?" Broman replied. "We don't even have a vodka."

After the pasta feast, the trio drove up to Princeton to meet with Ayer's former CEO, Neal O'Connor.

Neal O'Connor told Broman and Brindfors how Wayland Ayer, when the agency was formed in 1869, had named the company N. W. Ayer & Son, after his father Nathan Wheeler Ayer. Wayland, at twenty-one, was afraid that clients wouldn't take him seriously because of his tender age. "This demonstrates," Neal concluded, "that deception was part of this business from day one."

The year before Neal O'Connor was appointed executive director of N. W. Ayer, the agency had lost two of its old clients, Hills Brothers, the coffee maker, and Dole pineapple. They lost the United Airlines account that summer, after Neal O'Connor had been in charge for less than three months. The following year, 1966, they lost the $30 million Plymouth account, representing half of Ayer's turnover and more than half of its profits. Basically there was only one profitable account left, and that was AT&T.

One year later, Neal O'Connor received notice that AT&T intended to take their business elsewhere.

Through a heroic creative effort by Ayer's legendary copywriter, Pat Gallagher, and his team, the agency managed to put together a campaign that saved the AT&T account. So exciting was the pitch that the people from AT&T doubted at first that it was an in-house Ayer job. Neal O'Connor, who personally attended the presentation, had to stand up and read out loud the names of the people involved.

That campaign saved Ayer. One of the twenty-seven names was Jerry Siano.

After the enormous transformation that Neal O'Connor had orchestrated, Ayer found itself way behind the other Madison Avenue agencies in two respects. First, they had almost no household consumer goods accounts: canned food, soap, shampoo, toothpaste, soda, beer, cigarettes, liquor—everything the admen considered to be major league.

Ayer's second shortcoming was its lack of foreign affiliates. Without foreign affiliates Ayer could never attract the multinational companies and, without multinationals, no strong brands. It was a vicious cycle.

Then suddenly, in 1977, Pan Am Airlines announced that it was considering leaving J. Walter Thompson and N. W. Ayer was one of ten agencies that would have a chance to compete for the $32 million account. The catch was that Pan Am required its new agency to have an international network.

Neal O'Connor had just replaced himself with Lou Hagopian, the big-nosed Armenian from General Motors. He launched himself on a global buying spree. O'Connor soon found that there were very few good independent agencies up for sale.

Throughout the winter and spring, scores of Ayer associates visited the agency at Blasieholm's Square in Stockholm. Neal O'Connor left one offer after another. He was prepared to do almost anything to convince a local hero to part with his agency, or at least a piece of it.

But the Swede stalled. Gunnar Broman wanted to see how well they could work together on the bottle.

• • •

"Why is it, really," Gunnar Broman asked Neal O'Connor, as the four men wandered back through Princeton, "that you who are so incredibly big are so interested in us, who are so incredibly small?"

"Because, Gunnar," answered Neal, "you just make people feel so good. You put everyone you meet in such a damn good mood."

Everyone who met Gunnar Broman just started laughing. Everyone except Myron Poloner.

Myron just smiled.

After the presentation at Ayer had been proclaimed a victory for the funny little medicine bottle, it became a matter of finding an importer right away. They called in Joe Tomassi, the liquor consultant. And Curt Nycander and Peter Ekelund were ready to return to the City of Dreams.

In order to receive a new group of American liquor executives in style, Curt Nycander rented a room at the Royal Swedish Consulate. The Ambassador and his wife had promised to make an appearance. Four elderly American gentlemen turned up, shook the hand of the royal ambassador, and settled down to watch the latest Swedish slide show. Nycander felt like he was back at his graduation. He described the glorious history of the Monopoly and praised the quality of Swedish booze. From Ekelund spouted optimistic sales predictions. Tomassi enlarged upon the American liquor market. "Vodka is a fast-moving product," the liquor man explained. "And that is why a vodka bottle must make an impact."

Coming to his point, Tomassi looked a little queasy. A vodka bottle, he proclaimed, must stand tall. It should have a large red label, a number of royal crowns, lions, and unicorns, and preferably a Russian name. Tomassi pointed at the screen.

The four old men stared up at the bottle. It was short. It had no label. The name was impossible to make out.

The bottle was practically invisible.

CHAPTER 4

MONOPOLY GAMES

Lars Lindmark attempts to sweep the old bureaucracy out of the Wine and Spirits Monopoly's gloomy corridors.

Rolf Arfwedson had been part of the management team at the Wine & Spirits Central since 1949 and had served under its new boss, Lars Lindmark, for the past three years, but he still couldn't understand why the man was so angry. He was like a seven-year-old kid. He had a seven-year-old's curiosity, a seven-year-old's sulks, and, when he didn't get his way, a seven-year-old's rage.

And hidden under the man's desk was a dachshund, a little black devil, ready to jump out and bite an honest Swedish official on the leg.

Old Kinna-Erik Eriksson, who had run the Monopoly for more than twenty years, had never even raised his voice. Not once in two decades had that noble old gentleman been bad tempered for a single day, and yet the operation had run as smoothly as port wine in fine old casks. The Swedish people got their Renat. The upper class got its French wines and Scotch whiskey. The state got its hundreds of millions of dollars in tax revenue, and that was the end of the matter. Everybody was very happy.

The Liquor Monopoly's real mission since the day it was founded was, according to Arfwedson, to see to it that the Swedish people got their liquor without being fleeced by the farming community.

In the grand old days, the voice of the farmers had been Pontus De la Gardie, Count of Borrestad, Chairman of the Society of Distillers, as well as head of the National Society of Little Piggies. De la Gardie was a magnificent opponent. He spoke on behalf of the country's eighty-two private distillers, most of whom were to be found on the plains of Skåne in southern Sweden, and all of whom ganged up together and every year tried to squeeze a few extra pennies per liter out of the Monopoly, which to Arfwedson was synonymous with the Swedish people.

Count De la Gardie and the other distillers mass-produced potatoes, which they fermented into raw aquavit. The end result was in part the aquavit that was, after lengthy negotiation, sold on to the Monopoly for purification, and in part the dregs, a sloshy, bubbling, protein-rich mess that was fed to the cattle. It was a great combination, so ingenious that, according to De la Gardie, only the Lord Himself could possibly have come up with it.

Besides the actual reimbursement, the farmers had bargained themselves into a special allowance for repairs, with the result that private stills were utterly decrepit. The buildings were barely standing. Arfwedson himself had spoken on several occasions on the necessity of repairs, but the distillers just grinned. No chance they would repair anything. "We've already spent all the repair money," they said. When he pointed out that they had to take care of the distilleries, paint them, and make sure rot didn't set in, they just said, "Well, then, we'll just have to raise that repairs allowance, won't we?"

Negotiations with the farmers were often contested to the final penny. De la Gardie would say that there was no point in bringing in an arbitrator to haggle over a measly penny at this stage. Surely Arfwedson could grant them that much. But that last penny would be multiplied by fifty million liters of raw liquor, so there was a good deal of change on the table.

One year the board of the Society of Distillers decided it was time to celebrate a jubilee, with appropriate festivities. De la Gardie declared his intention to preside over the rank and file at the Freemasons Hotel in Kristianstad, in the deep, deep south of Sweden. Arfwedson was duty bound to travel down to represent the Enemy and pay his respects to the Count. He brought a grandiose gift: a large silver cask of fully five liters capacity, with taps at all points of the compass.

De la Gardie was delighted when he saw the gift. The order was given to have it filled to the brim with champagne and placed by the count's cover at the dinner table. Every time there was a toast, De la Gardie lifted the cask to the rafters and drank straight from the tap as from a shining silver teat.

But the lid of the keg was not fastened, it worked loose, and to the farmers' merriment a torrent of champagne gushed over De la Gardie's shirt. The count smiled magnanimously, for he took such misfortunes in his stride. He slammed down the cask from the Monopoly, this Trojan horse from the capital city, and his laughter echoed through the the Freemasons Hotel in Kristianstad.

That same night at the Freemasons Hotel, Arfwedson ran into Nils Petter Mathiasson, the second Liquor King of Sweden, who had created a liquor trust in 1910, establishing control over every purification plant in the nation. Mathiasson had governed a private monopoly from his Reimersholm base outside Stockholm until 1917, when the infamous reformist Ivan Bratt bought him out for the incredible sum of two and a half million dollars, all of which he later lost on the stock market.

At the age of ninety-one, Mathiasson was still active, and wasted no time in expressing a desire to exchange a word with the emissary from the Monopoly. The old man, who was quite deaf, beckoned Arfwedson closer and screamed in his ear that he intended to sail for the United States of America soon. He was going to establish a factory for the production of Swedish schnapps. Arfwedson wondered how he meant to accomplish this. Well, replied Mathiasson, he had the answer to that one. Producing the liquor in Sweden and shipping what was essentially water across the ocean was not good business. The liquor would be produced over there in the United States of America. And he leaned over to Arfwedson, so none of the farmers would hear what he had to say: "I have the recipe right here in my pocket," he yelled. "It's all I need. A piece of paper in my pocket, no bigger than a playing card, and I'm ready to go!"

• • •

The people of Stockholm would stop on the street and stare up in puzzlement at the Liquor Monopoly's high walls, wondering how this gigantic brick fortress could have been erected right in the middle of their city. There were lions rampant in alcoves and lush clusters of grapes hewn into the cornerstones. They had laid a railroad track from North Station all the way in through the main gate. They liked to boast that they had the biggest elevator in Europe, so vast you could lift a freight car in it. There was an enormous cistern, a reservoir really, into which the wine was emptied. It was then fed through a complicated series of pipes and taps to the bottling plant.

It was all extremely well planned, a miracle of engineering, as perfectly thought out as the country's social structure. Except, of course, that the wine came in by boat.

The building could have done with a wharf, a waterfront, and an ocean.

Entering the Liquor Monopoly was like stepping into a cold and moldy sepulchre. Huge drapes in leaden velvet hung from the ceilings. A newly recruited young man nervously drew back the drapes to make sure the world was still out there. On the windowsill was an old percolator from the 1920s covered with spider webs.

No one was allowed to leave the building during his shift without written permission. After all, they were producing liquid social dynamite. In a little sentry post down by the gate, the guard, who rather fittingly came from East Germany, scrutinized all those who passed. There was something wrong with the poor man's arm. He used to place the dysfunctional limb on the table, regarding it as though it were an alien fish plucked from the sea of wine behind his back. Patiently he waited for it to jerk into life. The only time the German could wrench his eyes from the offending appendage was to pore over a pass, suspiciously examine its owner, then grab the rubber and, with his good arm, stamp.

Sweden may have been a country that had got modernity and change on the brain, but the Liquor Monopoly was frozen in time. It was a ship on its way to the North Pole, abandoned among the ice floes with its precious cargo.

The wine was in the basement. Up in the musty attic passages you might run into the museum curator, rooting among the ancient stills and eighteenth-century spirit bottles. It was from the third floor that the Kingdom of Liquor was ruled. The corridor there was steeped in constant gloom, with red and green lamps glowing dimly in the corners. Outside the office doors bellboys sat panting and waiting until a bell tinkled somewhere within and one of the boys would disappear into one of the rooms before reappearing in a rush, clutching a piece of paper.

Behind each and every door sat an intimidating secretary who dealt with unwanted telephone calls and unwelcome visitors. And behind the secretaries' rooms—the three directors.

The administrative director's secretary had received orders that five minutes before the director arrived in the mornings his window should be opened and the top drawer of his desk pulled out exactly fifteen centimeters, measured with a ruler.

The technical director had instructed his secretary to see to it that his room was always locked when he was not in. The technical director did not like visitors.

The financial director was waiting for an important phone call.

They were all waiting for news of Kinna-Erik's foot. Kinna was strapped to a bed at Ersta Hospital, with gangrene gnawing away at his leg like a hungry predator.

At lunchtime, the three directors would enter the directors' dining room, where each director had his appointed place. There they found cotton tablecloths, silver service, and well-starched napkins, with home-baked bread and butterballs set on crushed ice. The food was served with the noblest wines in the land by sweet old ladies in starched white aprons. Excluded employees would peer in enviously on their way to the staff cafeteria.

"Well, you're certainly living the good life here," joked one of the department heads as he passed by, making a clumsy attempt at conversation. The three directors were having none of it.

"We drink wine only when we have guests," they informed him stonily.

"But, er, there aren't any guests today," stammered the nervous manager.

"You are the guest." The wine was poured. There was a deathly silence at the table. Eventually, an incredulous whisper: "Chateau Blanc Forty-nine!"

But it wasn't the unbelievable amount of Renat they had to produce, or the running of the seven big liquor factories, or the farmers' private distilleries, or the wine importing, or even the complicated distribution apparatus that was their greatest challenge.

The most sacred mission of the Monopoly (and this was something only the initiated knew, something only they *should* know) was the compilation of the Confidential List.

The Confidential List was a secret assessment of international wine production, compiled by the most distinguished tasters in the country. Every year they stuck their sensitive olfactory equipment into the wine-tasting bowls, slurped, spat, and pooled their resources in the execution of another list. Every year the Monopoly's best noses came together for a trial by taste, sampled the season's best wines, and recorded their findings in the form of a list.

The physical manifestation of this list might have seemed rather ordinary, a flimsy pamphlet a few pages long, with fifteen wines to a page, no more (it slid easily, not to mention discreetly, into an inside pocket). Yet that list was as sought after as the key to the vaults of the National Bank.

It was distributed in three different versions. In the first, the wines were completely unclassified. There were no check marks. On the intermediate list, the very best wines were indicated with one ✔.

But the most exclusive list had up to three ✔✔✔.

This was the Confidential List.

The Swedish people didn't like wine. The Swedes drank their Renat. There was nothing the Monopoly could do about that. Let them drink what they wanted. The task for the Monopoly was to keep its nose out of alcohol policy, produce cheap liquor, and compile the Confidential List.

But compilation was just the first and easiest phase. The list then had to be distributed.

The version with no check marks was distributed at departmental level, to chairmen of county councils and tenured professors. The ✔ list went to government officials, prominent businessmen and local governors.

No more than fifty copies of the inner Confidential List were printed. One copy was personally handed over to His Majesty the King. The list was then sent out to members of the cabinet, mighty bank directors, captains of industry, judges of the Supreme Court, and, it goes without saying, to the members of the board of the Monopoly. These were citizens who knew the true worth of such information, persons who had a use for it, who could appreciate three checks.

Having the List was like being on the list. It was like having ✔✔✔ after your name.

One day the chairman of the board showed up looking grave. He called for the three directors and explained to them that he'd spoken to the minister of finance himself. Kinna-Erik's successor would not be chosen from within the organization. The new managing director would be an outsider.

Silence.

"Well!" hissed the technical director. "So it's impossible to advance in this organization."

"Hmph!" exclaimed the administrative director. "I shall have to review my position."

"Exactly!" agreed the financial director. "Isn't the Monopoly like any regular organization?"

"Yes, yes," sighed the chairman. "But this is the way the minister wants it."

And then someone demanded to know the name of the intruder.

"Lindmark," said the chairman. "Lars Lindmark."

• • •

Lindmark couldn't believe it. It was as stuffy as an English gentlemen's club. Bellboys, red and green lamps, so gloomy he had to feel his way along the wall. Lindmark couldn't even think about discussing a modern business strategy with bellboys bustling in the perpetual dusk outside his office.

He threw the three directors off the board. He just didn't like them. The administrative director was mean, the technical director hostile, and he thought the financial director was just plain stupid.

Instead, he took in consultants. That was how he got hold of Curt Nycander, who had once written an eighteen-inch-thick report for him in less than six months.

"I give you Curt!" he had proclaimed to the three directors. The Amazing Curt, Curt the Eighteen-Inch Man. He recruited Leif Öberg, the fighter pilot, who had *a whole year's experience* in the private sector. He took in Gunnar Broman, the laughing adman. This was the same Broman who had caused an alcohol epidemic in Sweden with his beer campaign that was so successful it had become a matter of parliamentary debate. These were the kinds of men Lindmark wanted on his team. He brought in twenty-four-year-old Magnus Lagerkvist, who smoked cigars in the office, wore a sober three-piece suit, and had an unshakable faith in his convictions, whatever the subject under discussion. These were the sorts of people Lindmark wanted treading the corridors of the new, modern Monopoly.

Lindmark explained to his consultants that his goal was to modernize in true American fashion. They would modernize, mechanize, computerize. They would build a mammoth of a company. He wanted the Monopoly to be the textbook example of how a state-run enterprise could be effectively led while increasing productivity.

A *model,* one might say.

Lindmark told the Monopoly's financial director exactly what he considered to be the foundation of good economic policy. Budgets. Nothing was better suited to the creation of order and discipline than a carefully planned budget.

To the financial director, budgeting seemed completely unnecessary. There was, after all, nothing to budget *for.* The profit margin at the Monopoly was not decided by the board, or by the sales, but by the government, when they set the level of alcohol tax in *their* budget. It wouldn't matter a damn what Lindmark did, *because the government didn't want sales to increase.* Lindmark's careful planning would collapse around him like a house of cards.

The three directors were baffled by Lindmark's obsession with sales. Was the man a moron? If sales increased even a fraction of a percent, the government strangled consumers with higher taxes until they returned to normal. So why bother trying? It upset planning, production, and politicians. It created chaos. The prime minister got pissed. The entire fabric of the structure groaned.

•

The volatile Lindmark had probably never been more furious during his entire career than when ousting the three directors from the Monopoly. He threw official folders at the fleeing executives, trying to smack them in the neck as they exited his office. He stormed out of board meetings, slamming doors off their hinges. And Sträng had thought that the job would be such a nice rest for Lindmark, allowing him to sail calmly toward retirement. Not if Lindmark had anything to do with it. He turned savage, exploding in magnificent displays of anger.

And he loved it. He could sit for hours just waiting for one of the trio to poke his head around the door. Once he'd been sitting on the toilet planning a broadside, and it was so good that he just couldn't wait. He had to vent his venom without delay. He hauled up his pants and with suspenders trailing treacherously around his knees, rushed into the administrative director's office to deliver an exquisite harangue. The very windowpanes shook. Jesus! He felt so alive! It was a moment to cherish.

And then he came to young Magnus Lagerkvist's smoky office with that idea. They should do something—big. They should have a look at the export market. Have a look at it? What did that mean? What it meant was, Lagerkvist should get off his ass and find a consultant who'd say exactly what Lindmark wanted him to say.

So Lindmark's men found him a consultant. A refugee from the Soviet Union, he'd fled his Baltic homeland during the war. Ilmar Roostal was his name. He was a giant of a man, with nervous gray eyes. He looked like he was waiting for the ghost of Stalin to appear, to demand a personal retribution.

They sent Roostal on a round-the-world trip. "Have a quick look at the export market," they said. "Just a look."

•

And that's when loyal Rolf Arfwedson, that paragon of faultlessness since 1949, decided he'd had enough. Lars Lindmark was starting to sound like old Mathiasson, that dark night at the Society of Distillers party, when the old fool came up to him with the recipe for schnapps in his pocket.

Rolf Arfwedson had become more and more convinced that the new head of the Monopoly had come down with a bad case of megalomania. And eventually Arfwedson had to do his duty as a civil servant. He had to force himself to be completely straightforward and tell his superior the truth.

So he laid it all out for Lindmark. Export, yes, well, that had been tried. And it had been a catastrophe, a sorry chapter in the illustrious history of the Monopoly. The question had been taken up before the board back in the fifties, because Sträng—Gunnar Emmanuel Sträng! *God Himself!*—had thought that selling some of Sweden's liquor abroad would be a good way to bring in some foreign currency. The directors had investigated the possibilities and concluded that they could, perhaps, export small quantities of aquavit and Swedish punsch—the classic products. The problem was, of course, that no one outside Sweden drank aquavit or punsch. They got as far as printing labels in English and shipping a few cases to Swedish embassies. They had a meeting with Ambassador de Besch from Washington and suggested to him that it might be worth exporting aquavit to the Midwest, where the Swedish immigrants had settled. De Besch thought it was a great idea, but he pointed out that if they were serious, they'd have to spend at least a million dollars in advertising. Otherwise, forget about it.

A million dollars?! They forgot about it.

Toward the end of the fifties, though, the Americans discovered that they could use vodka as a base for cocktails, and what was aquavit if not a kind of vodka? Someone at the Monopoly had the bright idea that the Swedes could have a slice of the pie after all by furnishing thirsty Americans with a little quality Swedish alcohol to put in their drinks. They came up with a schnapps that they christened Explorer Vodka.

All went well at first, but then a terrible tragedy occurred, a tragedy that shook the Monopoly to its foundations. Arfwedson forced himself to recount the shocking story for Lindmark, to illustrate the folly of his plan. A week after they registered the trademark Explorer Vodka, the Americans sent up a satellite called *Explorer. Explorer.* My God, they delivered twenty-five thousand liters of the stuff to the United States of America, and every liter disappeared in the course of a single afternoon. The importer called from Los Angeles, screaming for more. The satellite orbited Earth, Americans were dizzy with national pride, and they wanted to drown themselves in Explorer Vodka from Sweden. It was a nightmare.

Rolf Arfwedson tried to break all this to Lindmark as gently as possible. He talked to him as though to an impressionable child. He left out the details. But even so, he could see immediately that Lindmark had not grasped the point.

"Ah!" said Lindmark excitedly. "Reeaalllly? Is that what happened?"

"Yes. We tried. And it brought the Monopoly to its knees."

CHAPTER 5

GUNNAR FIRED

Myron plots Gunnar's exit from the project, William Burroughs gets lost in the invisible bottle, and Absolute loses an e.

It seemed like Myron Poloner didn't get it. When Jerry Siano, Ted Regan, and Al Wolfe got together, that meant work on the Swedish vodka had been given the highest priority at N. W. Ayer.

Finding an importer for the Swedish Liquor Monopoly required high-performance American advertising. Because—if the Monopoly got its importer, Broman and the Swedes would all be happy. If Broman was happy, he might sell his agency to N. W. Ayer. If Ayer bought Broman's agency, that would mean yet another step toward seizing the gigantic Pan Am account. With the Pan Am account, Ayer would be back in the game.

How come that Myron the politico, the master gamesman, didn't get this? It was a simple scheme. It was Myron's own game.

Instead Myron Poloner showed up in his two-thousand-dollar suit, waving his extravagantly expensive Swiss watch in front of Broman and his silent companion, Hans Brindfors. And every time there would be some cocky new comment, like "Booked any space in *Rolling Stone* yet? Ha, ha." Worse yet, Myron had started to refer to Broman as "the Swedish design company." Now he was telling people that the Swede didn't actually deal with advertising. Broman was just a run-of-the-mill designer. Broman had designed a liquor bottle, which frankly speaking looked like shit, and he wanted it introduced in the United States—with Ayer's help, of course. End of story.

Gunnar Broman's friends had warned him about Ayer CEO Lou Hagopian. Broman had better watch out, they cautioned, because Hagopian was a heap of accumulated aggressions, a real son of a bitch. But Broman had met the man in person, and he hadn't noticed anything unusual.

No one ever said anything, however, about Hagopian's right-hand man.

Myron Poloner had gotten Dr. Margaret Rodgers down in research on the thirty-ninth floor to build a simulation of a liquor store. There he sat down to ponder once again upon Vikings, kings, the Swedish countryside, and the strange transparent medicine bottle.

His analysis went like this: It would be a premium vodka for well-educated people in the high-income bracket. That much was pretty obvious. People with class. And—this was important—people with aspirations. A Jaguar or a Rolls-Royce cost a fortune. But for ten bucks you could drink the vodka Rockefeller drank. So, why not show it?

The American bottles all had big, red splats of color for labels—in imitation of Smirnoff, obviously, which everyone thought of as Russian. And the imported brands had labels that imitated the American brands. (Myron had even done some investigation down in Philadelphia, Pennsylvania, where alcohol advertising was regulated and sales more or less hung on how the bottle performed up on the shelf.)

He contemplated the fake wall. What did the Swedes actually know about vodka? That was the question. The longer Myron thought about it, the longer he pondered the wall, the more certain he was: Swedes didn't know dick. There shouldn't be any

Vikings, kings or countrysides on the label. Not even a crest or a czar or The Big Red Russian Label. What they wanted was something different.

It hit him like a thunderbolt right out of the blue: *the bottle should have no label at all! It should be completely invisible!*

A throng of typical American consumers was led in front of the one-way mirrors, behind which sat Myron Poloner, barricaded with notebooks. The consumers were actually his own colleagues, the people he normally kept tabs on. Well, they fulfilled his demands: they were well educated, maybe not high salaried, but they liked vodka.

They looked at the labels and turned the bottles. And the result was always the same. They did a double take as soon as they caught a glimpse of the medicine bottle. They hated it. Or—they loved it. The researchers held up new bottles, with emblems and ornamentals and crests. But the respondents continued babbling on about that crazy plasma bag, they couldn't get it out of their system. Well, you can't see it, they said. Okay, said the researchers, but now look at this one. Look at this one with a crest. Yeah, but that other one, the one without the label. It's so, so . . . *different.*

And that's how Myron discovered the medicine bottle. Actually, the bottle in itself had been nothing. It might have been a passing fancy, just another crazy idea. But now Myron had positioned the bottle.

Now there was more than a bottle. Now there was strategic analysis.

N. W. Ayer was making a steady comeback after the catastrophes of the sixties. Four years earlier the agency had moved its last department from Philadelphia to New York and was now planning to go head to head with the best on Madison Avenue.

The problem was that Ayer still had no household consumer accounts. For years they had done advertising for United Airlines, but United was more like a retail shop. They had worked on prestigious accounts like De Beers diamonds and Steinway pianos, and on big accounts like AT&T and Plymouth. And they had worked on the Army account. They had helped recruit boys from the suburbs to fight in Vietnam by offering them a free education, paid for by the U.S. Army. *Be all you can be*— that was the slogan, and it seemed to be as close to a household consumer goods campaign as Ayer ever came.

It is selling products on the strength of the packaging and the advertising alone that is the true measure of the adman's genius. And that means selling consumer goods, because most consumer goods are pretty similar. And none are more similar than the various brands of vodka.

Vodka is by law odorless, tasteless, and colorless. In a blind taste test the average person would find it near impossible to distinguish among the different brands. The quality of the product means little. It is the ultimate test of the advertising man.

It is something out of nothing.

The Ayer team was determined to give the Swedish vodka its best shot. But there were obvious problems. For starters, the text on the bottle wasn't there. So far, it was only a mock-up in the form of a long list for DOCTOR BÖGER and his German chemicals. The silent Swede, Brindfors, had tried to explain that they didn't know what the finished text would say, but that it would be in silver. The laughing one, Broman, declared that the text shouldn't just be a regular name with an accompanying tag line. He wanted the long copy normally used in an ad, but this time printed directly onto the bottle.

One of his proposals started out, "This vodka is produced

from pure Swedish grain. In order to maintain the grain character in its flavor and aroma, it has been produced by a carefully controlled distilling process that is based on four centuries of Swedish tradition and experience." The Ayer people thought it sounded almost like a declaration of contents. "Yup," Broman agreed with a little satisfied nod, "it did." The old honesty trick. He felt that the most sophisticated way to sell was not to sell at all.

Ted Regan, the copywriter on Hagopian's dream team, started to work over the text. He tried to insert small signals that he felt the American public might understand. You just couldn't say "in order to maintain the grain character . . . produced by a carefully controlled . . . ." That didn't sound American. It sounded like they were sent out from the Department of Health to take test samples in a restaurant kitchen.

During the following weeks, Regan would show one suggestion after the other to Siano. The copy on the bottle then volleyed back and forth across the Atlantic. Regan stuffed American adjectives in on one end, and Broman took them out on the other.

When Ted Regan started out in the 1950s, he loved to read *The 100 Greatest Advertisements* by Julian Lewis Watkins. Ted Regan had read that book until it fell apart, and he knew most of the headlines by heart. One ad in particular stuck in his mind: "Imagine Harry and me advertising our pears in *Fortune!*" It was about two brothers—Harry and David—who ran a pear farm up in Oregon. They had been selling their pears by mail order, but had then turned to the wizards of Madison Avenue. When the admen suggested that they should expand their operations and run ads in *Fortune*, David was overawed. "Imagine Harry and me advertising our pears in *Fortune*," he said. It was almost too good to be true. The admen looked at one another. The customer had just done their job for them.

That copy from 1936 had everything Ted Regan looked for in a good ad. There was something folksy, something that Regan considered to be human in the deepest sense, a warm, noble feeling, but at the same time it was dramatic, and it grabbed the reader. So you'd clip out the coupon at the bottom of the page and order a box of juicy Royal Riviera pears, swaddled in tissue paper and delivered directly to your door.

Regan loved the old advertisements with their long texts and short stories. But he was under no illusions. Times had changed. His favorite author nowadays was one of the younger and more laconic men. His name was Julian Koenig. Koenig never needed a whole page. One sentence and a picture was enough.

When Ted Regan was young, Ayer used to send him to the advertising convention up in Chicago, and there he met a bunch of executives who exchanged business cards with each other. One of the old geezers once asked Ted what his name was, and since Regan didn't have any business cards of his own, he turned the card over and wrote "Julian Koenig."

Regan told Jerry Siano that he thought they should use Absolute Vodka to do a "fill-in." They should intentionally make a small mistake in the name or on the label, a minor–major mistake that would make it impossible to forget the product. Regan thought they should take away the *e* in Absolute.

It was a well known psychological fact, he explained, that if you started to draw a circle, but ended the line before the shape was complete, so that there was still a small opening, most people would experience it as a full circle. They unconsciously completed it. By leaving that little opening, you slyly involved them in a creative process.

Regan remembered that Broman had mentioned that in Swedish, *Absolute* was spelt *absolut,* without any *e.* At their first meeting the Swedes had confidently—but incorrectly—proclaimed that they could always use the Swedish name if there was any problem with American registration laws. Regan strongly felt that they should use the Swedish name. Every single American who saw the bottle would silently put an *e* on the end anyway. The perfect fill-in.

And besides, the English "absolute" was way too obvious. He didn't like that at all. Everyone would immediately understand what the Swedes were getting at; they were claiming to have created the ultimate vodka, and now they were going to flat out say so—whether it was in good taste or not.

Absolut without the *e* was more cunning.

Absolut was more absolute than Absolute.

Gunnar Broman had taken the official name of the Swedish workingman's booze classic, *Absolut Rent Brännvin*, and made a quick translation. It came out as Absolute Pure Vodka. But from day one Broman called it Absolute Vodka, or The Absolute Vodka.

Jerry Siano thought this was the name they should use. He had never liked, or understood, the "pure" part. It was just as redundant as the *e* in Absolute.

When "Pure" disappeared, Hans Brindfors felt he needed something to soften up the brand name on the front. Siano explained to the Swedes that he had considered using Broman's other platform, the "Country of Sweden Vodka" line, because it had everything that Absolute Pure Vodka lacked. Heritage. It showed that there was a background, the product had a history.

Siano wanted background without losing simplicity. And he thought Sweden was good. True, not many Americans might have any idea where it was, but "Country of Sweden" was nevertheless a description of quality, Siano said, not a name. Sweden is polar bears and purity. "Exactly," Broman said. "It's a platform."

Brindfors returned with:

ABSOLUT
COUNTRY OF SWEDEN
VODKA

And Siano liked that.

Myron Poloner had experienced a revelation. Gunnar Broman was not Ayer's client. The client was the Swedish State Wine and Liquor Monopoly represented by the walleyed visionary, Peter Ekelund, and his boss, Curt Nycander (who appeared from time to time and, some of the suits thought, looked remarkably like a gun-shy hound dog; one prominent liquor boss thought Broman was the Monopoly man, Nycander his house-trained adman). Peter and Curt were the client.

Regardless of how much Ayer respected Broman's *design* firm, and regardless of how much they appreciated the fact that the Swede had brought the vodka bottles over to show him, Myron felt that it was still Ayer's duty to give the client the best work they possibly could. All of these Vikings and kings . . . Poloner shook his head. Amusing enough in their own way. But it would definitely not cut the mustard in the United States.

Poloner shared his thoughts with N.W. Ayer CEO, Lou Hagopian. Lou totally agreed. Ayer couldn't do the work for other agencies, certainly not for a Swedish design firm. The Monopoly was the client, and Ayer needed to sort out their loyalties.

When the assistant to the boss of one of the world's biggest, and certainly oldest, advertising agencies announced that he would help them, the Swedes were ecstatic. They certainly needed help. The presentation that Curt Nycander, Peter Ekelund, and Joe Tomassi had given at the Royal Swedish Consulate in New York had led to nothing. Myron Poloner explained that the Ayer agency could provide them with a finished bottle, sketches, even complete ads. Everything perfectly positioned and produced by America's finest. No effort spared.

A tectonic shift was imminent. Effective immediately, the Swedish vodka project was American territory. It belonged to Ayer—*alone.*

Lou Hagopian suggested that Jerry Siano should sort this out with the guys from the Swedish agency. After all, Jerry was the one who had been working with them. Myron immediately fired off a warning. It might be unwise for Jerry, who had built up such a good rapport with the Swedish designers, to risk it all by reading the riot act to them. That could become uncomfortable. But who should do it?

Before Lou had even asked for a volunteer, Myron volunteered.

Myron reminded Lou of the time when the two of them had had a little heart-to-heart about the fact that it was always Lou who gave the orders and Myron who cracked the whip.

"You know, Myron," Lou had said, "either you trust me as your only constituency, or not. If people come in here and tell me how wonderful you are and how nice you are, you're not doing your job. Cause you cannot be well loved and do what you have to do for me."

Clear as a bell.

Myron would clear things up with Broman. A dirty job, but somebody had to do it.

So Lou Hagopian's right-hand man explained to Gunnar Broman how incredibly grateful everyone at Ayer was that Broman had taken the time to bring his bottles over. But the Monopoly and Ayer had come to an agreement. The Monopoly was the client, not Broman, and from now on the Monopoly wanted Ayer to run the show. Myron presented this new theory in a calm and philosophical way. No screaming. No harsh words. It was a quiet little thing.

When he was finished, Broman turned to Jerry Siano.

"Hey, Jerry," said Broman. "What the hell do I need him for? I don't have any use for these board guys. I need creative people."

I need creative people. Wait a minute. This was supposed to be a clarification of the fundamental relationship between Ayer and their client. And this Broman adds insult to his own injury by tossing in a malicious reference to all that other stuff.

Creative people!

Not very smart of Broman. To put a silver bullet between the eyes of Lou Hagopian's right-hand man.

The hick would have to pay.

• • •

Peter Ekelund and Curt Nycander's dismaying failure to sell the idea of Swedish vodka to America's liquor establishment may have been explained by the fact that they still had no real bottles (or any real vodka to pour in the nonexistent bottles). This understandably affected the impact of their presentations.

During that spring of '78, the Swedish admen had been invited several times to sample vodkas at the Monopoly's newly built plant outside Stockholm. The director of the laboratory poured the transparent liquid into small bowls and contentedly watched the admen sip. Broman and Brindfors sniffed and drank, drank and sniffed, but never noticed any differences. "It doesn't have any flavor," they sniffed. "Exactly," said the director of the Monopoly's laboratory, and looked even more smug. "Exactly."

Hans Brindfors made it his personal duty to furnish the Monopoly with the missing bottles. He turned to another well known Swedish monopoly: the bottle monopoly, PLM, and its Hammar plant in southern Sweden. An engineer took a good look at Brindfors's sketches and shook his head. As far as being a bottle was concerned, he explained, it was wrong. Neck too short, angle between neck and body too sharp, surface too uneven. Maybe one of the old glassworks in Småland, where the old-timers blew bottles by hand in front of an open furnace, could help. Although at their pace it would take about two years to blow the first batch.

The engineer clucked his tongue and studied the sketch. Besides, he said, it was impossible to turn it out in clear glass. The glass at PLM was recycled, so there was a slight green or brown tint in it. A totally transparent bottle was out of the question. Then he noticed that there was supposed to be silver on the bottle. Silver? He didn't like silver at all—that would create dangerous gases, and the union would never accept that. No, no, no. That bottle would never see the light of day. His advice? Trash the sketches and revise the whole concept.

But Brindfors had heard of a French glass manufacturer, Saint Gobain, outside Paris, who had a small specialty workshop for perfume bottles. He flew down, and a woman in a white apron carefully studied his sketches and explained that it would be a great honor for Saint Gobain to produce this highly unusual, but still—bottle, in a special series of twelve.

For a week Hans Brindfors lived in a boarding house near the giant glassworks while the French craftsmen produced a special wooden mold and then, with great precision, cast twelve completely transparent bottles with extremely short necks, sharp angles, and silver lettering. Brindfors paid for an extra seat on the plane and flew home with one arm protectively cradling a well-sealed box.

Next time Gunnar Broman went down to the glassworks at Hammar, he brought one of Brindfors' bottles. The engineers looked at it and patiently explained that they had already tried to get Broman's colleague to understand that taking the step from such an incorrect prototype in plastic to a real bottle in glass was technically impossible. Broman lifted the bottle over his head and slammed it down onto the table. Shards of glass rained down over the experts.

The Liquor Monopoly's in-house American researcher, Dr. Stanley Noval, had returned to New York for an extended visit. To find an apartment, Dr. Stanley put an ad in the *New York Times*. He received dozens of replies, mostly from stubborn old ladies offering him "one of the best apartments in New York City," complete with flaking wallpaper, a bare light bulb dangling from the ceiling, and a view out over trashcans. In the end, Dr. Stanley gave in and accepted his fate. The chosen landlady demanded ten references, three months' notice before moving out, and two months' rent in advance. Only a certified check would be acceptable. Dr. Stanley promised to return the next day with the money. "If it's still available," she warned.

A message was waiting for him at his temporary residence. After some deliberation he returned the call, and a voice explained that it concerned a penthouse on Park Avenue. Dr. Stanley could never afford that, he regretted. But the money was no problem, the voice urged. He just had to take care of the apartment and answer the phone.

When the elevator operator in the old brick building pulled open the doors, Stanley stepped right into the lobby on the top floor. From the penthouse's wraparound balcony he could look toward the East River, the southern tip of Manhattan, Grand Central Terminal and the Pan Am Building to the north, and to the west, right in front of his eyes, the Empire State Building's bar.

The proprietor, a literary agent leaving for Europe, explained that Stanley could pay $450 a month if he liked. The money really didn't matter. The only important thing was to answer the phone and forward the mail.

During the coming days and nights, Stanley took calls from Allen Ginsburg, Peter Bogdanovich, Patti Smith, and a cross-section of pop culture's stars. The researcher dutifully jotted down messages and filtered stacks of celebrity-studded mail.

When Peter Ekelund heard about Dr. Stanley Noval's new lifestyle, he asked if they could use the Park Avenue penthouse for receptions. Dr. Stanley was glad to oblige. One evening when Peter had taken the Monopoly's guests out onto the balcony to enjoy the $450-view of the Empire State Building, Broman happened to notice a letter on the mantelpiece. The envelope was addressed to Mr. William S. Burroughs. Dr. Stanley explained to Broman that the owner of the apartment was a literary agent who, among many other things, handled business matters for the famous author. Broman got all fired up.

"My God, Stanley!" he exclaimed. "Without William S. Burroughs I wouldn't be here today."

Broman explained that Burroughs had introduced "free association" in American writing, and that was a literary school Broman had also dabbled in. Before becoming an advertising man, he had thought a lot about stylistic matters. He had investigated the complicated problem of reducing a text to its essence. He had studied his Hemingway. He had read the old Icelandic sagas. But Broman had never really felt he was getting anywhere until he found the works of William Burroughs. Then Broman saw what could be done with the written word. Burroughs had taken the language apart and put it back together. By doing so, he had reinvented it.

Dr. Stanley had to swear on his grandmother's grave that he would do everything in his power to arrange a meeting between the Swedish adman and the great American wordsmith.

Gunnar Broman had the greatest respect for Dr. Stanley Noval's professional abilities, but he could never understand why ordinarily sane people gave money to a bunch of harebrained statisticians who came up with answers that nobody understood. A company would pay out fifty thousand bucks to find out that consumers preferred one brand over another by a factor of 2.153. It was 100 percent scientifically produced proof. The problem was just—what the hell did it mean?

"Basically, my profession is about invading people's integrity," Broman said. "I get them interested in things they are not interested in, and I get them to long for things that they didn't know existed. That's why it is fundamentally meaningless to ask people what they want. I have to rely on my gut feelings."

Dr. Stanley, an understanding scientist if ever there was one, used to say that "I have my quantitative models and my computer, and Gunnar Broman has his qualitative models and his gut." "And it is a most substantial one," Broman would add, patting himself on his qualitative model.

During his time at the Monopoly, Dr. Stanley Noval had built up the largest statistical model of consumer drinking habits the world had ever seen. He had constructed a questionnaire more than fifty pages long, and more than two thousand Swedes had answered it. The investigation touched on every kind of beverage the Swedes could possibly absorb into their bodies. In the end, Dr. Stanley could tell down to the last centiliter what the Swedes drank, how much they drank, when they drank, and why they drank.

Stanley naturally knew from his own experience that Swedes drank in a completely different way and for completely different reasons than his own countrymen. One Nordic researcher had complained to him about how frustrating drinking in the United States could be.

"You have one or two drinks," the man sighed, "and then it stops. For a Scandinavian, that's worse than torture. It's like sex: what's the point of starting if you're not prepared to go all the way?"

Lars Lindmark had once asked Stanley Noval to attend a board meeting at the Liquor Monopoly and give a report on consumption projections for the next fifteen years. He explained to the nine board members, the six deputy members, and four rapporteurs what it meant to make a scientific forecast. A scientific forecast was not necessarily more accurate than ordinary guesswork. There were in fact people—and Stanley had met one or two of them—who had an uncanny ability to guess right, because they had the model in their guts. But in a scientific forecast, Stanley continued, you can specify the exact conditions that would have to be met in order for certain events to occur. For example, for Halley's comet to land on their heads or for ordinary Swedes to give up Renat for French wine.

When Dr. Stanley was finished, it was the chief technician's turn to deliver his report. The chief technician said that, based on the scientific forecasts Dr. Stanley Noval had just outlined, we must make the following multimillion dollar investments over the next five years. All of the board members nodded. Then the chief financial officer said that, based on Dr. Stanley's scientific work, we must build two new factories. After that, the union representative requested permission to speak and explained that, based on Dr. Stanley's prognoses, the parking lot in front of his factory had to be enlarged. All of the board members nodded.

In the end, the board approved a program of investment that would cost tens of millions of dollars. Dr. Stanley tried to persuade them that he had never said anything about those things. He was no oracle, he was a *scientist.* All nine board members, six deputy members, and four rapporteurs nodded. They patted Dr. Stanley on the shoulder as they filed out of the boardroom:

"You spoke well, Stanley."

"Good job, Stanley."

"You did it, Stanley."

Only once had Dr. Stanley told anyone about the real reason he had come to Sweden. It wasn't that Sweden had the most complete set of statistics on liquor consumption in the world. Not at all. It was something much more disturbing.

It was chance.

In his youth Stanley Noval had made a trip across Europe. At that time, before he became *Doctor* Stanley Noval, Stanley didn't speak much. Essentially he had traveled from one end of Europe to the other in silence. One evening in London, he ended up in a pub full of laughing students, where he heard a girl behind him say: "*Vendredi le treize.*" Friday the thirteenth.

"Oh!" Stanley turned around, because he felt that now was the right time to break his long silence. "Friday the thirteenth."

"Don't talk to me about Friday the thirteenth," the girl blurted back.

"I was actually born on Friday the thirteeenth," Stanley proudly explained.

"Me too," she sighed.

That's how Stanley got to know Patricia, who was the daughter of the Belgian Ambassador. Patricia shared an apartment with Margaretha from Sweden, who had a friend, also a Swede, named Bengt. That summer Stanley made a little detour to Sweden, to meet Bengt, and through Bengt he met Karin, with whom he lived for many years.

Bengt once asked Stanley if he could identify the ultimate reason why he had come to Sweden in the first place.

"Well, you see, Bengt," Stanley answered, "there is a scientific reason, which is the fact that this country has the best statistics on alcohol in the whole world. But the real reason why I came here is so improbable that I am afraid it doesn't even exist."

"And what's the real reason?" asked Bengt.

"I was born on Friday the thirteenth."

"So was I," Bengt replied.

One day Lars Lindmark asked Peter Ekelund to show Broman's bottles to Dr. Stanley Noval. (Noval was the only available live American, and Lindmark wanted to know which bottle would work in the U.S. market.)

Dr. Stanley reviewed the Country of Sweden Vodka, the Blonde Swede Vodka, the Royal Court Vodka, the Damn Swede Vodka, the Black Vodka, and the Absolute Pure Vodka.

For once Stanley had no statistical models to rely on. He might have done a survey. He could have sent out a questionnaire. But it so happened that the day before he had read an article by

Lord Kelvin in *Scientific American* about absolute zero, –273°C. And that was the first thing that came into his mind. It was strange, and it was utterly unscientific. He wrote that he thought Lindmark should go with the funny little apothecary bottle. He should go with Absolute Zero.

Strange coincidences just happened to Stanley. And since he was a constant victim of chance, he tried to make sense of it. To no avail. One day he received a call in his Park Avenue apartment from his landlord, the literary agent.

William Burroughs was in town. A Belgian avant-garde theater group was visiting New York to give a performance based on his work and Burroughs planned to be there.

It turned out that the author of *Naked Lunch* had a small, but fortunate, quirk. Burroughs refused to drink anything but vodka. He would therefore consider meeting with the Swedes on condition that they be well supplied with samples.

In preparation for the big night, Broman grabbed one of Brindfors' French bottles and stole away, casting a furtive shadow on the city streets. The bottles were intended for corporate America, but Broman figured that if there were exceptions in life—and there were—then this was one of them.

And so Gunnar Broman, Dr. Stanley Noval, the literary agent, and the distinguished author made a night of it. Entering the room, the writer pulled a revolver out of his pocket and placed it on the table. Broman, in turn, put down the bottle. The creator of modern prose scrutinized the fruits of Broman's labors. It was a rare example of modern business poetry. Then that stubby ice-clear apothecary bottle with the silver lettering and no label disappeared under the lugubrious shadow of the Burroughs hat brim. It did not emerge for a while.

The avant-garde performance—Burroughs' own, that is—confirmed Broman's high regard for the man. The celebrated writer slept through all three acts. Even when a dozen stark naked Belgians rushed onto the stage hooting enthusiastically, Burroughs' only reaction was a deafening storm of snoring.

America's great son made Broman think of a Midwest farmer, a dried-out wretch who for weeks had stood, hat on head, out in the fields, staring up at a cruel sky, waiting for that liberating rain.

But it wasn't water Burroughs needed.

It was only fitting, the adman thought, that William Burroughs should be the first American to taste a nonexistent Swedish vodka.

• • •

Myron Poloner was out of the creative loop and distinctly pissed off by the treatment "the Swedish designers" had bestowed upon him.

But he had established that the Swedish Liquor Monopoly, not Broman's Stockholm agency, was N. W. Ayer's client. He started taking Peter Ekelund out on little field trips to New York's liquor stores. To the great astonishment of the storeowners, Myron ordered them to rearrange their shelves. He placed Ayer's own clear Absolute Vodka bottle alongside the old, beloved hits—Smirnoff, Stolichnaya, and Wolfschmidt—to see how the thing stood up visually. Poloner and the big Swede strode around the store admiring their work from various angles, hemming and hawing like visitors to one of the city's more exclusive art galleries. Then they asked the storeowner to move the bottle an inch or so and walked a few more laps in deep concentration.

After that, Myron investigated caps. He ordered up bottle caps in every shape and color: black, red and gold, big, small, high, low, glass, metal, cork. He changed the caps and placed the bottles up there on the shelves, next to Smirnoff, next to Stolichnaya.

The whole time Myron had a sense of secret happiness.

Gunnar Broman and his taciturn collaborator Hans Brindfors continued to work on the project with Jerry Siano in his Bucks County garage. They discussed different approaches for a future ad campaign. Two years earlier, the Soviets had invaded Afghanistan. Research at Ayer pointed to a remarkable fact: a Russian image might actually hurt a vodka. Siano thought that this was the time for a breakaway campaign—emotional arguments for the American vodka consumer to take leave of the Russian heritage.

Then there were other interesting possibilities, known as the Absolut Something option: Absolut Dry Martini, Absolut Bloody Mary . . . . Broman's partner in Stockholm had sent them a couple of simple sketches that were turned into regular ads at Ayer's studios, just showing a filled glass and Absolut One Drink or Another.

All the time, and sometimes at great length, Broman explained that he didn't want to jazz it up. The copy was on the bottle, not in the ad, so just show the bottle.

Then, going even more minimalist, Broman and Siano came up with: The Absolut Perfection, or just Absolut Perfection. Two words—no more—and the bottle.

Poloner presented the Monopoly representatives with five campaign proposals, all based on the clear bottle. (When Myron told Lou Hagopian about it, he said that the Swedish designers really wanted to stick with their Vikings and hills, but Siano and the others had finally argued them around.)

The copy on the Ayer bottle was based on the "ancient traditions" of Swedish vodka. Although the American admen still had not been able to taste any Swedish vodka, they couldn't resist a fine old story, especially if it was new.

On a bottle that resembled the original molded plastic prototype, Poloner had put a transparent acetate film taped with dark lettering. It read:

ABSOLUT
COUNTRY OF SWEDEN
VODKA

THIS SUPERB VODKA IS MADE
FROM THE GRAINS GROWN IN THE
RICH FIELDS OF SOUTHERN SWEDEN.
DISTILLED AT THE FAMOUS OLD
DISTILLERIES NEAR AHUS,
IT HAS BEEN PURIFIED 10 TIMES
IN ACCORDANCE WITH TRADITIONS
DATING TO THE YEAR 1498.
IN PERFECTING SWEDEN'S
NATIONAL REFRESHMENT, IT
HAS BECOME KNOWN BY THE NAME
ABSOLUT RENT BRAENNVIN,
ABSOLUT VODKA.

It was Broman's copy. Not only had Broman put the five-hundred-year-old traditions of Swedish liquor on the label, he had put the Swedish workingman's cheap potato brew up there in capital letters: ABSOLUT RENT BRAENNVIN. *Renat.*

The ad read:

History

1350

First historic document about distilled alcohol in Sweden.

1494

First prohibition to sell liquor.

1498

License to distill and sell liquor given to Cort Flaskedragare.

Ca. 1575

Introduction of grain vodka

1869

Trademark and label registered for Sweden's all-time market leader.

1978

Decision to start major export venture.

Another ad just showed the bottle. The accompanying copy was:

1498

for

$8.00

The second line of approach was referred to as "The Spirit of Sweden." A pun. Cute. Here was that new and distant homeland of vodka, Sweden, but since they had abandoned Broman's felt-pen sketches in favor of real photos, and since they didn't have any real photos of Sweden, they had abandoned the Swedish countryside.

One of the pictures featured a sleek speedboat crossing an open American waterway. Another showed a group of people dressed in white and draped over a chalk-white veranda. It looked like a scene from *Gone With the Wind.*

Above the imagery, it read:
The Spirit of Sweden.

The third approach was Siano's head-on attack on the Russian enemy:

RUSSIA
MAKES
BETTER
TANKS.

Another ad declared that

WHILE THE
REST OF THE WORLD
WAS MAKING
ABSOLUTE WAR
WE WERE MAKING
ABSOLUT VODKA.

The only image accompanying these slogans was the peace-loving bottle.

The fourth campaign propoeal was a single sentence: THE ABSOLUT OF VODKAS.

In the fifth and last campaign, the Absolut with its missing *e* was joined by some other amputated buddies.

ABSOLUT
DISTINCTIV

and

ABSOLUT WELCOM

Suddenly, everyone at Burlington House started to feel pretty uncertain about what they were seeing—or rather, what they were not seeing.

It had been fun playing the rebel for a while with a bottle that bore no similarities whatsoever to the competition, but now that they had done it, there was a creeping feeling that something was missing. Were they deluding themselves? Hadn't someone suggested the very first time Broman showed up that this wasn't a real bottle? That it was a non-bottle? Now that they thought about it, one statement had emerged from every consumer group and in every liquor store they had visited. Someone always blurted out, "But you can't see it!"

The emperor's new clothes. Facts could no longer be ignored. The bottle was naked. It would disappear the moment it landed on the liquor store shelf or in front of a bar mirror. It might be an adman's wet dream—purity, clarity, and all that—but they had forgotten the most important thing of all: *you had to be able to see the goddamned thing!*

Even though Curt Nycander, the Liquor Monopoly's cautious vice president, knew that the bottle was supposed to be clear as ice, have no label, no colors, just—silver, he was forced to conclude that Brindfors' French bottle was so completely transparent that the text was unreadable. To see it, you had to hold it against a dark background, preferably at a distance of less than fifteen inches from your face.

After the unsuccessful presentation at the Swedish Consulate in New York, Nycander simply didn't dare bring the French bottle to the States with him. The Monopoly's good name had to be protected, not to mention his own. Instead, Nycander had the bottle photographed with a strong backlight, so that Brindfors' elegant silver lettering stood out like pitch-black newspaper headlines screaming of war and murder. In the picture, the bottle's contours had been softened, and it looked like an unidentified flying object cruising through space.

There were people who insisted that they had seen the Loch Ness monster. Nycander knew this. There were those who had met God. Fine. But Curt Nycander—who had recently been promoted—was not going to travel to the United States of America with an invisible bottle. No way. If there was anyone who doubted the existence of the Swedish vodka, well, he had the evidence. He had the photographs. But he did not intend to stand up in front of a bunch of American liquor executives one more time and show them a bottle that they just couldn't see.

Broman had had a special wooden box built to hold three of Brindfors' French bottles. It looked like of a crate of grenades. When the Swedes were boarding the plane from Stockholm to New York, the adman asked Nycander to take one of the boxes. Nycander stiffened. "No," he said. "Quite impossible." He didn't have room. He had to carry his briefcase with the all-important export memos. Broman seethed, then he booked two first-class seats on the Monopoly's tab, one for himself, the other for the bottles.

Neither man uttered a single word to the other throughout the flight.

When Broman realized that Curt Nycander actually listened to what the people at Ayer said, and that alternatives to the French-manufactured label-free bottle had to be produced, he knew that his grand plan was falling apart. Somebody else was grabbing the wheel. He had a good idea who it was.

In order not to have the whole project slip into Ayer's hands, Broman announced that he would produce new alternative bottles in Stockholm—and he would do it on his own.

In his report to the Monopoly, Broman now presented Brindfors' silver-etched bottle as the "completely consistent" Absolut. Then there was his new variation, the "modified" Absolut, with ornamentation and dates, followed by "heritage" Absolut: lots of ornament, silver foil around the neck, dates, background, tradition, and all in *fin-de-siècle* lettering.

Finally, in order to show that he was willing to try almost anything to keep control over the creative process, Broman promised to put a label on the bottle. The label could be done in leather, he explained, or (why not?) in silk.

"So that you can *see* the bottle."

Jerry Siano had seen it coming. Gunnar hated bureaucrats, and he couldn't handle the management people. Something had been cooking for a while. Jerry just couldn't figure out what it was until Neal O'Connor stood in his office one day looking grim.

"Well, I guess the whole deal's off," he said. "It's not gonna work with Gunnar. We're pulling out."

In a way it was nothing to be upset about, just another affiliation on the other side of the globe that was never going to happen. Just another line that would never go on Ayer's letterhead. But this time it was his garage group.

Jerry tried to change Lou's mind.

"No way!" retorted Ayer's CEO. "No way we're gonna do business with that guy!"

That lucky guy, Gunnar Broman, who could have had it all. Could have sold his agency to N. W. Ayer of New York and headed straight for the golf course.

He shouldn't even have been there with his crazy bottles.

All because he couldn't listen to the right people, let them run the show. And now he had gotten nothing.

There was of course one person at Ayer who held an unshakable belief in the undecorated bottle. Myron Poloner. It might not have filled shelves (after all, it was invisible). But it certainly filled Myron's own empty space.

Myron could sit for hours, sunk down into his chair in front of the fake wall with the mock-up shelf, with its plastic prototypes, with the screaming American brands and then—that bottle. That transparent entity.

Finally, Myron Poloner knew how creativity *felt.*

And if you looked very carefully at the bottle that had been used in the Ayer advertising campaigns, you would discover, all the way down at the bottom, under the long text about the extraordinary grain in southern Sweden and the five hundred years of proud liquor traditions, printed in very small letters, two words:

POLONER IMPORTS.

CHAPTER 6

ROOSTAL'S THEORIES

All vodkas are created equal. Ilmar Roostal explains why selling "Renat" is just a matter of subliminal imagery.

As long ago as the 1950s, Ilmar Roostal had read about an American company that had started marketing vodka as a premium product. Roostal thought it was a superb idea. Vodka was one of the purest forms of alcohol, and it cost no more than a couple of cents a liter to make. People in his Estonian homeland had made their own vodka before World War II, before Ilmar had been forced to flee to Sweden. Everyone in Estonia drank moonshine. Vodka was really nothing more than base liquor, the result of distilling grain, or potatoes, or molasses. The more Roostal thought about it, the more he liked it. Sweden produced copious quantities of vodka, right? It made no difference that the Swedes insisted on calling it Renat. Why not load up a tanker with Renat, ship it across the Atlantic, and sell it at a huge markup?

One of Roostal's old classmates from the School of Economics was now head of sales at the Swedish Alcohol Monopoly. When Roostal was passing through Stockholm he called him up and presented his idea. He pointed out that the Monopoly could earn a little pocket money by exporting surplus liquor to the United States. Roostal's classmate asked if he'd been drinking. How the hell could they sell Renat to the Americans?

The Americans didn't drink Renat. Roostal attempted to explain what was going on over there, that everything in America came down to marketing. If only the Americans were told that Renat was vodka, which of course it was, they'd gladly drink it. And if Renat were marketed as a premium product, an expensive, exotic luxury from a faraway land near the North Pole, they'd pay a fortune for the privilege. It was a simple, fundamental principle of profiling. It was easier to create an image for a product with fewer distinguishing qualities, and Renat had virtually none—no taste, no smell, no color. No anything. When it came to the history of the product, well, as far as Roostal knew, Swedes had been drinking Renat since the dawn of time and exporting it since the Vikings pushed out their longboats.

Roostal proclaimed himself willing to conduct a study at no cost to the Monopoly. But his classmate remained unimpressed. No, sorry, Swedish liquor in America? It was the craziest thing he'd ever heard.

For some years before he hatched his vodka export scheme, Ilmar Roostal had been aware that things weren't what they used to be. People still bought cars, and refrigerators, and cigarettes, and kitchen appliances, and cosmetics. But it wasn't the things themselves that interested them any more. There was something else.

Roostal had an American friend who was the editor of *The Journal of Marketing*. His name was Steuart Henderson Britt. Britt was a trained psychologist as well as a professor of marketing. Every time Roostal and his wife traveled to the States, they visited the Britts at their home outside Chicago, and they were always welcome to stay the night. Britt's large house on Lake Michigan was a shrine to the practical joke. When you opened a drawer, springy snakes whacked you in the face. Turning on a lamp got you a water jet in the eye. In the evenings, Roostal used to settle down with Steuart Henderson Britt before a crackling fire in the library and discuss the future of marketing.

On December 27, 1949, Britt had given an address at the American Marketing Association's annual convention. Some hailed it as the speech of the year. Britt tried to answer a question that had confounded marketers for years and went unanswered still. What made the American consumer consume? Some suggested that it was extremely simple: people always needed new things. Britt didn't believe that. There had to be more.

According to Britt, the preceding decade had seen real progress in research into marketing and consumer behavior, but the greatest strides had been in the field of statistics. Researchers could now ascertain the significance of an experimental result to many figures after the decimal point. They had learned to cross-reference their data, and their questionnaires were more precise; but no one had asked the most important question of all: why? Why did they buy? Britt told the gathered marketers that he'd read dozens of studies of beer and soda sales. He knew everything about seasonal variations in sales, which brands sold best, what kind of family bought which kinds of soda, and what the average family consumption was. But, he explained, he still had no idea what complicated, hidden motives provoked them into "sipping, swallowing, and guzzling" twelve billion bottles of carbonated drinks every year. The marketing people just didn't seem to care. The only thing they were interested in, Britt said, was head counts.

Britt had planted a seed that would grow into the big debate of the coming decade. Hundreds of textbooks were written on the subject. Leading universities were forced to reorganize their marketing courses. Research institutes sprang up, and advertising agencies were faced with a whole new way of thinking. And all because Britt gave voice to a thought in the winter of 1949: consumers didn't work the way marketers thought they did; they had hidden, complex motives, and head counting was not going to reveal a thing.

So what were these hidden and complicated motives? Britt's surprising answer was that it was impossible to tell. Human reasoning was so complicated, so hidden, that it was futile to try to interpret it. Well, almost. There was a way. Britt told the marketers the fable of the toothpaste.

Admen had always assumed that people bought toothpaste to have nicer teeth. This belief was so fundamental that no one questioned it. Every toothpaste ad showed happy boys and girls with even, shiny white smiles. They were like movie stars in a world of flashing teeth. But one stubborn researcher refused to believe that it was a desire to be beautiful that drove consumers to brush their teeth twice a day. He was William A. Yoell, and Britt called him a voice crying out in the wilderness. William A. Yoell had devoted himself to the study of consumer behavior, and he claimed now that the real reason people brushed their teeth was that they were afraid to die. The consumer used his toothbrush to banish the microscopic remains of his last meal, which were trapped between his teeth, filling his mouth with a fusty, rotting sensation and reminding him that we are all walking in the valley of the shadow of death.

At the end of the forties, a new toothpaste was launched in which the active ingredient was ammonia. It didn't make teeth the slightest bit whiter, and it was an immediate success. No one but Yoell understood why millions of people would suddenly abandon their faithful old brand and start scrubbing their teeth with ammonia. The answer was that the manufacturers claimed their ammonia toothpaste was antibacterial. Brushing with the new toothpaste left your mouth feeling *really* clean. William A. Yoell was the only researcher who had managed to unearth consumers' complex hidden motives. And the explanation was, according to Britt, that Yoell had not confined himself to simply counting heads. He had conducted—and now Britt uttered a phrase that would soon be very familiar to American marketers—*in-depth interviews.*

Britt confronted his audience with psychological truths in direct contradiction to what they had taken for granted. First, said Britt, everyone is driven by a feeling of insecurity. Insecurity nourishes fear, hate, prejudice, and desperation born of helplessness. Second, the fear leads people to subconsciously build up reservoirs of aggression and hostility that must find some form of expression. And finally, he concluded, all people are searching for status symbols to bolster and inflate their beleaguered egos.

When Britt stepped down from the podium, the romantic dream world of the marketing men had been obliterated. Instead of a happy consumer searching eagerly for further happiness, Britt had given them a new animal: a terrified psychopath, hopped up on adrenaline, ready to protect his ravaged self-esteem by any means necessary.

The American Marketing Association assigned a committee the task of scrutinizing the new method. At first, the committee had trouble deciding what term should be used to describe the new interviewing technique. The members tried several variations: intensive interviewing, detailed interviewing, noncontrolled interviewing, conversational interviewing, informal interviewing, and in-depth interviewing. Eventually they decided to call it the qualitative method.

The qualitative method, the committee reported, aimed to achieve a complete, exhaustive account of every subject's innermost secrets and desires. Instead of asking three thousand respondents if they preferred one or two breast pockets on their suits, as scientists using the quantitative method had been doing for years, the qualitative method aimed to establish what function pockets performed in the life of the individual consumer. How did double pockets affect his personal prestige, or his sex life?

The qualitative method used techniques researchers had always deemed sloppy. There was no statistical selection of subjects. There was no standardized questionnaire. Furthermore, the responses were impossible to convert to numerical results, since the subjects never answered yes or no, or filled in a cross on a Lickert scale from "I agree strongly" to "I disagree strongly." In fact, the responses could be, well, just about anything at all.

The qualitative method, the committee went on, consisted of an *unstructured, undefined* and *investigative* style of interview. The market researchers were no longer observational scientists. Now they were expected to behave like district attorneys. If someone described a certain wrapping paper as "pretty," the interviewer immediately asked what he meant by "pretty." If the subject said he "liked" a product, the DA would instantly probe for the meaning hidden behind the concept of liking. The subject would be mercilessly grilled, steered all the while closer to his innermost self, inside which his complex motives lay.

While researchers using the traditional method were taught that it was a fatal mistake to show any reaction to the subject's responses—the ideal was to use college undergraduates to read the questions tonelessly from a preprinted form—it was "anything goes" in the qualitative method. The interviewer could, if he was entering a particularly sensitive area of questioning, indicate with a gentle nod that he agreed with the respondent's opinion. Yes, of course, colored people *were* different.

If the researcher considered it appropriate, he could even provoke the subject into an answer, a technique that had previously been considered unthinkable.

Sometimes it was regrettably necessary to torture the subject. The committee stated that it was a near impossibility to force someone to talk about a painful topic, but weren't the painful topics the most revealing? A woman who was interrogated as to her reasons for watching TV answered that she thought it was "useful." The interviewer pounced. What did she mean by "useful?" What exactly was it in the TV shows that she considered "useful?" The woman didn't want to answer at first, but the interviewer refused to back down. Eventually she was forced to admit that she had plagiarized a line from a TV show when comforting her sister at her son-in-law's funeral.

It was no longer enough to answer "yes" or "no" or "I agree strongly with this statement"—*everything* the subject said or did was interesting. If, instead of replying to a direct question, the subject burst into tears, the advocates of the qualitative method declared this to be an excellent reaction, worth a thousand standardized questionnaires. Everything the subject did was therefore thoroughly recorded: nervous ticks, yawning, involuntary laughter, evasions, quick glances at the watch, blushing.

Since it was considered that the presence of a stenographer, scribbling frantically in a notebook, might upset the subject as he unraveled his complex hidden motives, it was necessary to construct special rooms for the in-depth interview. Two-way mirrors and tinted glass concealed secretaries, technicians with recording equipment, and specially trained psychologists, as well as bemused, soda company executives.

The qualitative interview caused such a rumpus among the market researchers that the American Marketing Association had to appoint yet another committee to look into the opposition it aroused. A subcommittee was ordered to sort out just precisely what conclusions the original committee had presented in their report. The qualitative method was unstructured—anyone could see that—but it surely couldn't be *that* unstructured.

The members had difficulty agreeing on what they meant by an in-depth interview. The problem was whether the important part was *in-depth,* as half of the committee claimed, or *interview,* as the other half advocated. To avoid embarrassment, the committee sought the help of thirty distinguished members of the Association. The answers they received made them even more confused. Some market researchers were of the opinion that an in-depth interview could take just about any form you liked, so long as the purpose was to uncover the subject's underlying—complex and hidden—motives. Others defined it strictly as any interview that was unstructured, undefined, and investigative in nature. But only if the subject's reactions were closely observed, of course.

Unhappily, stated the committee in their report, the members of the Association were not particularly consistent in their definitions of the in-depth interview. There were, in fact, as many definitions as there were market researchers. The conclusion was that the concept should be discarded for good. The in-depth interview, the committee wrote, could from that day on be forgotten on the dusty shelf of Terms That Didn't Make It, together with other misapplications of social science such as "instincts," "underlying social factors," and "the free market."

But the committee also had a serious warning to issue to the members of the American Marketing Association. It had come to their attention that some researchers had made groundless statements to the effect that their special in-depth techniques were able to reach "deeper" into the mind of the consumer than anyone else's. Some of them claimed *never* to have engaged in head counting at all. Unfortunately, some members of the Association had been taken in by these scurrilous claims. The committee especially wanted to caution against the application of *so-called* analytical psychology in the blessed realm of market research.

Both Roostal and Britt were fully aware of which particular hidden motive lurked behind this danger signal. The red flag was warning about a redheaded Jewish refugee from Vienna currently spreading terror throughout the ad agencies of New York City.

His name was Ernest Dichter.

• • •

Britt was well acquainted with the work of Ernest Dichter. The ideas expressed in his speech at the 1949 convention were in fact culled from an article by Dichter. Britt had quoted Dichter extensively in the speech. Six months before Britt's address, Dichter had made his debut with a manifesto which, though it was only five pages long, would come to be as important to American marketing as Martin Luther's theses were for the Catholic Church.

Dichter claimed that an advertisement could be well written, it could be well designed, it could receive as much attention as you liked, but none of that mattered in the slightest. The aesthetic value of advertising was irrelevant. As a matter of fact, the consequence of professionally designed advertising, he said, could be to strengthen a person's distaste for the product being advertised. It may even encourage that person to purchase a competitor's brand.

This statement sent a chill through the world of American advertising. The big American corporations—Procter and Gamble, Philip Morris, Nabisco, Coca-Cola, Ford, Chrysler, and GM—were, in other words, throwing away hundreds of millions of dollars a year to infuse consumers with an even stronger dislike for their products. That sort of stuff was not nice to hear.

Actually, there had long been an unvoiced opinion that the superexpensive agencies on Madison Avenue were perhaps, just perhaps, not delivering on their promises. It was more of a joke, really, something the marketing chiefs at the big companies would say to each other for comic relief. They were trying to laugh off the nagging feeling they had that it wasn't quite clear who the ad agencies were conning more, the consumers or the clients. Now Dichter had turned up, and he was telling them that American marketing was less than successful. The companies were spending their money on nice pictures and witty copy, and the admen were winning their impressive awards, but were they actually convincing anyone to buy products?

No, said Dichter.

He compared the American advertising industry with a door-to-door salesman, greeting a housewife in one of the shiny new suburbs with the cheery pitch: "Good morning, ma'am! I'm from Woodhaven and Sons, manufacturers of quality ashtrays. Are you in need of an ashtray today?" only to turn on his heel and skip off like a cheery idiot, not waiting for an answer, and never an ashtray sold.

Advertising was not based on scientific research, Dichter reminded them. It just wasn't scientifically defensible. When Dichter spoke of science, he always meant analytical psychology. Historically, advertising was concerned only with the superficial rationalization driving the consumer's behavior: why consumers themselves *thought* they bought or did not buy a certain product, not the hidden reasons actually driving them. Asking people straight out why they preferred one product to another was, in Dichter's eyes, completely meaningless. Consumers had no idea why. And if they did happen to know the answer, there was a big chance that they'd lie about it. Dichter liked to tell the story of a brewer who had canvassed his customers in an attempt to find out which of his products they preferred—the normal beer or the high-class low-alcohol variant. Everyone professed to prefer the light beer, which surprised the brewer, since it had been an unmitigated flop. There was no shortage of similar studies, and Dichter seemed to know them all.

Dichter explained that two things were required to get under the consumer's skin. First, the researcher had to be properly—scientifically—educated. (Preferably a doctor of analytical psychology.) Second, he had to be professionally trained in the qualitative method.

Luckily, Ernest Dichter met both these requirements.

Dichter owed his early fame to a study that came to be known as "The Mistress or the Wife," that had been conducted on behalf of Chrysler. Car salesmen had long been aware that they could entice male customers onto the lot by putting a sports car in the showroom window. They also knew that open-topped cars very rarely sold. For some reason, folks usually went for the good old-fashioned sedans. Dichter had his assistants analyze the phenomenon in a series of in-depth interviews and came to the conclusion that the male customer's subconscious sexual desires were at play. The open-topped sports cars symbolized the men's mistresses. The absence of a roof made them dream of illicit trysts and forbidden sex, and these dreams drove them into the salesrooms. Once there, they awoke to harsh reality, and in order not to reveal their planned infidelities they quickly chose a practical, everyday sedan. In psychoanalytical terms, one could say that male consumers marry sedans, but they dream of having sex with sports cars.

According to Dichter, Chrysler should not be alarmed by the strangely inconsistent behavior of the American male. They should exploit the sexual fantasies of their customers. They could, without trouble, heighten the horny males' forlorn hopes by subtly transferring some of the qualities of the sports car to the normal sedan models.

A short while later, Chrysler launched the hardtop, a car with a removable hard metallic roof. The hardtop was an instant success. Dichter took all the glory. It was inevitable, he explained.

According to Dichter, all products have an individual personality in exactly the same way as human beings, a wholeness into which their individual qualities melt. A Ford has a different personality than a Chrysler, and every car owner knew that.

He spoke of the products' *gestalt,* a term he had taken from Carl Jung's *Gestalttherapie*, which Dichter regarded as one of the most important books of the century. But when he opened his New York practice, Dichter realized that he would never be able to use the word *gestalt* in the United States. He was a Jewish refugee from Vienna. He'd lived across the street from Sigmund Freud for ten years. He held a doctorate in analytical psychology. He didn't want to make things worse by spouting technical jargon in German.

To adapt analytical psychology to the world of American advertising, Dichter needed an English equivalent to *gestalt,* and what he came up with was *image.*

Other advertisers battered consumers with superlatives or dazzled them with technical data, but Dichter and his disciples tried to create a mental image. They no longer regarded themselves as marketing or advertising men.

They were image makers.

The differences among products was now so minimal, said Dichter, that the only possible way to introduce a new product on the market was to exploit subtle, preferably sexually charged, symbolism. By systematically controlling symbols in the name, packaging, and advertising, marketing men could give the product qualities that did not, and never would, exist.

Unfortunately, it was all too easy to choose entirely the wrong symbols. One campaign showed a plain station wagon in a luxurious setting, with the effect that the target group—the working class—felt themselves mocked for their meager bank accounts.

A candy store owner redecorated his entire chain in hospital white, hoping to evoke purity and quality. When Dichter's team assessed the hidden motives of candy eaters, it became apparent why the stores were now standing empty. Customers had come there intending to stuff themselves with junk, to indulge in an orgy of chocolate and jellybeans. In the new clinical environment, their gluttony was cruelly exposed as simple gluttony

Dichter stated that image could not be manufactured to the marketers' liking, not even if they conducted an infinite number of in-depth interviews. It was as futile as attempting to influence a human being's personality through sheer force of will. *The gestalt of the product was a result of history.*

In Germany, several brands had been beaten into extinction when Allied bombers blew the factories to rubble in World War II, halting production for several years. After the war, they rose like a flock of Phoenixes from the ashes, and quickly regained their previous market shares. Brand names had an iron grip on the people. This was a problem for new products, like instant coffee and frozen food. Simply put, they had no history. Such products were as scary as a person with no past. The only solution, Dichter said, was to invent a past.

• • •

Every year, Ilmar Roostal used to organize a seminar on modern marketing for Swiss executives in Geneva. To give the Swiss a breath of fresh air from the outside world, he flew in Steuart

Henderson Britt. Britt tried to bring the concept of image to the Alps, but it wasn't easy.

The Swiss were a practical bunch, obsessed by their precisely ticking clockwork and hermetically sealed vaults. Britt thought the best approach would be to illustrate his point by explaining how a product's nationality affects its image. What foreigners were really paying for when they bought Swiss watches, said Britt, was not any advanced technology that was unavailable elsewhere, but a mental image of Swiss perfection. In a way, you could say that the Swiss had been exploiting imagery for decades, even if they didn't know it. Britt warned them not to be too self-assured. One day someone else might appear, maybe someone from Japan, and copy their watches and cameras and sell them at half the price. The Swiss executives had a good chuckle at that one. Even if it did happen, Britt continued, it would take the usurper an additional period of decades to establish a mental image of perfection. The important part was the difference a consumer *felt* existed between two products, not actual technical discrepancies.

The Swiss always enjoyed Steuart Henderson Britt's little performances. Listening to Britt was like watching a fantastic magician in action. He made it look so easy. He pulled white rabbits from his hat and the audience cooed in appreciation. He could have gone on for hours, everyone loved to listen to him. He strengthened their mental image of the USA as a nation of devil-may-care crackpots.

And then one year Britt turned up with a full beard.

"But, Steuart," exclaimed Roostal, "What's this supposed to mean? You've completely changed your image."

Britt had intended to lecture on the five levels of the ego. There was the "true" ego, the person "I" really was. He used to say the "true" ego with a generous dollop of irony. Since it was all about mental perception, there was actually no place for true or false. Then there was the *"I"* that *I* thought I was. Then there was the "I" that *other* people thought *I* was. So far so good. Now we come to the *"I"* that other people thought I thought I was. Bit more complicated, there. And finally, on the fifth level, was the "I" that I thought that other people thought I was. When he got that far, Britt was usually confused himself. Why did Roostal make that comment about the beard?

Everyone knew that Dichter had also grown a beard, a full, wild, ginger beard.

• • •

Ilmar Roostal grew up in Tallinn, Estonia. When he was eighteen years old, the Russians marched into Estonia, but in the fall of 1941, the country was occupied by the Germans. The following year the German army started conscripting youths of Roostal's age to fight on the eastern front. Roostal and a few of his classmates decided to make their way to Finland and to try to reach Sweden from there. A fisherman promised to take the boys in his boat, but when they arrived at the agreed time, they found he had changed his mind.

For three days Roostal and his friends sat in the back room of the fisherman's shack playing cards and waiting. German border guards occasionally came by, and the boys could hear their heavy boots on the floorboards as they spoke to the fisherman in their loud voices, trying to make him understand German.

Ilmar's family had to stay behind in Tallinn, but they promised to catch up with him when it was all over. Then the Russians came back, and they conscripted every male over the age of seventeen who could lift a rifle. Roostal's father, a doctor, was accused of writing false sick notes for young Estonians, and the accusations were probably true. He was sentenced to seven years hard labor, and he lasted a year. Roostal never found out what happened to his mother and sister. Before he'd reached the age of twenty-two, he was alone in the world. He didn't even have a homeland.

In Stockholm, Roostal learned to speak Swedish and was accepted at the Stockholm School of Economics at the first attempt. As soon as he graduated, he left for the United States and didn't return for fifteen years.

Toward the middle of the sixties, Roostal's wife thought they should go back, so he took a job at one of the consulting agencies in Stockholm, where he led a number of projects with Sweden's leading exporters. One day someone asked if Roostal had heard the latest. The Wine and Liquor Monopoly was going to start exporting, and they were on the lookout for a consultant. Would Roostal be interested? He knew both the European and American markets, and even though no one seriously thought they could get the Americans to drink Swedish liquor, it could be interesting to investigate the possibilities.

At the Monopoly, a young man in a three-piece suit explained to Roostal through a haze of cigar smoke that they wanted a clear analysis of the major liquor markets. This was to be a full-scale report on the potential for selling Swedish liquor throughout the world.

No one at the Monopoly remembered that Roostal had told his old classmate, the head of sales, exactly what to do fifteen years earlier. Ship the clear stuff to America. When Ilmar Roostal accepted the job, he had an ulterior motive.

He wanted to meet Ernest Dichter.

CHAPTER 7

HAGAR'S HISTORY

Helmut Hagar tells the strange story of Swedish liquor, and how the teetotallers ended up selling the alcohol.

The men from the Monopoly climbed the stairs up to the lair of Helmut Hagar, curator of the museum. They needed academic expertise, and they had come to ask Hagar if he could put together a short but comprehensive history of Swedish Spirits.

"We are going to export our liquor," they proudly announced. "To the Americans."

Hagar stared at them incredulously.

"To the . . . ?"

"Yes indeed." And, they wondered, could he maybe keep the text to the minimum? Pictures were the main thing, they told Hagar. "So the Americans can look at it without having to read it," they explained. "You know how they are; always in a rush."

The first time Helmut Hagar had tried to buy a bottle of liquor in Sweden was back in the 1940's, in a store on Norrland Street. When the clerk asked him for his Liquor Pass, he told her he didn't have one. Where he came from, they had never heard of liquor passes. Terrified, she gaped at him as though he had just dropped his pants.

"Liquor Pass!" she screamed. "LIQUOR PASS! *Must* have Liquor Pass!"

As he sat down to work on his easy-read book of liquor history, Hagar thought that of all the peoples of the world, none had such a complicated relationship with alcohol as the Swedes. The first thing they say when you visit is always, "have a drink and be human."

Thus began Helmut Hagar´s picture book of Swedish Spirits:

In the time of the great plague, one third of Stockholm's population perished. In some parts of the country there were not even enough men left to bury the dead.

To alleviate the horror, King John III turned to the royal pharmacist, Simon Berchelt, and ordered him to concoct a remedy. The result was Aqua Vitae Oppositum, the Water of Life to Cure Everything. This medicament was a purified alcohol distilled from Rhenish wine, to which had been added ground horn of unicorn, one part crushed red coral, one part ground ivory, one small part burnt elk-antler, as well as an unknown quantity of spices and herbs.

Archbishop Petrus Gothius blessed the royal medicament. Benedictus Olai, the respected physician-in-ordinary to the King, proclaimed, after having tasted the concoction, that in the pernicious throes of pestilence, men should strive to delight in life's bounteous joys and dwell not on the mortality of the flesh.

Drink to keep death at bay.

After tasting the royal elixir, King John and his queen, Catherine Jagellonica, were stricken by thirst. This was a thirst unlike any other they had ever known. No matter what they tried—water, cow's milk, goat's milk, or the blood of a freshly slaughtered sow—the thirst remained. A burning dryness seared their guts, as if a fire was destroying their innards. Only by imbibing more of the royal medicament could they find relief.

In the Beginning was the Thirst.

•

Every morning the king and the queen sat down at the great council table in the royal palace, and they downed fourteen liters of the royal medicament a day. Still, this was not enough.

Soon the thirst had spread throughout the court. Depending on the season, Princess Elisabeth drank two-and-a-half liters a day. The Catholic monks in service to the queen demanded a fixed ration of 1,700 liters a year. (To his Lutheran chaplains the king, wisely, did not grant a drop.)

The French envoy wrote that at the palace in Stockholm he had, with his own eyes, seen the royal couple raise to their eager lips a five-foot-high goblet, so big a child could have drowned in it.

All who drank of the royal elixir soon felt the onslaught of all-consuming Thirst. At first, imbibers of the potion felt a certain lightness buoy up their chests. It was as if the soul was a palace whose doors had been flung wide open. Soon afterwards, though, a great hole opened at the very core of each one's being.

• • •

It was not until the boldest of all the great twentieth-century reforms was enacted that the Swedes' unfortunate and ancient love of the bottle was ended, at a stroke, by the alcohol regulation system.

The leaders of the Social Democratic Party made a significant discovery in the early 1900s: public enemy number one was neither the capitalist nor the aristocrat. What did people have to fear from them now that they were to have the vote? Although it could never be declared openly, the real problem was in their own ranks. People just weren't coming to party meetings. They didn't have what it took to see a general strike through. They had no desire to read books and improve their minds, and until they were prepared to do so, the labor movement would never gain power over the means of production. It would never govern the social structure.

Labor movement activists spoke gloomily about the way things were. Down in Malmö the transport workers' union would post a notice of meetings to be held at eight in the evening, but not a soul would show up. Why? Because the workers were drinking in the beer halls. One bright young man suggested opening a bar in the labor movement's own community center to attract the men to union meetings. So they rolled in a few barrels and the next meeting degenerated into a tidal wave of fury. Fights broke out in the hall, and one burly man fought his way to the podium, raised his fist, and declared that all capitalists should be shot at sunrise. Another worker reeled on unsteady legs, face to face with the chairman over a pitcher of water that stood between them on the tabletop. When he was told to go back to his seat, he yelled in the chairman's face, at the very leader of the transport workers' union in Malmö, the man who was in the process of creating the New Swede. "What the hell are you looking at?" the New Swede shouted. "Do you think I'm gonna piss in your pitcher, you asshole?"

This problem weighed heavily on the minds of those legendary leaders of the workers' movement. How could they ever separate the Swede and his bottle? If they failed (God forbid!), the entire reform program wouldn't amount to a hill of beans.

And so, Hagar mused, as he worked on another drawing for his history book, their irrefutable logic gave rise to the most illogical system of control and regulation that the world had ever seen.

• • •

At the Medical Council's debate on alcohol in February 1908, a young man took the floor and claimed to have the solution to the alcohol policy problem.

His name was Ivan Bratt, Dr. Ivan Bratt. He was thirty years old, and he had looked the victims of alcohol abuse in the eye at Katarina Hospital in Stockholm. Dr. Bratt's position was clear. He did not deny the adverse effects of alcohol abuse, but he did not believe in total prohibition. "Alcohol use is not our enemy," he declared, "our enemy is alcohol abuse." Only those who could not drink in moderation should be prevented from drinking. The rest had nothing to fear.

In 1913, Bratt started a company he called The Stockholm System Ltd. in order to apply for the exclusive license to sell liquor in the capital. Director Rubensson, current holder of the license, fell over laughing when he heard about it. "Bratt? Bratt? Who is this Bratt?" It was ridiculous. What the hell did Bratt know about selling alcohol? Bratt was granted the license, and at thirty-five years old, overnight he became the new Liquor King.

Bratt's original idea was that some form of identification card was all that was needed. Those who couldn't handle their booze would simply be denied access to it, and everyone else could buy as much as they liked. It soon became apparent that such a scheme would depend on establishing where use disintegrated into abuse, and that could be difficult. Bratt then toyed with the idea of coupons, but this scheme also had problems.

It was theoretically possible for someone who drank in moderation to sell their surplus coupons to an alcoholic. Finally, he issued a special book to every citizen of Stockholm and he called it the liquor pass. The first pillar of the Bratt system was in place.

Bratt decided that those in full command of their senses would be allowed to indulge in sixteen liters of hard liquor per quarter. Or, in other words, about a liter and a quarter of Renat a week. This was considered a generous but by no means extravagant amount. For the next thirty years, the liquor pass was the most important document most Swedes possessed. It was more important than a passport, more closely guarded than a last will and testament, more cherished than a marriage certificate. It was holier than the Bible.

Without the liquor pass a God-fearing Swede could not get his hands on a drop of legal liquor.

When Bratt had established a stranglehold on the consumption of domestic alcohol in Stockholm, the private wine importers in the city's more prosperous neighborhoods experienced an immediate surge in sales. Bratt realized that he would have to take control of these expensive imported beverages, too. The result was an upper-class revolt. Bratt, whom they had regarded as a noble man of medicine with a mission to save the misguided, hard-drinking hoi polloi, had turned on them! The editor of the conservative *Swedish Daily News* almost had a stroke. Ivan Bratt was nothing more than a socialist in disguise!

Bratt quickly saw that it would be impossible to solve the alcohol problem as long as the market was controlled by private businessmen. He decided to rewrite the rulebook once more. He entered into talks with the distillers and wine merchants, explaining to them that he was their only hope of avoiding a catastrophe. His argument was compelling. The teetotalers were well on the way to forcing through a total ban on alcohol. If they succeeded, the market would disappear overnight. The distilleries, the bottling plants, the licensed stores, all would be forced out of business, and not a penny would be paid in compensation. Bratt made them an offer they couldn't refuse.

Simultaneously, he informed the Treasury that in the event that he should take complete control of the production of alcohol in the nation—and he didn't doubt for a second that he would—all profits would be channelled directly into the state coffers. The Treasury thought it was the most reasonable proposal they had heard in a very long time.

In the first year, Bratt bought out forty-four companies, fifty-four the following year. It became apparent that he was more than just a doctor, lobbyist, and promoter of alcohol policy; he was a polished businessman, a natural. He paid with borrowed millions, conducted mergers, and made deals. It took him four years to piece together a private monopoly.

In 1917 he founded the Wine & Spirits Central—the Monopoly—and gave the state the right to buy out the shares unchallenged. The company consisted of five warehouses, two realty companies, eleven sales agents, a distillery, the largest brewery in the country—the Carnegie brewery—and the pharmaceutical company Astra (today the Swedish–British giant AstraZeneca). It owned the classic Grand Hotel in Stockholm and a chain of dispensing pharmacies.

The Monopoly was, besides being the ultimate arbiter of liquor sales in Sweden, the second pillar upon which Bratt's national alcohol policy rested. All profit would henceforth be eliminated from sales of alcohol.

It took five years for the government to realize what had happened.When the politicians came around, they could only declare that there was a state of monopoly. But the Treasury had already been reaping the rewards. Two years previously, Bratt's company had taken home five million crowns. That was 10 percent of the state budget.

Just months after taking over the capital city, Bratt had been possessed by a new insight. It was, of course, entirely pointless to have the city of Stockholm in a state of siege if there was no control in the rest of the country. People were simply traveling outside the city limits to buy their booze. The new goal, he declared, must be to establish a structured system of control over sales throughout the nation. The entire population could not be overseen by a couple of civil servants in Stockholm, naturally. An army of controllers was therefore assembled. The control of alcohol consumption was entrusted to a small department originally intended to ensure that alcohol was of the proper strength: the Control Agency.

Bratt had issued more than a million liquor passes. In the summer of 1920, the Control Agency revoked four hundred thousand of them. Nationwide registers were compiled listing the names of alcoholics and those at risk of becoming alcoholics. People's marital status was recorded, along with information about their place of residence, income, and tax details. Misbehavior could result in a note in the register, and much prized information was gathered about suspect individuals in small towns by asking their neighbors. Not paying tax, questionable morals, unemployment, almost anything could be proof of an unhealthy relationship with alcohol.

Bratt himself now warned that the system could be interpreted as an infringement of human rights. But the wheels of bureaucracy were turning. The Bratt system had a life of its own, with or without its creator.

The Control Agency demanded that details of all liquor sales should be kept in a personal register—permanently. The bureaucracy reached new heights. In Gothenburg, eleven people were employed full time on the allocation of passes. The head of System Company in Uppsala declared that his register would never be completed—and that was exactly the right attitude.

Control agents showed up in the middle of the night and demanded to be shown the registers. They raided warehouses and inspected the contents of the barrels. If you were holding a party, you were permitted to buy more than your standard allowance. So the Control Agency ordered the liquor stores to inform them of every party taking place in the whole country. Every one. With all the details. Fiftieth birthdays, wedding receptions, office parties. Who was there, and how much did they drink?

And Bratt's original idea had been so straightforward: the abusers would be stopped from drinking and no one else had anything to fear. Out of that simple idea had sprung a tangled jungle of rules and regulations, exceptions to the rules, and rules for the exceptions. In the end, the Bratt system became so despised that Bratt was forced to move to Paris.

The museum curator Helmut Hagar thought, "What that man had done was unforgivable. He had succeeded."

When the old distillers were forced to sell out to Bratt in 1917, they all became quite rich. But they still demanded that their offspring should enjoy the same privilege their fathers had had: free access to alcohol.

One dispossessed mother had personally called on the head of the newly created Monopoly, boasting that her son had such an acute sense of smell that he could, just by sticking the tip of his nose in the children's pillowcases, determine who had slept on which pillow. The Monopoly appointed the manufacturers' sons as official wine tasters. Hagar had glimpsed them in the holy inner sanctum of the Monopoly's tasting room, hunched over their little tin casks trying to make contact with the wine's spirit.

Swallowing was not allowed. Not even the Monopoly's world-renowned wine tasters were allowed to actually drink. The winetaster general was a big Buddha of a man who could easily have filled one of the old oak barrels in the cellar. On the day of his retirement he asked for permission to go all the way. And from the highest authority came the dispensation—you may swallow. His colleagues watched him expectantly. But that foreign liquid must have gone to the winetaster general's head, because he fell headlong and heavily, made a flailing attempt to get up but again collapsed, tumbling through an office divider, dragging tables, chairs, and fellow workers into one big howling pile, until he la,y motionless on the floor.

• • •

Hagar the curator had often gone out to the old nineteenth-century liquor factory on the Reimersholm island to collect artifacts for his museum. The whole area reeked of alcohol-rich fusel oil. It seemed to seep from the walls and practically drip from the ceiling. There were bottles everywhere, cans and barrels in every nook and cranny.

But the workers looked as if they were mulling over some deep philosophical problem. "Liquor?" they asked, in deep denial.

• • •

After World War II, a commission was appointed to investigate the possibility of reforming the Bratt system, to reduce the red tape and end the Big Brother policy. The chairman of the commission declared that he would liberate the masses from the tyranny of the Liquor Pass. The socialist prime minister responded by saying that if he'd known the outcome of the commission's report, he'd have appointed a different chairman. The champions of the working class had come round to Bratt's way of thinking. The socialists knew the workers made a lot of noise about the Liquor Pass, but they also knew that many of them were secretly content—a liter a week was, after all, not too bad; it was almost *lagom*. And they knew that in almost every Swedish home was a housewife who blessed the pass for an orderly budget and a quiet life.

These were the years during which Sweden rose from poverty to become one of the richest countries on earth. And all the wealth the workers had created, the schools and hospitals, bridges and roads, all that could just as easily have been invested in rotting the livers of the people. As it was, working-class families could suddenly afford to keep their children in school. Swedish industry was at the cutting edge of technological development. They were making progress faster even than the United States, and it was all due to the newfound sobriety of the average Swedish worker, formerly so devoted to the demon drink. The love affair was over. The workers turned up sober in the morning, and they were every bit as clear-headed when they went home in the evening.

The socialists knew that the popularity they would gain from abolishing the pass would be a poisoned chalice. If they relaxed rationing, allowing two or four or eight liters a week, they'd win the hearts of men, but the cost would be measured in collective misery. No amount of popular support was worth that. Besides, there was a higher price to be paid. It wasn't just the newfound material wealth of the country that was at stake. They had created a whole new social structure. Nowadays, when the unions held their meetings, the workers were no longer angrily demanding that capitalist overlords be strung up by their intestines. No, they had begun to talk of *their* Sweden. They were pioneers; they had laid the foundations for their new social order. And they had no intention of abandoning their baby on the doorstep of the management.

In its forty-year reign, the Liquor Pass had made a powerful enemy, an enemy devoted to the destruction of the Bratt system, whatever the consequences. This hostile force was neither the distinguished old readers of the *Swedish Daily Times* who had campaigned for Ivan Bratt's deportation, nor was it the country's heavy drinkers and hapless winos.

The enemy was, oddly, the Temperance Movement.

The teetotalers despised the pass and its inventor to such a degree that they refused to sit on the board of the system. They declared the Liquor Pass to be a cancer on the kingdom of Sweden.

The implementation of the Liquor Pass had been nothing less than a catastrophe for the Temperance Movement, for it had ended all debate about a total ban on alcohol. Wasn't it bad enough, the people argued, that an honest working man was limited to one liter a week? Was he to be deprived of even this small pleasure? Nowadays, few men and women stood up at temperance meetings swearing never again to touch a drop. It was heavy drinking that had driven the men to the meetings in the first place, the misery of alcoholism had been their motivation, and the Liquor Pass had cured the epidemic. No alcoholics, no teetotalers. This was the terrible reality facing the total abstainers. And what was their conclusion? The Liquor Pass was the major stumbling block on the path to prohibition.

During the forties and fifties, the soldiers of sobriety embarked on a new crusade, once more galvanized by a common goal—the Bratt system must go. They claimed that the pass had had the opposite effect to the one desired; it had created a suggestive influence. It gave people the impression that they had a God-given right to get roaring drunk. As long as they didn't drink more than their fair share, they had the blessing of the government. The Liquor Pass was a drinking license. No, said the abstainers, alcohol must be set free. So that it could be abolished. It was the only reasonable conclusion.

Slowly but surely, support for the Temperance Movement grew. Leading liberal newspapers editorialized on the movement's new pragmatism and the strength of their arguments. The suggestive influence became an accepted phenomenon—suddenly it was so obvious. The people thought of nothing more than how to get their hands on more liquor. What did people talk about at the office and on the street? Drink. What was the first thing a Swede brought up when he met a stranger? As surely as the Englishman talked about the weather, the Swede spoke about booze. In the early 1950s, the movement claimed to have scientific evidence that the abolition of the Liquor Pass would not lead to increased alcohol abuse. Rather, removing the suggestive influence would actually *decrease* consumption. And so the party folded. The legendary heroes of Swedish socialism, so supportive of Bratt in the preceding decades, hung him out to dry. Why should they preserve a system so evidently unpopular, a system, furthermore, responsible for this powerful suggestive effect that turned decent Swedes into hardened winos?

On 1 October 1955 the Liquor Pass was abolished.

From Monday to Friday of the first week after abolition, alcohol sales increased fivefold. On the Saturday, the traditional night to party, there were three times the normal number of drunk and disorderly cases. By the end of the month, there were more cases than in the entire preceding year. After two months, levels exceeded the record set in 1912. The first cases of delirium were recorded in November, and the trickle of patients became a steady stream, then a flood. A couple of people died from acute alcohol poisoning each month. The press reported that people weren't just drinking at home, in the bars, at work, in parks, on the streets; they were drinking in hospitals, nursing homes, drying-out clinics.

Gunnar Broman *credit: Hans Gedda*

Dr. Ivan Bratt (1878–1956); social reformer, founder of the Wine and Spirits Corporation and the Swedish liquor control system, or "the System." *Credit: Reportagebild.*

L. O. Smith (1836–1913); "The Liquor King." With his best-selling product, the "ten-times refined or absolute pure vodka," Smith took control over the Swedish liquor market. He later became one of Europe's largest producers of unrefined spirits. Smith died a poor man after having been twice wealthy and twice bankrupted. *Credit: Reportagebild.*

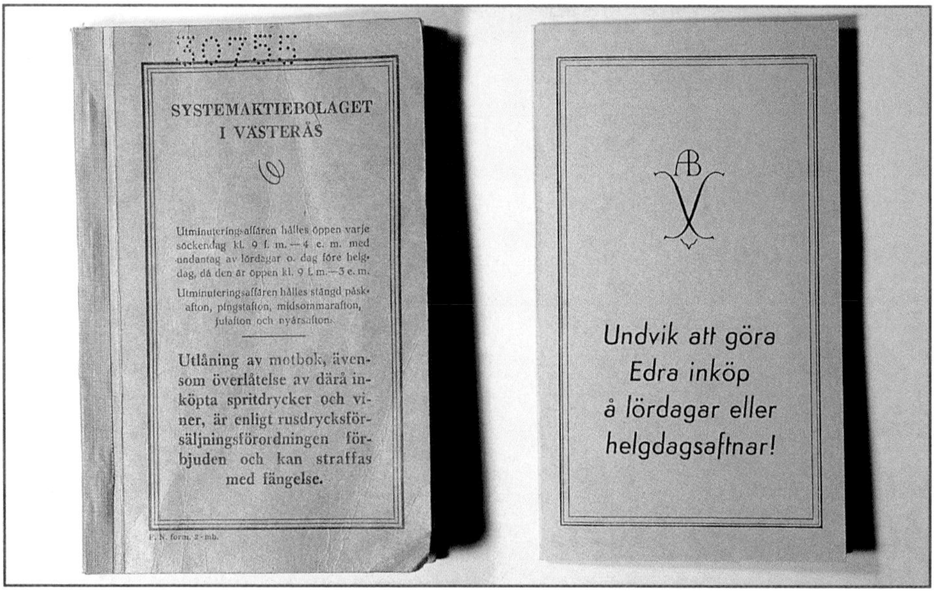

Swedish Liquor Pass
Credit: Pica pressfoto.

Hans Brindfors, art director at Carlsson & Broman agency, photographed today with the first bottle: Brindfors refused to budge from the silver lettering. *Credit: Gunilla Welin.*

Absolut Original: The first bottle was made at the Saint Gobain glassworks outside of Paris. *Credit: Brindfors Enterprise.*

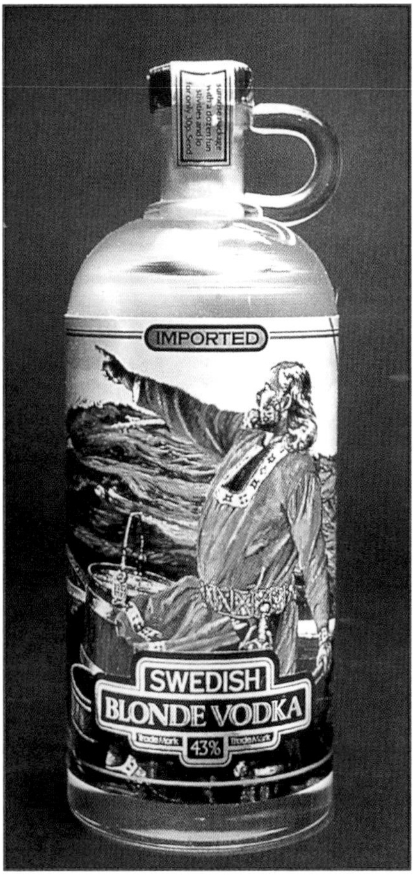

One of the first prototypes of the bottle for the Swedish vodka—quickly abandoned.

Jerry Siano, chief creative officer of N. W. Ayer.

Gunnar Broman and Lars Börje Carlsson: The Carlsson & Broman agency billed the Monopoly $157,000 for its work on the Absolut account (expenses included). Today more than 80 million are sold worldwide each year (50 million in the U. S.). The Swedish Liquor Corporation is rumoured to have been offered more than $3 billion for the Absolut brand alone. *Credit: Victor Lenson Brott*

left: Arnie Arlow, creative director of TBWA from 1984 to 1994, headed the team that made Absolut Vodka one of the most successful campaigns in advertising history.

right: Myron Poloner, the young assistant to Ayer's powerful chairman, wanted the stylishly designed Swedish bottle. He did not want the Swedish designers.

Original sketches, calligraphy, seals, and bottles from Asp & Jönsson design shop.
The American admen wanted more ornamentation and merry colours.

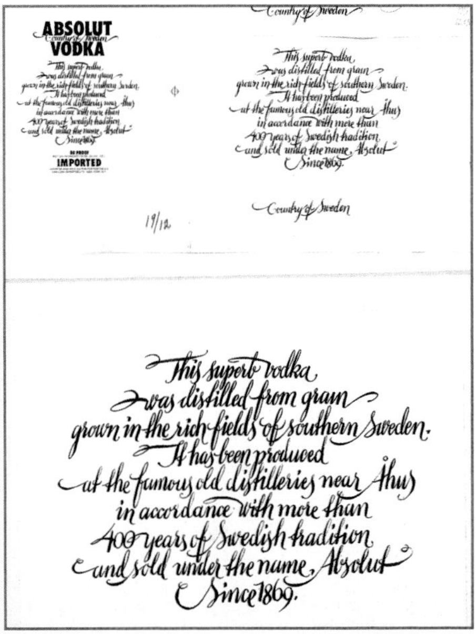

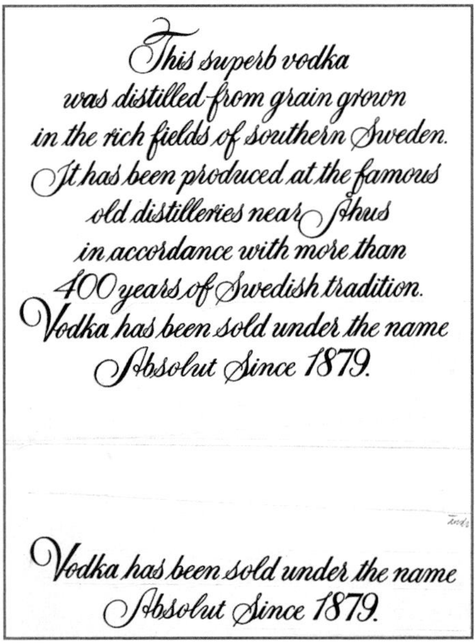

Country of Sweden seals 1869

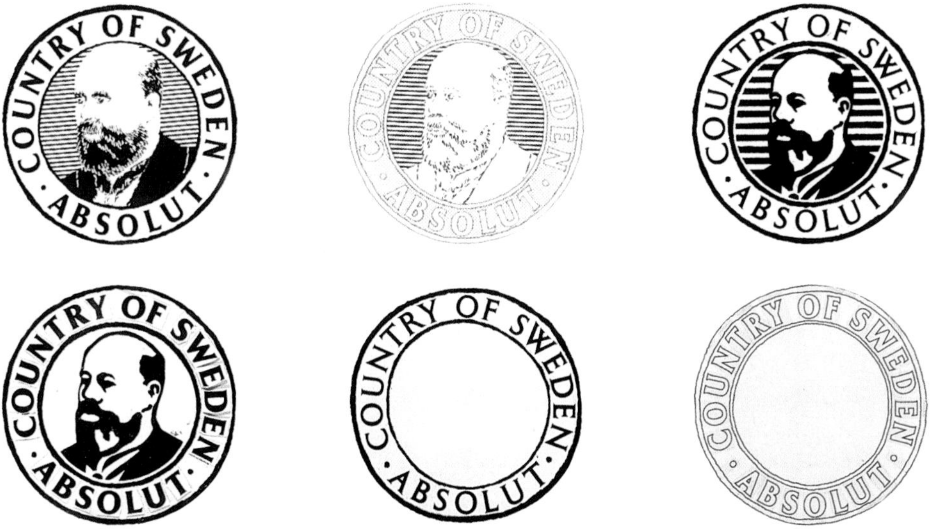

L. O. Smith seals

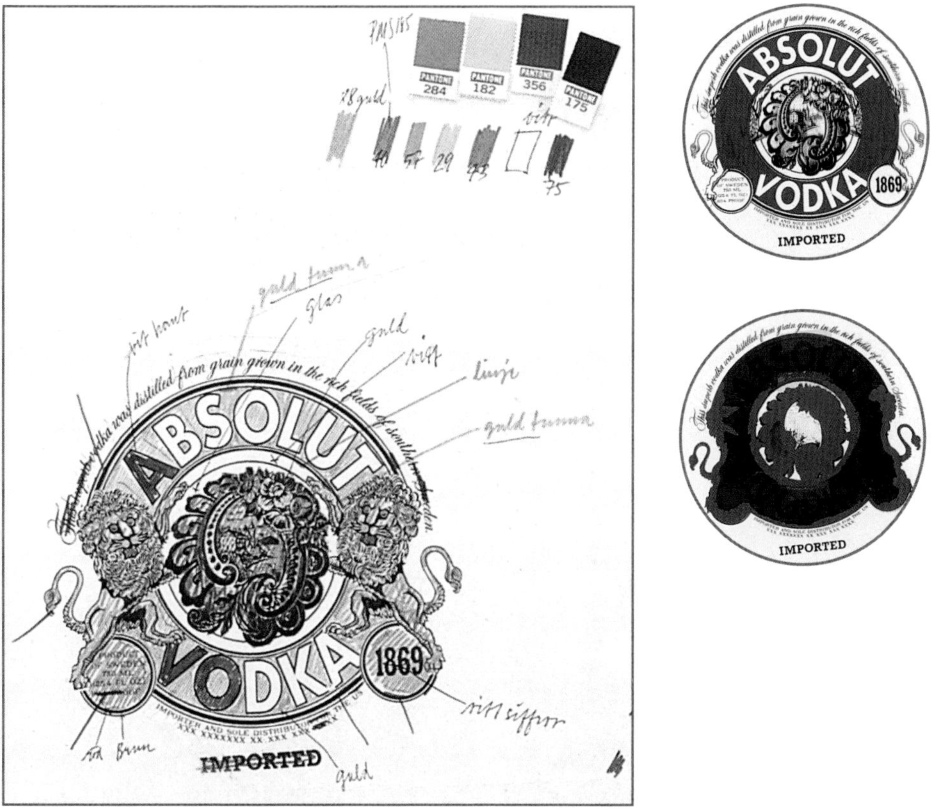

Absolut Vodka lion & heraldry seals

Manilla script samples

Colored Absolut mockups

As the number of bottles grew at the Carlsson & Broman agency in Stockholm, so did the Americans' impatience.

Curt Nycander: The cautious consultant soon became executive vice president at the Swedish Liquor Monopoly.

Lars Lindmark, CEO of the Swedish Wine and Spirits Corporation: Lindmark came from the State adminstration and wanted to turn the old liquor Monopoly into a model state-owned corporation. *credit: Pressens Bild*

Peter Ekelund: Straight out of school, the young maverick Ekelund started to work for Lindmark; to everyone´s amazement he chose to devote himself to the "export project."

Bill Tragos and Michel Roux: A Greek American, and an American Frenchman.

Titi Wachtmeister and Olof Tranvik: Titi never married her teenage sweetheart, the King of Sweden, but she became the Queen of New York. *Credit: Petter Oftedal.*

Provisional ads for the Swedish vodka by Jerry Siano´s group at N. W. Ayer

Ayer used the same picture with three different two-word slogans:
Absolut Everything, Absolut Distinctiv, Absolut Welcom

The classic Absolut ads by art director Geoff Hayes and copywriter Graham Turner of TBWA. They are a client´s wet dream, consisting only of the product and a line. The baseline is two words. One of them is the brand name. *credit: Steve Bronstein, photographer*

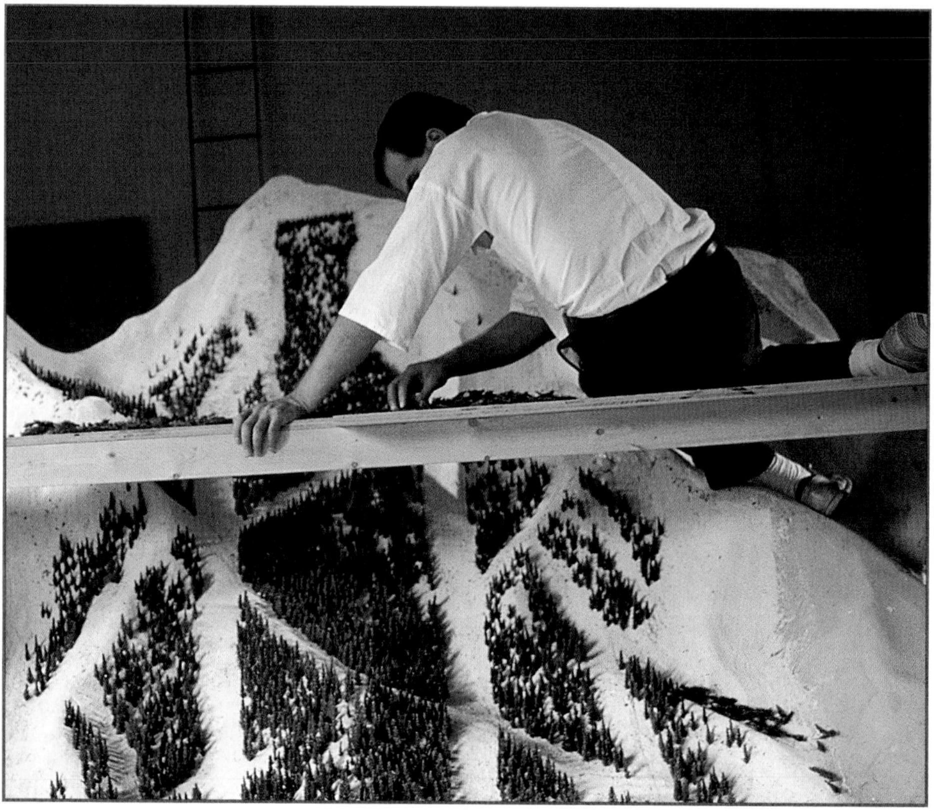

Steve Bronstein constructs the set for Absolut Peak: Preparations sometimes take weeks. Pictures for the Absolut ads are always shot in a studio with a minimum of post-session computer manipulations. *Credit: Steve Bronstein*

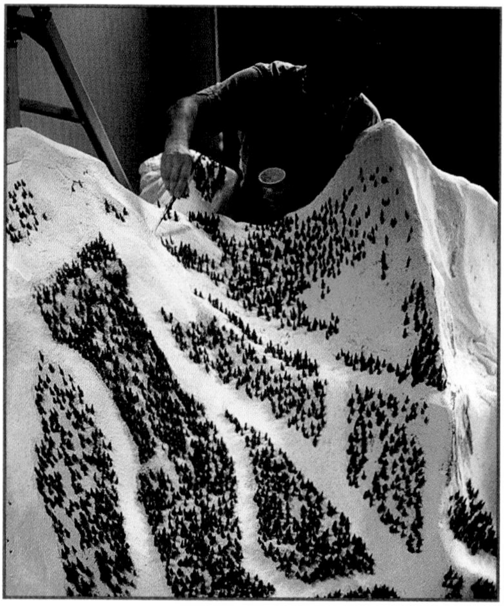

ABSOLUT PEAK.
ABSOLUT® VODKA. PRODUCT OF SWEDEN. 40 AND 50% ALC/VOL (80 AND 100 PROOF). 100% GRAIN NEUTRAL SPIRITS. ABSOLUT COUNTRY OF SWEDEN VODKA & LOGO, ABSOLUT, ABSOLUT BOTTLE DESIGN AND ABSOLUT CALLIGRAPHY ARE TRADEMARKS OWNED BY V&S VIN & SPRIT AB. ©1994 V&S VIN & SPRIT AB. IMPORTED BY THE HOUSE OF SEAGRAM, NEW YORK, NY.
THOSE WHO APPRECIATE QUALITY ENJOY IT RESPONSIBLY.

Absolut Warhol: the famous pop artist asked Roux to ask him to paint the bottle.

Now that the catastrophe was a reality, the *Daily Times* dryily observed that anyone with a modicum of foresight should have seen it coming. Everyone knew that the working class had a love affair with the bottle.

At a triumphant conference six months later, the chairman of the Temperance Movement declared the alcohol debate to be more alive than it had been for half a century. Liquor, he enthused, had become a national concern once again. A leading light in the movement announced that they had more money than ever. Government grants were pouring into their war chest and drunks were rolling into their meetings. More than eighteen thousand new members had been registered. The months following the abolition of the Liquor Pass were indeed a golden age for the Temperance Movement.

As early as November, the government had realized its mistake, but there was no way back. The poor gullible socialists who had swallowed the fable of the suggestive influence decided in their rage to let the movement take responsibility for the monster they had created. The government merged the Bratt system stores into one company, called it the System Corporation, and placed the teetotalers on the board of directors. And they put them on the board of the Liquor Monopoly as well.

On that day, Hagar wrote, Sweden became the only country in the world where the teetotalers sold the booze.

CHAPTER 8

SMIRNOFF COUNTRY

The Swedish contender will have to fight the world champion—Smirnoff—in the American market. In Sweden, Lars Lindmark battles The System.

By the time Roostal's world tour reached San Francisco, he was more convinced than ever that the whole venture was a joke. The Liquor Monopoly had officially sent the consultant on a global search for ripe export markets, but every time he tried to report to the three directors, they just turned a tired gaze his way and said: "Some other time, Roostal. Some other time."

Ilmar Roostal checked in at the consulate in San Francisco and was granted an audience with the consul general, Cecilia Nettelbrandt. The morning he arrived, the consul was dressed in green—green dress, green jacket, green stockings, and, something new to Roostal, green glasses. At the reception that evening, here she was again, but this time in cornflower blue. Roostal made a quick visual check. Yep. Cornflower glasses were planted on her nose. Roostal had never seen anyone with such a distinct personal image as the Swedish consul in San Francisco. She was as easily recognizable as a Coca-Cola bottle on a soda stand.

Speaking of which. At the reception Roostal was introduced to a representative from Pepsi-Cola. Pepsi ran the Stolichnaya agency in the United States, which basically meant they received

Russian vodka instead of hard cash in exchange for the Pepsi sold in the USSR.

Roostal quickly pulled out Hagar's famous picture book of liquor history. The man from Pepsi-Cola studied Hagar's masterpiece with great interest. He found it amusing that the Swedes had called liquor "medication" for hundreds of years.

That's when consul Nettelbrandt jumped on the Monopoly's traveling consultant and ordered him in Swedish "Put away your picture book, Roostal. There's no point in you coming here and blabbing on about liquor, because the parliament will never approve of any exports."

She turned to the Pepsi man and spoke soothingly to him in English.

"He's just an old fool with foolish dreams. The Swedish parliament will never allow this. You see, alcohol is very dangerous."

There was a new administration in power in Sweden, loaded with teetotalers. Maybe that's why Nettelbrandt got so worked up.

Roostal had to understand, the consul told him afterwards, that this was nothing personal. "I was an accountant at the Monopoly for six years. I know what I'm talking about. Kinna-Erik, poor man, was a very close friend of mine. And I can tell you, Roostal, that no liquor will ever be exported from Sweden."

• • •

When Kinna-Erik's replacement at the head of the Liquor Monopoly, Lars Lindmark, was trying to lure young Magnus Lagerkvist over to the Monopoly, he understood that the hook would need some juicy bait.

"I've decided to look into our export possibilities," Lindmark confided. "We're going to sell some liquor abroad."

He stopped himself short.

"Magnus, for God's sake, not a word of this to anyone. It's a bit of a sensitive issue, if you know what I mean."

Lagerkvist found that he had landed in a strange business. At the Monopoly they talked endlessly about tradition, production expertise, and their goddamned taste buds. So he did a small experiment. The Monopoly sold a whiskey called Standard Selection, which was considered to be of very poor quality. At Lagerkvist's home town of Luleå, way up north, close to the Arctic Circle, a family acquaintance was always going on about how the only thing he ever drank was Ballantine's scotch. All other whiskies were donkey piss, and the worst among them was that damned Swedish Standard Selection.

In the interest of science, Lagerkvist had therefore served Standard Selection out of a Ballantine's bottle. The whiskey expert of the Arctic sniffed and tasted and affirmed that it was the real thing, until Lagerkvist informed him of the switch.

The man then stood up and threatened to beat the crap out of Lagerkvist.

From this experiment, Magnus Lagerkvist was able to draw the conclusion that liquor affected everything in the head except the taste buds. A short time later, Standard Selection was replaced by a new whiskey, named Selection of 1923, which became a huge success. Finally, the experts declared, the Swedes have learned the difference between cheap donkey piss and whiskey.

But, as Lagerkvist used to point out, it was neither the customers, the donkey, nor the drink that had changed. Just the label.

Magnus Lagerkvist sat down in a cloud of cigar smoke and set up the "Export Project."

Solely for the sake of research, Lagerkvist then made a couple of really long trips to the major liquor companies in the United States. He was received like a king: a helicopter when he landed at the airport, a red carpet when the helicopter came to rest. He shook hands with the CEOs, and they exchanged views over cocktails. Lagerkvist lit his cigars and nodded. The Americans gave him all the information he asked for and more. Even classified information they would not share with anyone else was now laid out at the feet of twenty-seven-year-old Magnus Lagerkvist, representing the world's largest importer of brewed and distilled beverages. The CEOs nodded and lined up in a row when Lagerkvist was about to helicopter away. But, they always added, this is a very tough business. No foreigner has ever succeeded in earning any real money selling liquor to Americans.

It was Lagerkvist's idea to move the whole project over to a big American advertising agency. An exploratory meeting was set up with the heads of N. W. Ayer. Lagerkvist explained to the American admen that he had analyzed the marketing problem and concluded that Sweden was a salable concept.

"When we say Sweden," Lagerkvist lectured, "Americans think clean environment, clean water, blond girls. That's not a bad start."

"Bullshit," one of the admen barked. "The typical American has no idea what Sweden is. It's like part of the Soviet Union or Switzerland or something."

• • •

When Ilmar Roostal asked the three directors at the Monopoly about earlier efforts to export alcohol, they explained that as early as the 1950s an attempt had been made to export the classic Swedish products. Dressed up in newly printed labels in

English, bottles of glogg, punsch, and aquavit were sent off to the Swedish communities in Minnesota. What a goddamned stupid idea! Roostal had met the second generation Swedes, the immigrants' children. Conservative as granite. And half of them were teetotalers.

Roostal quietly cursed the fact that they hadn't listened to him in the early sixties. That's when the vodka train had left the station. In 1966 whiskey sales accounted for two thirds of the American liquor market. Now, ten years later, it was only 50 percent. Vodka had become fashionable, just as Roostal had predicted. A whole new group of customers had appeared: women and young people who wanted to have a lighter and whiter product. They used it as a mixer, of course. Americans blended vodka with orange juice and tomato juice and God knows what else. They had even begun to make their martinis with vodka.

And every year the whiskey executives declared that vodka was just a fad. It would soon die out, because why would people drink something that had no flavor, no smell, and no color? Only alcoholics drank that. A fad.

But vodka continued to grow, year after year. And Roostal thought that it was important to enter a market as it was growing, because then everything would be so much easier. The established firms were not as aggressive, customers were more interested, the advertising threshold was lower.

Roostal set up a meeting with Heublein, who produced the great American vodka classic, Smirnoff. The meeting was to be held at the main office in Hartford, Connecticut. Monopoly boss Lars Lindmark flew in from Sweden. It was a real show of force. On the American side Hicks Waldron, the president of Heublein, was present with fifteen officials who were not supposed to say anything, just sit in and show respect.

And Lindmark pitched like there was no tomorrow. Aquavit and Swedish punsch and spiced wine—he even started pitching *Kir,* a sickly sweet dessert wine. That was the breaking point for Roostal. They shouldn't be wasting valuable time talking about unsellable Swedish favorites.

Roostal knew what they needed Heublein for. The guys in Hartford knew the market inside out. If anyone could sell a Swedish vodka, it was them.

• • •

The origins of Heublein's achievements could be traced back forty years to a hotel bar in Paris. Rudolph Kunett, a Russian émigré, had met with a fellow countryman who had fled the revolution. His name was Vladimir Smirnoff, and Smirnoff was the heir to what had once been one of Russia's great fortunes.

When the family's distillery on Pjatnitskij Street was confiscated, Smirnoff was captured by the Bolsheviks and imprisoned in the Ukraine. He was dragged out of his prison cell five times to face a firing squad, and five times the guffawing soldiers finally lowered their rifles and led him back to his cell. Then the White Army unexpectedly occupied the town for a week, and Smirnoff managed to escape.

Vladimir Smirnoff claimed that since 1818 his family had produced the greatest vodka in all Russia, perhaps the greatest vodka in the world. Smirnoff had been the official supplier to the crown, with the seals to prove it. Czar Alexander himself had come to the company's pavilion at the exhibition of 1886 and patted little Vladimir on the head. And here they were, fifty-something years later, Vladimir Smirnoff and his brother, old and broke in Paris. Now they wanted to sell the recipe for the Smirnoff vodka, along with the rights to use the family name in the United States.

Kunett started producing the Smirnoff vodka in the U.S., but success never came. Americans simply did not understand how they should use the drink. Drinking vodka like the Russians did, as a shot with dinner, demanded Russian food: *pelmeni, blini* with sour cream and caviar, *soljanka* soup, above all *zakuski*—meat zakuski, fish zakuski, vegetable zakuski, all of those dishes so rich in fat and spices that ice-cold vodka cuts like a knife.

In 1939, Kunett turned his company over to Heublein, a small liquor producer up in Connecticut, for fourteen thousand dollars and a job with the company. For ten years Heublein sold its Russian liquor like *white whiskey,* without success. At the end of the forties, Heublein's owner, Jack Martin, thought he would try teaching Americans to use vodka in mixed drinks; the eastern drink would meet western drinking habits. One of Martin's friends imported ginger ale, and he used to mix it with lime and Smirnoff vodka, pour it into a copper mug, and call it a "Moscow Mule." Jack Martin advertised the Moscow Mule, and it became popular in bars all over the United States. Heublein had demonstrated to the American drinker that Smirnoff worked just fine as a cocktail ingredient.

In 1953, Jack Martin decided to invest $150,000 in a national advertising campaign. The idea was simple. He hired one of America's leading photographers, Bert Stern, to take a picture of a vodka martini in the sand in front of an Egyptian pyramid—*driest of the dry.* For several years afterwards, Stern traveled the world shooting that glass in exotic locations. They were not just tourist pictures. They had style. They had that sophisticated Cole Porter feel that gave Smirnoff its profile.

In the sixties, the admen at the Lawrence Gumbiner agency came up with a new slogan: Smirnoff leaves you breathless. This was imagery at its best. Not only did it hint that the drink was so fantastic you lost your breath, it also taunted the whiskey lovers.

Everyone knew that whiskey stayed on your breath. An entire bagpipe orchestra started to play when you opened your mouth. Vodka, on the other hand, was silent.

Jack Martin realized that the sixties had ushered in a more open lifestyle. All those young people coming out of school, getting good jobs with the big American companies, they all wanted to try new things. Heublein started using women in its ads, in spite of the fact that the Distilled Spirits Institute had told Jack Martin how inappropriate that was. The Heublein boss even went so far as to have the odd black or Puerto Rican in the Smirnoff ads.

Each month, Heublein launched a new cocktail recipe. In 1976, Dr. Boston included sixty-one vodka drinks in his big cocktail calendar. True, Dr. Boston had more than one hundred whiskey drinks, but sixty-one meant that something tasteless, odorless, and invisible (basically only drunk by alcoholics) was well on its way up.

When Lindmark showed up and presented himself as the biggest wine and liquor importer in the world, Hicks Waldron responded by saying that Smirnoff was the biggest liquor label in all categories.

Everyone wanted to jump on the vodka bandwagon. First, there were the vodka labels in about the same price range as Smirnoff, and all with made up Russian names. Some even insinuated that they really were Russian, but all were fakes. Wolfschmidt and Kamchatka and Crown Russe in the United States, Cossack and Vladivar in Great Britain, Puschkin in West Germany. None of them had been anywhere near Russia.

Then there were the truly cheap vodkas with phony Russian names. They were marketed without any advertising, almost like generic goods. Roostal couldn't understand how you could make any money on those vodkas. You had to achieve such unbelievable sales volumes before they became acceptably good business.

A third category consisted of local vodka substitutes. There was Kornbranntwein in West Germany, Viin in Estonia, Shochu in Japan, and you could put Rent Brännvin, Renat, from Sweden in there, too.

Renat was made from industrial potatoes of the worst quality, potatoes you wouldn't even feed to a pig. But for political reasons the Monopoly was forced to buy the raw materials at unfavorable prices from the Farmers' Cooperative.

Vodka could be made from potatoes, or grain, or molasses, or from just about anything else. Impurities gave pretty much all vodka a slight taste of fusel oil, except for the Finnish domestic vodka, Koskenkorva, which was almost completely pure. The Asians often tried adding some spices. The Turks and the Poles put a blade of grass in theirs, and in Japan, Roostal had seen a vodka with a snake in it. But for the American market, it wasn't the additives that gave it flavor, it was the image.

The last category was imported vodkas: the real Russian vodka, Stolichnaya, and the Polish and Finnish vodkas, Wyborowa and Finlandia. But the Americans didn't drink real Russian vodka; they wanted American Russian vodka. Rudolph Kunett had figured that right when he decided to make the deal in that Paris bar forty years earlier.

Thirty-five percent of the whiskey market consisted of imported products. The vodka market was only a half percent imported. There were plenty of liquor pushers who contemplated those figures and asked themselves: If Scotch whiskey had to come from Scotland, shouldn't Russian vodka come from Russia, not from Hartford, Connecticut?

• • •

The executives at Heublein listened politely. Then they warned Lars Lindmark that imported vodka was a tough business, one of the toughest. Success was near impossible. The Chinese had made an attempt at launching the market's most expensive vodka—it flopped.

If you listened to the executives up in Hartford, you got the picture pretty fast: They had positioned Smirnoff so perfectly that it had cornered the entire market. First of all, it was Russian, which meant that it took up the domestic and import market shares. Second, the ad campaign that was still rolling along after three decades beat the brains out all of the knockoffs. And third, Heublein's distribution was so well organized that you could find Smirnoff in every single bar in the entire United States, taking up valuable shelf space.

The executives in Hartford, Connecticut, explained to Lindmark and Roostal that in America, vodka *was* Smirnoff. More than 20 percent of all the vodka sold in the United States was Smirnoff, in spite of the fact that they were competing with thousands of local vodkas, hundreds of copies, and dozens of imports. When Americans thought of Smirnoff, they were still left breathless.

Then the Heublein executives politely ruminated that Scandinavian aquavit might work in the States. Somerset had invested in Aalborg Aquavit from Denmark. They had put significant sums into advertising, and now they were established in the American market, even if they didn't sell more than twenty thousand cases. And there was the food angle; that hadn't been used in liquor advertising before. The execs had understood that you drank aquavit with food, and the American people were not aware of this. If you could just convince a million Americans not only to take a drink before eating but to have one with their food as well, well, anything could happen.

Roostal had heard the same argument from a well-pickled adman in Chicago. The Swedes should skip vodka, he affirmed, and create a whole new drink category for the American market. The new drink should be called "diluted Aquavit," or "Aquavit Light." If Roostal had understood rightly, it would be an aquavit somewhere between a vodka and a real aquavit, so mildly spiced that it could be used as a mixer.

"Diluted aquavit is an item that people will think of as Swedish vodka, but that they will remember much better," he said.

There was a fairly simple reason behind his assertion: "Swedish vodka . . . hey, what's that?" exclaimed the alcoholic adman. "I'm gonna tell you something very important, Mr. Roostal. Vodka is Russian. Swedish vodka doesn't even exist."

The Heublein executives declared that they would be happy to include some of the classic Swedish quality products in their sales program. But—and here was an important issue that Paul Dohl, head of Heublein's Spirits Group, had wanted to discuss with his Swedish counterpart for quite some time—there was this delicate problem. Heublein's distillery in Hartford was running "24, 7, 365." Big rigs loaded with Smirnoff were pulling out day and night. "And in order to fill the colossal appetite of the American people for our product, we have built and bought distilleries and processing plants all over this great country, and in spite of this, we can't get out enough liquor. And besides, we have the whole European market to think of as well."

So it was perhaps unsurprising that the CEO of the largest vodka producer in the free world now turned to Lars Lindmark, representing the planet's biggest importer of distilled spirits, to ask him, well . . . if the Swedes could consider distilling Smirnoff on Swedish soil.

Roostal thought this was the logical end to an insane discussion: distilling Russian vodka for the Americans *in Sweden*.

•

After eight months and four continents, Ilmar Roostal was back where he started. This absurd world tour touting crazy proposals to export all Sweden's products to all the world's markets was, thank God, coming to naught, and it should never have begun.

The question had been clear to him from day one. It had never been a matter of what they should sell and where they should sell it, just *how* they could sell that pure stuff to the Americans.

Vodka was the most extreme example of Ernest Dichter's old ideas on the importance of image. Back in April of 1949, the master had explained it all. "Although every manufacturer will disclaim any similarity of quality and service between his and other products, it is small wonder that the consumer has great difficulty in distinguishing one brand from another."

In the end, everything was just image.

• • •

Problems were mounting for Lars Lindmark in Stockholm, too. Swedish liquor history was on the move again, for Rune Hermansson, general manager of the System, had announced that he was paying a visit to the Monopoly's new boss, Lars Lindmark. The heads of the two liquor superpowers were to meet face-to-face for the first time.

The System was born in the mid 1950s, when all the liquor retailers in Sweden were merged into one company after the disappearance of liquor passes. The new entity was named The New System Corporation, but was pretty much always known as "The System." Even individual liquor stores were called "The System." When Swedes mention The System they aren't talking about the government, they are referring to their local liquor store.

•

Rune Hermansson was considered by officials at the Monopoly to be the Darth Vader of Swedish spirits, a fanatic. When the gaunt, ghostly figure entered the mighty stone fortress, he was ceremoniously ushered upstairs and into the executive dining hall.

Hoping to soften Hermansson's dark mask, Lindmark had asked his assistant to select one of the noblest wines from the Confidential list—a ✔✔✔ wine.

Hermansson carefully studied the dusty old bottle with its softly glowing, honey-gold contents, while Lindmark and his assistant watched, grinning like a pair of cunning pimps. A good relationship with the dark lord of liquor was crucial.

The System's director broke their reverie. Speaking in a throaty whisper from behind a thin smile, he said, "You know what, Lars, I think I'll just have a beer . . . alcohol free."

Sadly, the Monopoly men followed the rejected bottle's retreat out through the swinging doors.

Some years before Lindmark's arrival at the Monopoly, The System began to focus its activities on a newly created wine department. The decision sent ripples of uneasiness through the Monopoly.

One bit of bad news soon followed another. The System started recruiting its own wine tasters. The System opened up its own wine information department to the general public. The System sent employee delegations across Europe to sample new wines.

At first, vice president Rolf Arfwedson at the Monopoly could barely believe this bad news. After all, the Monopoly was the importer. The System was supposed to be a retailer and nothing more. Touring the vineyards of France and Italy in early fall, when it was down to forty degrees back home, with rain in the air and no sun for weeks, wasn't that a burden the Monopoly had shouldered for decades? And those infinitely subtle palates so necessary for tasting a wine in a truly professional manner, did not they belong to the Monopoly, too? But now, among the sun-ripened grapevines of Provence, there was suddenly a risk of running into an intoxicated employee from The System, struggling to hold himself upright and yelling: "Hullo! Are you Swedish, too?"

When alcohol consumption soared after the disappearance of the passes, the liquor stores were moved to back streets in remote parts of the city in an attempt to discourage this trend. Local businesses were invited to advertise their products in the windows. Bicycles, mopeds, clothes, and lawnmowers were put on display, disguising the business that went on inside.

It was no help. Sales of Renat rocketed.

Finally, the teetotalers on the System board remembered their old pal, "suggestive influence." If people must drink, couldn't The System at least suggest them into drinking some less poisonous . . . poison?

They came up with the idea that after four hundred years of drinking the clear stuff, Swedes would be suggested into drinking wine. The System had finally discovered their New Swede. The New Swede was a Frenchman.

Out went the mopeds and the lawnmowers. In came clusters of plastic grapes. That awful opium of the people—Renat—that had always been placed out front, was tucked down under the counter, and up went the wine bottles. Now the Swedes would become Frenchmen, assuming their newfound freedom—with responsibility, naturally.

The System even went so far as to run ads in the papers. Yes, they hired admen, the devil's henchmen. Although the teetotalers were unshakably opposed to liquor advertising—"only on the back of matchboxes"—consumer information against Renat was another matter.

This was no longer an issue of alcohol policy. This was exorcising Satan.

"Why pay five or six dollars for a bottle of liquor," the admen wrote, "when you can get a GOOD WINE for around one dollar. Liquor doesn't belong here. Wine is much better. New times, new customs."

Unfortunately, what happened was—nothing. The power of suggestion, that trusted old ally of the teetotalers, had apparently gone fishing. The Swedes calmly continued drinking their regular Renat.

Could it be that the Swedes couldn't quite get their tongues around the French language, that they could not or dare not order these noble products when they were in "The System?"

The System printed up new catalogues. The French wine names were written out in Swedish.

Well, folks, how about a *van blonk demmy seck,* or a *casstello dell monty,* or how about a classical *bar-dough row-shh?*

After ten years of intensive ad campaigns, wine sales gradually began to rise. The admen were intoxicated with joy.

But consumption patterns for Renat remained unchanged. The statistics refused to budge.

The teetotalers at The System had merely managed to make Swedes drink wine—*too.*

One day, Lindmark's assistant had visited System headquarters. The beaming director of information greeted him with a big bear hug and told him that the admen had come up with a slogan that would fundamentally change Sweden.

"Flush the booze, Leif!" he screamed. "Flush—the—booze!"

The assistant grimly related the scene to Lindmark.

"That asshole," he responded, "that asshole is going to run a multi-million dollar campaign to destroy our best product."

• • •

In the Monopoly's executive dining hall, Rune Hermansson ate in silence, while Lindmark and his assistant fidgeted thirstily in their chairs. During preparations for this unprecedented liquor summit, technicians at the Monopoly had asked Lindmark to present Hermansson with a new way to handle empty bottles. This was a sensitive issue with The System.

Lindmark's technicians had developed a machine that could sort the empties in the System stores. But The System refused to install it. Staff complained that the machine made so much noise it might interfere with their descriptions of the international wine selection.

"But it's not noisy," Lindmark smiled. "We've actually measured the sound level, Ivar. If only the bottle-sorting machine could be installed, the whole system of returns could be made more efficient."

The overlord of The System sipped his alcohol-free beer.

"The System is no glass-crushing plant, Lars. The System is a guardian of drinking culture."

Hermansson embarked on a long and elaborate presentation about the two organizations, their common interests, the possibilities for cooperation, coordination . . . . A great deal had already been done, "and further significant gains could certainly be achieved from increased efficiency, if they could just . . . ." At this point Hermansson's voice dwindled to little more than a whispering breeze drifting over the tabletop. Lindmark and his assistant leaned forward.

"If we could only take the necessary decision, Lars."

Lindmark and his assistant looked at each other. The necessary decision?

"Yes," Hermansson continued. "Yes . . . ."

The head of The System suddenly smiled warmly at Lindmark.

"If we simply merged."

He wanted The System and the Monopoly to merge.

Through their joint efforts, Hermansson explained, the two superpowers of liquor would finally be able to change drinking patterns. Hermansson had even decided on a name for the new company.

"New Spirits Inc." He smiled. "A beautiful name."

Hermansson's optimistic presentation from the other side of the table shifted into a muffled mumble, not unlike the sound of a glass-crushing machine in full swing. It all became horribly clear to Lindmark. He couldn't sell liquor in Sweden because he had an asshole for a retailer. In every liquor store they were running a campaign against his bestseller—Flush the booze!—while the Monopoly had been given the back side of a matchbox. And if, against all odds, he should actually manage to increase sales, the teetotalers in parliament raised the alcohol tax until he was back where he started.

He had dragged the Monopoly out of the Ice Age and steered it into the 1970s. But for what?

"You understand, Lars," said Hermansson, as he stretched contentedly in his chair. "We have to let the market decide. And the market—that's me."

• • •

Ilmar Roostal met Lindmark's right-hand man, Magnus Lagerkvist, in New York, along with one of the three old directors from the Monopoly who had tagged along as a retirement present from Lindmark. Roostal proposed a meeting with Ernest Dichter, the marketing guru. He had asked Dichter to come up with ideas for the Swedish export project, and they had arranged to have lunch at the Pierre.

"It would be wise," Dichter began, "to recall the background behind the success of vodka in the United States, specifically the success of Smirnoff. In the beginning, it was all a kind of revolt against whiskey. Whiskey was the normal, the commonplace, what everyone drank when they came home from the office. But Smirnoff changed all that.

"Smirnoff made vodka sophisticated. There is therefore a great danger in copying the Smirnoff theme. Every time you do so, you run the risk of selling more Smirnoff. I think therefore," Dichter continued, "that you should take advantage of the fact that you are small. Emphasize the idea that this is a label for individualists, a special vodka only appreciated by those in the know.

"Advertising people have always thought that we drink for social reasons. They are fumbling in the dark. Everyone rationalizes their reasons for drinking alcohol, but in reality we are secretly seeking change. Change from one mood to another, change from one social class to another. Alcohol makes rich and poor equals. It is the great revolutionary leveler. But there is an ultimate reason for drinking, a longing after an even deeper change—we are searching for another person within ourselves. Once intoxicated, we say, 'Is this really me? I didn't realize that I could be that other person, too. Then I'll just drink and—reinvent myself.'"

• • •

On his return from New York, Ilmar Roostal presented his large export study. In order to fortify the spirits of the Monopoly's board members, Lindmark's men had asked a representative from the Swedish Tobacco Company to tell them about the small, but important, success they had had selling a Swedish pipe tobacco in the United States.

The tobacco man never showed up.

Roostal's report was met by a giant wave of objections. Obviously the consultant was ready to explode, but Lindmark with a Caesarian gesture showed how important it was to keep one's composure. The situation called for calm and dignity.

After that, Peter Ekelund reviewed the project's finances. The Monopoly would invest four million dollars for four years in a row. They would see the first positive returns on their investment after nine years. This implied that they needed to sell two-and-a-half million bottles a year. If they sold five million bottles, they would be rich.

The representatives from the business community looked at the costs and were horrified. The politicians saw the profits and were terrified.

Lindmark verified that they would not be risking more than four million max. Then Gunnar Broman, the adman, got up and presented the various product proposals. There was Country of Sweden Vodka, Royal Court Vodka, Blonde Swede, Damn Swede, and finally, Absolute Pure Vodka.

At that point, all hell broke loose. The chairman of the board stated that he didn't want to stick his nose in this matter, since it was about advertising, but that "Absolute Vodka" was inappropriate. It would be confused with "Absolut rent brännvin," Renat. The clerks at the System stores would not know what people actually wanted—absolute this or absolute that. That would damage the Monopoly's delicate relationship with The System.

Torsten Bengtson was the appointed teetotaler on the board of the Liquor Monopoly. Bengtson had been a UN delegate for twenty-five years and had lived with an American woman for three years. ("A pureblood American woman," he liked to add, to emphasize that she wasn't just some European immigrant. Pure settlers' blood ran in that woman's veins.) Torsten Bengtson thought he knew Americans, and Americans, he explained, have very strong opinions. They either like something or they just get rid of it.

In all the years Bengtson had spent in New York City, he had never seen one single person order Swedish liquor. Three Japanese people had once asked for Danish aquavit in a restaurant, but they had rapidly set it aside once they had tasted it. To Bengtson, Lindmark's export venture was clearly a folly, and he wanted to warn the board against it. But he had an even more important motive than business logic for opposing the investment. It was a matter of principle.

"Are we going to export sin?" Bengtson vehemently asked his colleagues around the table. "Is this really what you intend to do?"

Torsten Bengtson had been a teetotaler since his youth. When he became speaker of the parliament, the king had told him: "You are a teetotaler, Torsten. And so am I. I became one in 1911, and not even you have been sober that long." He always liked to inform younger colleagues at the Monopoly that a young man who flirted with drink would cost society two million dollars during his lifetime, and that didn't even include the sufferings of friends and family. A bottle of liquor should cost a hundred bucks. Only then, declared Bengtson, would it cover the real costs.

When the government chose Bengtson as a board member,

the old minister of finance had called him into his office and told him: "Your responsibility is quite clear, Torsten. The Monopoly is not a sales organization. Under no circumstances should the Monopoly engage in advertising its products."

It was also clearly stated in the contract between the Monopoly and the government that any alcohol advertising the Monopoly came across was to be forcibly removed. Occasionally, they unearthed some hidden advertising on corkscrews and sportswear, but now they themselves were going to engage in advertising. An adman was standing in front of the Monopoly's board of directors, holding up bottles! It was downright antisocial. And Bengtson and Lindmark had always agreed on this point. Bengtson supported Lindmark's modernization, and Lindmark backed Bengtson's policy, that the Monopoly should not be commercialized.

Bengtson summarized his position. "Economically, it's a travesty, and morally, it's wrong. Is it seriously the intention here to export Sweden's alcohol problem to the third world?"

"Third world?" the confused chairman asked. "I thought we were talking about the United States."

"We should export our alcohol policy instead," Bengtson asserted.

"I have to agree with you there," the hearty Gunnar Broman burst out, "'cause it's sure not needed here!"

"And if Broman absolutely must hawk liquor," Bengtson shot back, "then he can just call it something else. The Black Death would be a more appropriate name."

"Black Death?" Broman considered the name. "*Black?* But that's actually very good, Torsten!"

•

Later, when the meeting adjourned for lunch, Bengtson congratulated Gunnar on his ingenious suggestions. He held no grudge against the adman, he said, but—and here he raised his voice so everyone could hear—this whole folly would be stopped by parliament. Because he, Torsten Bengtson, would bring it to the floor himself!

Curiously, Bengtson was usually the one to approve the wines served at Monopoly lunches. The Monopoly's own master blender verified that there was no one on the board who had such a thorough knowledge of the company's products as Torsten Bengtson, the teetotaler. A newspaper had once challenged him to prove that he could tell the difference between cheap and expensive wines. He agreed, since he wanted to demonstrate that smelling the wines was adequate, you really didn't need to swallow them. He started by selecting the most expensive wine, then he arranged the rest according to quality, all the way down to the humblest two-dollar bottle.

When they reconvened after lunch, Lars Lindmark gravely explained to the board that the Monopoly was a state-owned corporation and the export project was therefore classified.

He tried not to look at Bengtson as he announced that until their next meeting, it would be a crime to breathe a single word about their plans outside that room.

CHAPTER NINE

ELUSIVE IMPORTERS

Doors are closing in Lars Lindmark's face, and only old-timer Al Singer bothers to listen.

At Monopoly headquarters in Stockholm, people were growing nervous. They spent a hundred million dollars on a new plant on the West Coast without batting an eye. But when a hundred thousand disappeared on Roostal's report and on Broman's plastic prototypes—well, that was another matter altogether.

Lindmark wondered if it was all going to turn out to be one horrible, expensive flop. His troubleshooter, Curt Nycander, kept mumbling sourly about those "Swedish advertising geniuses." One American after the other had confirmed Curt's suspicions about that bottle: it would be a hard thing to sell because you could hardly see the damn thing. The unsettling thing was that this was exactly how the board had reacted, too. And when the administrative director from the old regime had seen the bottle, he was brutally frank: "It's goddamned ugly."

He had even said it looked like a medicine bottle or a blood-plasma bag, which was word-for-word the American point of view, although Lindmark and Nycander kept that fact to themselves.

People were backing away from the project in droves. Nycander was getting a creeping feeling about who would end up with this mess in his lap. He decided to invite Broman down to the main office for a classic Monopoly champagne-and-two-wines luncheon. He would give the adman an offer he couldn't refuse.

Nycander let Broman stew through the whole three-course get-together. Little old ladies in starched white aprons appeared and disappeared while Nycander watched the adman's curiosity rise. Finally, coffee was served. The Monopoly exec put down his cup and gravely demanded that the adman take a sacred oath, there and then, to accept full responsibility for the introduction of the Swedish vodka in the United States.

It was no longer a question of Broman's taking care of just the "creative" end of the project. Who but Broman could see this project through to a happy ending?

Broman was surprised by Nycander's sudden change of attitude, but sure, he said, he would take care of it.

When Broman ran into Lindmark, the chief expectantly asked him, "You'll do it Gunnar, won't you?"

The Monopoly needed someone with a good marketing feeling, Lindmark explained, "an open-minded man, possibly even an advertising genius."

Gunnar Broman was touched. He swore he would not rest until Absolut Vodka had found its importer, and bottles were selling by the thousand all over the U.S.

But no one seemed particularly interested. Nycander and Ekelund had met with Seagram, Paddington, Brown–Forman, and Austin Nichols. The Swedes had been received several times in the Mecca of Vodka up in Hartford, Connecticut. They had presented their ideas, their photos, their prototypes, even the invisible bottle with a taste of its invisible contents. The Americans sipped, nodded, and exchanged meaningful glances with one another, before turning the offer down.

Heublein's domestic division had already taken on one foreign vodka: Finlandia. (Word had reached Sweden that Heublein had assured the Finns that they would sell their vodka, but that naturally, it would have to be done in a carefully controlled manner. Apparently they were keeping the "controlled" part of the agreement very well. "We've *buried* Finlandia," they chuckled contentedly to each other in Hartford, Connecticut.)

But now Gerry McNamara, head of marketing at Heublein's international division, thought that Heublein should take on the Swedish vodka and market it—for real. McNamara had written a couple of memorandums in which he claimed that the future belonged to premium imported vodka. He asserted that it was actually no longer even a matter of premium vodka, but of *super*-premium.

Gerry McNamara had looked at the transparent bottle and he thought that it looked interesting; those parts that he could make out anyway. The head of domestic sales, Charles Herbert, had been down to check it out and pointed out that the bottle would have to be redone since you couldn't see it.

Gerry McNamara felt he could have gotten Absolut Vodka from the Swedes anytime he wanted to, but McNamara didn't make the decisions at Heublein. International was so much smaller than domestic. At domestic they sold *six million cases of Smirnoff every year,* they had the world's strongest liquor label, and they didn't like foreign competition. They just plain old didn't like things that came from abroad. Gerry McNamara still thought that there was money to be made on an expensive imported vodka, but he couldn't convince management of the domestic group to take on Absolut. Charlie Herbert put an end to the matter: "If those Swedes come here and try to introduce one of those superpremium vodkas and threaten our Smirnoff, then I'll introduce the world's most expensive vodka, a Smirnoff de Czar and kick the shit out of them."

And the vice president of Heublein claimed that: "We spill more vodka up here in Hartford every day than those guys are going to sell in the entire United States."

Gerry McNamara was offered Absolut Vodka five times, and five times his bosses stopped him.

• • •

During the swinging sixties, Philip Morris asked Gunnar Broman to launch a cigarette called Saratoga. The adman started by ordering a consumer study in which people were asked when cigarettes tasted best. He received a pile of answers: with coffee, in front of the TV, in the morning, and so on. But the most common response really got Gunnar Broman excited: most smokers said cigarettes tasted best after sex. This was the answer he had been waiting for.

Broman had a photograph taken of a couple leisurely stretched out in bed, smoking their Saratogas. The woman in the picture was naked from the waist up, and Broman had a feeling that those breasts might cause a few heated discussions. "But," he said, "what the hell? The survey showed that Saratogas (or at least cigarettes) actually taste best after a good lay."

This was the first time in the history of advertising that someone had marketed a consumer product by openly suggesting that it was directly related to any sexual activity. Gunnar Broman had broken the sex barrier. The ad was incredibly successful. People were hoarding Saratoga cigarettes, supermarket shelves were emptied, and for a while it seemed like every smoker in the country was on their way home to see for themselves just when the Saratoga peaked.

From far and wide, study groups and tobacco dealers traveled to meet Gunnar Broman from Sweden, to look at the picture with the smoking couple and the naked breasts. The head of Philip Morris Europe hugged the laughing adman, declaring that Broman was probably the greatest advertising genius in history.

Everything was going great, and probably would have continued that way, if Saratoga had not had one peculiar quality—besides the sex thing. After the cigarette burned down about an inch, the glowing tip often fell off. This had a few unfortunate side effects, particularly for those who found themselves as bare as the breasts in Broman's ads.

After three months, sales of Saratogas just stopped. The packs lay untouched on the shelves. Nobody cared anymore about when a Saratoga was at its best. The executive director from Philip Morris showed up again and yelled at Broman: "Get the tits out of the ads!"

The Saratoga campaign was an experience that Broman gladly shared with his colleagues. He thought there was something important to learn from those breasts.

• • •

The Philip Morris people were not the only ones who had been following the cigarette campaign. People at the Ted Bates agency had also been tracking Gunnar Broman. Everyone in New York knew that the worst thing that could happen to a good adman was a bad product. Broman seemed to be genuinely brilliant, and he laughed all the time, which everyone at Ted Bates liked immensely. One night out on the town, they introduced Gunnar Broman to Gordon Werner, who handled money for the world's top advertising executives.

Werner was a very small, very smart, New York Jewish attorney who ate French fries and specialized in reinsurance in

Bermuda. Through the years, Werner had gotten to know admen around the globe, and he would always end up convincing them that they should let him take care of their money, which turned out to be an excellent deal for the executives and for Gordon Werner.

Many years into their friendship, Broman told Werner about his problems finding a U.S. importer for the new vodka. Gordon Werner remembered that he had placed a large sum of money for an adman who was now working with a medium-sized ad agency in New York called Martin Landey, Arlow. They created advertisements for foreign luxury firms, like Gucci. Among their customers was Carillon Importers, a small import company that sold French wines and liqueurs and was mostly known for marketing the classic French liqueur, Grand Marnier, in the United States.

True to his instincts, Broman had never really liked the big liquor companies that the Monopoly was pursuing. At Austin Nichols, Brown–Forman, or Heublein, Absolut Vodka would be one of several hundred labels, and the Swedes would never have any say in the ad campaigns. Broman thought the Monopoly should look for a business partner, not an importer. Lars Lindmark, the head of the Monopoly, understood Broman's point of view, but he would prefer a *major* business partner, he said, one that could instill a certain calm among the members of the board.

The head of Carillon Importers was an old guy called Al Singer. Even though Carillon's offices overlooked Rockefeller Center in Manhattan, Singer had made up his mind that he would live out on the West Coast. The weather was so much better there, and it was closer to Vegas. When the Swedes asked if anyone knew when Al Singer would show up, nobody at Carillon could give a definite answer. "It's down to luck," they said.

•

That summer of '78, Peter Ekelund took a friend with him to California to go surfing. When Ekelund landed in Los Angeles, he rented a car and set off to find Al Singer. Gunnar Broman, tipped off by his good friend Gordon Werner, had recommended the visit. And why not? One stop at Singer's and Peter could charge the entire trip as a business expense.

It was a hot summer day in California, and the car had no air-conditioning, so Ekelund decided to make the trip in his swimsuit. He had loaded Broman's presentation slides into the car, just to show the creative process. He had a few pictures of Brindfors's French bottles, taken with strong back-lighting, and—just in case things went really well, if this Singer was actually prepared to do business—he had also packed one of Brindfors's bottles.

Peter changed into his business suit out on the sidewalk. When the door opened, he realized that Al Singer had passed retirement age some years ago. The American had long, gray hair, a Hawaiian shirt unbuttoned halfway to his waist, and a necklace with a peace symbol. Al Singer laughed at Ekelund's suit. Life in California was so cool.

Singer had no slide projector, so Peter went to fetch one from the car. When he returned, he had already started to perspire in the California heat. Sweat had permeated his shirt and was seeping through his jacket, until a damp patch erupted under each armpit. As images of Broman's platforms flickered over the wall, and the big, blond Swede talked about his country's liquor traditions, dark patterns coalesced over his shirt.

When he came to the Absolut Country of Sweden Vodka, the little stream running down his back had grown into a major river flowing into a small lake around his abdomen. Al Singer smiled. He thought everything Peter had said so far was just so cool. Not only that, but he had always wanted a vodka in his assortment.

Ekelund opened the case and lifted out Brindfors's bottle. It would be so cool, he said, if Al Singer wanted to sell this Absolut Vodka in America. And, he added, if Singer wanted something more from the Monopoly's voluminous selection, then Ekelund could arrange that, too.

Ekelund figured that it would be insane to take off his jacket at this point, since his shirt looked like he had surfed over to Singer's office. Al Singer contemplated the bottle. Who else had the Swedes been talking to? Well, Peter answered, at the moment they were holding serious negotiations with several major importers, and Austin Nichols was particularly interested. Austin Nichols had just begun a big marketing survey to determine the quantities of Absolut that should be released in the United States.

Al Singer nodded. He congratulated Peter. He said the guys at Austin Nichols were very cool.

• • •

Martin Landey's office at Martin Landey, Arlow overlooked Third Avenue. He sat there, surrounded by classical French furniture, perched on an antique throne, thinking about the gestalt of vodka.

Landey had spent years developing his prophecy of a coming Europeanization of the American continent. In Europe there were two markets, Landey explained to those who would listen: there was a luxury market and a mass market and, consequently, one kind of advertisement for the rich and another for the rest.

Martin Landey was convinced that the United States was headed in the same direction. Well-educated middle-class Americans had begun to travel abroad. They were doing business in Europe, watching TV programs about Europe, and developing a taste for that fine, European upper-class lifestyle. American bankers had grown tired of putting on their bland Arrow shirts and their boring Brooks Brothers suits for a day at the office. They wanted a Pierre Cardin shirt and an Armani suit. Wall Street stockbrokers wanted to trade in their dull old Oldsmobiles for new Mercedes-Benz 350SLs. They didn't want to drink bourbon, they wanted to drink clear, refined vodka from Europe.

"I'm not talking details," Martin Landey said. "I'm talking about the big picture. I'm talking about the *gestalt* of things to come."

When Landey used the word *gestalt*—and he used it often—he pronounced it in German, with the *g* deep in his throat and with North America's longest *a*, like this: *ghestaaalt*.

The first time Landey did an ad for Al Singer's flagship, Grand Marnier, he had let his creatrive director pull the cork out of the French liqueur bottle. No one had shown a liquor bottle that way before. *"We took the cork out of Grand Marnier,"* Landey proudly proclaimed. He thought that the bottle without its cork had an unusually interesting and pleasing appearance. But the wet cork and the open French bottle provoked people into sending indignant letters. They said Landey's ad included a subliminal, supersensual penis, meant to drag them all down into a morass of sex and alcohol.

When the vodka bottle was sent over from Sweden, Martin Landey opined that it looked like a receptacle for urine samples. He had never laid eyes on such an ugly design in his whole life. The idea that this bottle would work in the United States was just laughable.

On the other hand, they had come up with a name that Martin Landey considered to be quite interesting. Absolut Vodka. Hmm, yes, more than interesting, actually. Absolut Vodka. The name was so good that there were moments when Martin Landey could have sworn that he had thought of it himself.

There were only two European vodka labels worth talking about in the U.S.—Finlandia and Stolichnaya—and both were small. Stolichnaya should logically have been a big success since it was a genuine Russian vodka, unlike Smirnoff. But the thing was, every time a political incident in any way related to the Soviet Union occurred, which was fairly often, the longshoremen out in New Jersey refused to unload the Russian liquor. The importer was forced to send out people from the Brooklyn office to try and coax them back to work. One or two cases would be opened during the negotiations, and they still wouldn't receive their products on time, or at all. The result of all this commotion was that Stolichnaya's sales went up and down like a yo-yo.

Martin Landey was convinced that there was a market in the U.S. for an expensive imported vodka. And if he could just redo the Swedish bottle, then Al Singer, who was a client and a friend, might take it on.

Landey presented his vodka vision to Al Singer, and Singer told him that he had actually seen the Swedish bottle, well, seen . . . the thing was, you couldn't see the goddamned thing. Anyhow, he hated it. If Martin Landey was so interested in Swedish vodka, Al said, he should take it to Abe Rosenberg, head of Paddington, which owned a quarter share of Carillon and all of Austin Nichols, and try to convince Rosenberg to take on the Swedish thing.

A couple of decades earlier, Rosenberg had introduced J&B Rare, blended by Len Jullian, a cockney in the East End of London. It had quickly become America's biggest-selling scotch. Rosenberg had been the CEO of Paddington since the beginning of time. When he saw the Swedish bottle, he called Martin Landey and said it was the worst piece of shit he had ever laid eyes on, and then he shouted for his secretary because he couldn't read the text—it was written directly on the bottle!—and she had to come in and read it out loud for him. The bottle was a crime against the first rule for how you introduced a new product, namely, visibility. You could see right through the damn thing—the label was missing, right?—and because of that, when it stood up on a bar shelf, the customers would see the bottle behind it instead—and magnified, too!—and what the hell good was that?

Abe Rosenberg wondered if it was really true that Al Singer wanted the Swedish vodka, because if he did, he could take it, but as far as he, Abe Rosenberg, was concerned, he wouldn't touch it with a ten-foot pole.

Of all the campaigns that Martin Landey had handled for Carillon throughout the years, not one had ever been approved by Al Singer. Martin Landey used to say that Al never says yes—that's just the way it is—but on the other hand, he never says no either.

When someone joked with Al about the trouble he had making up his mind, Al answered that, considering the bosses that he had seen in action, and considering the trouble they had caused, he thought the best thing a boss could do was to not make any decisions at all.

Al liked to gamble. He liked to see the dice dancing over the green felt down in Vegas. He liked to see the ponies burst through the gates at Aqueduct. It seemed as though Al Singer had a meeting scheduled with chance every single day. Maybe that was why he refused to make up his mind. He just sat and waited for his companion to come along.

Al Singer didn't like the fact that he had to tell Martin Landey repeatedly that he was not saying yes to the Swedish vodka.

Landey was constantly nagging. "Okay, okay, Al. I know it looks like a blood-plasma bag, but at least it's the only one of its kind." Al Singer grew more and more distressed. He didn't want to disappoint anyone; he just didn't want that bottle.

Finally Al Singer brought his sales manager with him to a meeting with Martin Landey. He was Michel Roux, a Frenchman who worked from Carillon's Manhattan office and who spoke the strangest English Landey had ever heard. It sounded like the man was gargling with mouthwash, and it was completely impossible to fathom what he was saying. Even Al couldn't understand him.

"What the hell's he saying?" he would bark at Landey. "What the hell's he saying?"

It turned out that the Frenchman was saying that he didn't like the Swedish vodka bottle. And besides, a vodka didn't fit in with the Carillon assortment.

"So, what did I say?" Al Singer concluded. "One—there's no market, two—I'm not into vodka, and three—the bottle looks like shit. Forget it."

• • •

Lars Lindmark had become so desperate that he personally flew over to the States again in order to try and convince someone—anyone—to take his vodka. He met with Seagram, he met with Schenley, he made a trip up to Hartford, Connecticut, once more.

They had talked to producers, then importers, then agents. The big companies all turned Lars Lindmark away. The whole thing was a nightmare. This was not something Lindmark wanted to report back to his board of directors.

The trip finally ended amidst the antique furniture in Martin

Landey's Third Avenue office. The last possibility was that little import firm, Carillon, a very small firm who, incidentally, didn't like the bottle.

Lars Lindmark explained to Martin Landey that the Monopoly had reached a crucial decision. They were determined to introduce Absolut Vodka in the U.S. and they were looking for someone who knew marketing inside out, "an open-minded man, possibly even an advertising genius." The Swedish Monopoly needed Martin Landey. If Landey would take on Absolut Vodka, Lindmark promised, he would get a dollar for every case sold.

These words made Martin Landey extremely suspicious. His intention was to do the advertising for the vodka, but he had no interest in *selling* Swedish liquor. Al Singer was going to do that. Martin Landey mumbled that he sensed a conflict of interest here. Possibly this was something they could do in Sweden, but not in the United States of America.

When Martin Landey saw the Swede's disappointment, he asked Lindmark to give him time.

"Listen," he said. "I'll work on Al. If we just redo the bottle so that it will sell in the States, maybe Al will change his mind."

Curt Nycander told Broman that things were moving forward at last. Al Singer and Martin Landey might handle the launch. Just one thing: a few minor adjustments would have to be made to the bottle.

"If changes have to be made," Broman answered, "we had better do it ourselves. After all, we designed it." Nycander could accept that, but he wondered what they should do about Hans Brindfors, who was always so touchy.

"Hans has gotten silver fever," Nycander complained. "He just won't listen to reason."

"I'll take care of it," Broman promised. "You know how Hans is."

They added a raised center in the base of the bottle, a little peak, and in that way managed to make the bottle half an inch or so taller. It was starting to approach a Smirnoff.

"They just can't swallow the idea," Broman said to Brindfors as they studied the result, "that we can sit over here in Sweden and design a good-looking bottle. It's like that story about the horse. Damn nice horse, but what if you made the neck a little longer? Then the next guy says, 'damn nice horse, but shouldn't the legs be a little thicker?' When they're done, they've created the perfect horse, but it looks like crap."

"I know one thing for sure," Brindfors said. "It's got to be silver."

One day Al Singer and Martin Landey went down to Thirty-second Street to have lunch with Marvin Shanken and settle the whole vodka thing once and for all.

Marvin Shanken knew everything there was to know about liquor in the United States. He had started a very influential magazine for the liquor industry, and every year he arranged a big convention for all the gentlemen in the business.

Shanken had known Al Singer forever, and when they sat down, he could tell that Al wasn't happy. This was probably, he figured, because someone was trying to force him to make a decision.

Al Singer outlined the vodka story to Shanken. Then he launched into a long and winding tale about how the Ligget tobacco company, who owned Paddington, who owned a quarter share in his own company, were pressuring him to take the Swedish vodka because they wanted to sell tobacco in Sweden.

The whole thing was one big goddamned conspiracy. The booze would come over the Atlantic, and the tobacco would go back, but in order for the whole thing to work out, they had figured that he, Al Singer, had to take the vodka. But before he did anything, Al wanted to hear Shanken's opinion, because Shanken knew the business better than anybody.

Martin Landey interjected that in spite of certain negative elements, there were also possibilities. If they could just sell twenty or thirty thousand cases, they could put together a little money to invest in marketing.

"So what?" asked Shanken. "That much money wouldn't get you anywhere, and Paddington isn't going to give you any money. You'd have to sell a hundred thousand cases to be in business. A half dozen Polish and Finnish vodkas have already tried it, and so far none of them have succeeded."

Then Marvin Shanken explained to Martin Landey what the liquor business was really all about.

"First you've got the wholesaler," he said, "and he only takes your product if you offer him a fat commission, because what he's really after is *your* profit. Then you've got the rep out on the street. He's got no loyalty to anyone. Do you think he cares about Chivas or Smirnoff or Absolut Swedish Vodka? He doesn't give a damn. He sells what the retailer buys. Then you have the bartender; he wants to be invited to fancy dinners before he'll even look at your bottle, and then he wants a little on the side for every bottle cap he can show you after three weeks. You have to call each and every bar, then each and every restaurant, then the owner of every liquor store in town. Tell your story, ask if you can come over and give him a sample case, and then you have to convince him about how many million dollars you are going to invest in advertising the label. And the only thing he does is to say, 'Yeah, that sounds pretty damn interesting.' He won't take a single bottle until people come into the store and ask for it.

"And as far as I know," said Marvin Shanken, "the world doesn't need a new vodka. Especially not a Swedish vodka. And especially not one that you can't see."

Around that time, Peter Ekelund was trying to find out just how old the new vodka was. Naturally, he knew that it was just a couple of months old, in fact not even that, since it wasn't quite ready yet. But he wanted to know how old it was in ad time.

The previous fall, the old liquor plant out on Reimersholm was being prepared for demolition when one night it caught fire. A number of heated arguments ensued about exactly how long the plant had really been out there, and which parts of it had been built by L. O. Smith, the Liquor King.

After speaking to Helmut Hagar, the curator in the attic, Ekelund felt pretty certain that liquor had been distilled out on the island since 1869. Hagar told him that it was Smith who had first advertised the liquor as being "ten times double-filtered," or "Absolut Rent Brännvin."

It occurred to Ekelund that they might put Smith on the new vodka bottle. He asked Kotte Jönsson, from the Asp and Jönsson design firm, to do a couple of sketches of the face from an old portrait. First, he painted the liquor king's profile in blue and placed him floating like a buoy near the bottom of the bottle. Then he featured Smith on a plastic medallion and moved him up above the name.

Kotte thought that there was something oddly disturbing about the picture. It reminded him of someone he knew. But L. O. Smith had been dead since World War I when Kotte wasn't even in the planning stage yet.

• • •

Lars Ohlsson Smith was born Lars Ohlsson, one of several sons of a poor farmer in Kiaby in Kristianstads County. When Lars Ohlsson's father could no longer support his family, the magistrate Carl Smith of Karlshamn took the boy in and promised to give him a proper education. Upon which Lars Ohlsson—age ten—promptly quit school and took a job with a local spice dealer.

Within two years, he had his own room and a fatter income than many of the adults in town. At fourteen, he sailed to Stockholm and landed a job in ship brokerage. At twenty, his annual income had reached two thousand dollars, an impressive sum for that time.

The economic crisis of 1857 hit the liquor shippers of south Sweden hard, and several wholesalers went bankrupt. Against everyone's advice, Lars Ohlsson took out a $60,000 loan from his old beneficiary, magistrate Smith, and established himself in Stockholm as a liquor wholesaler.

The peasant's son from Kiaby was ready to realize his grand vision. He would conquer and transform the Swedish liquor industry and in the process reinvent himself. Lars Ohlsson changed his name and became the international businessman, L. O. Smith.

Smith had decided to open a distillery outside the county limits in order to avoid the machinations of the county Bureau of Distribution. The factory, which was the most modern in the country, was built in 1869 out on Reimersholm, an island in Lake Mälaren, a stone's throw from Stockholm but in the next county.

Smith offered lower prices, but the Bureau of Distribution was sitting on a nice little monopoly and they refused to do business with him. Undeterred, he went looking for a loophole in the law, and he found one. The regulations required spirits to be free from fusel oil, which was considered unhealthy in high concentrations. Smith claimed that the traditional charcoal filtering method was incapable of removing all the fusel and should therefore be banned. If the Bureau of Distibution refused to buy his products, he would see to it that theirs got a bad name. A publicity campaign drove the point home to the general public.

In 1871 Smith found a sensational report by the French professor of medicine, Louis Marvaud. The Frenchman had proven that the fusel oil in distilled spirits was indeed harmful to health. He asserted that only hot filtering with column rectifiers could remove the ethanol pollution. Smith equipped the Reimersholm plant with the revolutionary equipment: two gigantic columns (one German and one French) with staged sections and a return pipe.

Using his columns in a public demonstration, Smith triumphantly extracted eight percent of impurities from the spirits sold by the Bureau of Distribution.

Smith publicly pilloried the old distilleries for selling "harmful spirits in direct violation of the law." In contrast to these mass poisoners, big advertisements offered the people "ten times double-filtered," absolutely pure spirits.

L. O. Smith's popularity was fortified when he arranged wine auctions out on Reimersholm island. His imported products were well known across the country, not least because Smith spiked the wine with good, decent Swedish liquor, which gave the drink its solid kick.

Perched up on a wooden platform, the Liquor King held the auctions himself, surrounded by a staff of notaries and clerks. Comfortable sofas and easy chairs were waiting for the prospective buyers.

The city officials were forced to surrender. The Liquor King was crowned.

L. O. Smith intended to use the profits from his monopoly in Sweden as leverage for an invasion of the broader European market. Each year Spain imported 75 million liters of distilled spirits for wine fortification. Fending off tough competition from the Germans, Smith managed to buy up large quantities of raw spirits in Russia, which he filtered at his own facilities and sold to Spain. To begin with, the Spaniards' gratitude knew no limits. Smith was given noble status and awarded the Great Cross of the Order of Isabella. He was soon selling more than sixty million liters of purified spirits per year and opened branches in Russia, Germany, Hungary, Italy, Spain, France, and Malta. The Liquor King of Sweden had transformed himself into one of Europe's richest men.

In 1880, when Smith was on an extended recreational trip to Egypt, his old enemies in Stockholm plotted a coup. The plan was to break up his Reimersholm company and appoint new owners in his absence. By pure coincidence, Smith got news of the plan. He abruptly ended his trip and hired a train car across Europe. He arrived in Stockholm in disguise and, to the dismay of the conspirators, appeared at the board meeting.

With his predatory business sense, Smith called their bluff. He demanded to be bought out. The jubilant board of directors, still reeling from the initial shock, were delighted to hand over the then staggering sum of two hundred thousand dollars.

L. O. Smith immediately started a new company and went into direct competition with his old one. He drowned Stockholm in cheap booze—again.

•

Smith's empire came to a sudden end. Towards the end of the 1880s, the Spanish economy was driven to the edge of bankruptcy by costly colonial wars, and the Spanish government decided to levy a tax on all alcohol sales, a tax that would be effective retroactively. Smith had a stock of sixteen thousand barrels of purified spirits on Spanish soil, all of which was confiscated. The loss ran into millions of dollars. Smith was ruined, his organization smashed. The Spanish decision went against all standing trade agreements. Not many tears were shed in the corridors of the Swedish parliament, however, and Smith received no help. The Swedish government did not lift a finger to help their countryman.

Within ten years L. O. Smith had earned another fortune, this time as an international banker, brokering large loans to the governments of China and Japan.

He lost it all again.

L. O. Smith's enemies saw in him only naked ambition and lust for power. His own daughters, whom he had married into the European nobility, called him an uneducated monster.

But one side of the L. O. Smith story was seldom told. He had a genuine concern for the living conditions of the working class. He supported the creation of a popular savings bank, spoke out for collective wage bargaining, and was a driving force in the formation of labor unions. And few people knew that the Liquor King also secretly financed several of the temperance organizations.

Above all, Smith had erected a monument to himself in the souls of the Swedish people. He had transformed a deadly fusel-producing brew to Ten Times Double-Filtered Absolut Rent Brännvin, the Swedes' beloved *Renat.*

• • •

Hans Brindfors, man of few words, keeper of the invisible bottle, went to see his boss, Lars Börje Carlsson, in August 1978, and quit. Brindfors was going to take four people from Broman's agency and start his own business. He was ordered to clean out his desk immediately, and before the working day was over, Hans Brindfors had left the Carlsson and Broman agency forever.

That evening, Dr. Stanley Noval, back from his life in the Park Avenue penthouse, stepped into the Opera Bar. He found Gunnar Broman hunched miserably over one of the tables. The adman told him that Hans Brindfors had quit. "What's going to happen now?" he asked Stanley.

At that moment, Brindfors and the four deserters entered the bar. Embarrassed, they sat down at the other end of the room. With a grand gesture Broman motioned to the head waiter.

"A bottle of the house's best champagne for the gentlemen over there in the corner!" he called out.

"Courtesy of Gunnar Broman!"

CHAPTER 10

BYE-BYE BROMAN

Martin Landey, Arlow take over as Absolut's advertising agency. Gunnar Broman tells Ayer's Jerry Siano he's off the case. Martin Landey tells Broman the same thing.

Thanks to Martin Landey's gentle coaxing, Al Singer still hadn't said no to the Swedish vodka. He just didn't like the bottle.

If there was one thing Broman was not going to accept, however, it was letting the Americans mess around with his bottle one more time.

Broman called Peter Ekelund in the States, where he was serving as the Monopoly's liaison, a couple of times a week. Ekelund could tell that the Americans were demanding radical changes. It was no longer a matter of the odd embossment or sticker, or simply trading Brindfors' silver letters for darker and bigger ones.

Applying all his powers of persuasion, Broman tried to make Ekelund stick to the original concept, the "completely consistent" Absolut, and to stop listening to the Americans.

Peter Ekelund was commuting between Stockholm and New York. He would spend three days at the Monopoly, where people took forty-five-minute coffee breaks, and asked him, amused but kindly, about the status of the export project. Was it still on?

Then it was back to New York for ten days at Martin Landey,

Arlow, where the admen shuffled in each morning straight from the nightclubs and headed for the bathroom to get ready for the day.

They went in listless and reemerged like turbo-driven rockets.

Creative director Arnie Arlow had decorated his studio like a space station. Everything was done in stylish gray; gray slate floor, gray-toned leather couches built into the gray wall, and a gray desk specially designed for the agency's creative mission control.

In the agency name—Martin Landey, Arlow—Landey got to have his first and second name, while Arnie Arlow was just Arlow. But inside the space station Arlow was never Arlow, simply Arnie.

If Martin Landey was a no-nonsense businessman prepared to fight bare-knuckled to make the United States more European, Arlow was an elegant and sensitive aesthete. Many on the creative side at the agency felt Arnie was the reason they stayed. Arnie had style, humor, and a sense of lightness—from his soft wavy hair all the way down to his tasseled Italian loafers.

Arnie Arlow thought the vodka project was great. Small, but great. He told the Swedes he was really happy to have this opportunity to work with them. And their bottle was—well, it was one of the most unusual things he had ever seen.

Creative, certainly, but . . . a bit unusual.

Arlow contemplated the three variations they had received from Sweden. They looked archaic. Even ancient. The text was written in Roman-style lettering in silver. *Silver?* It looked a lot like a medicine bottle from the 1800s.

It looked old.

This bottle is creative, Arnie Arlow announced from the bridge to the rest of the agency's creative team. Why? Partly because the bottle is so unusually short. So short, so stubby, and so much smaller than other bottles. If you look at it like this—Arlow measured with his hands in the air—then you clearly see the shortness. Plus, it doesn't have anything on it. No label, no red letters, no flags, no crests, no Russian name, nothing at all. Highly unusual, but creative.

But it looks old. Too old.

Commander Arlow sent the bottle off to the design firm of Appelbaum and Curtis. Their instructions were clear. Make it modern.

Under pressure from Martin Landey, Nycander's instinctive caution had been honed into terror. The whole thing would have to be reconsidered—nothing that the Americans said could be dismissed. Curt Nycander put his faith in the value of what was said over at Martin Landey, Arlow on Third Avenue. In spite of everything, Martin Landey knew the market.

According to Broman, the worst clients were the ones who couldn't make up their minds. Sure, they said "Great," nonstop. But that didn't mean that they had made a decision, just that they intended to take the sketches back with them to the office, so that they could mull over the campaigns. Or worse, start cutting and pasting them together themselves.

Nycander had started chopping up Broman's bottle labels and moving the different elements around on the bottle to see what might emerge.

"That man was born a nervous wreck," Broman hissed.

Nycander had once called Broman at home, a half hour after they had separated at Stockholm airport.

"You know what, Gunnar!" Nycander hollered enthusiastically down the phone. "I found an incredible deal on the way home. There was a suit on sale for forty bucks!"

"Wow!" Broman shouted back into the phone. "Pretty damn lucky, Curt! Congratulations!"

"I bet that suit's still hanging on the racks," thought Broman. "He will need to sleep on it before he actually closes the deal."

Curt Nycander could tell that the Americans were not satisfied at all. They wanted more hieroglyphics and royal crowns and bigger lettering—and more colors. They had even asked him why the Swedes couldn't put two fluttering flags, those pretty Swedish flags in yellow and blue, right across the bottle!

In the model world, where the systematic Nycander preferred to dwell, things didn't work like this. In the model world, you could examine all the variables, manipulate them and see what happened.

The trick was to shrink the unexplainable down to an insignificant factor, an unimportant random effect. If you made a tenth of a knot better than your competitor, you would win the Great Round-Gotland Race, a circumnavigation of Sweden's largest island, by a margin of—Nycander had calculated this—exactly forty minutes and thirty-one seconds.

Stuck in the middle, between the American and Swedish admen, Nycander sought his own compromise bottle. The thankless ad geniuses quickly dubbed it "Montezuma's revenge."

The work Broman had done with Jerry Siano at Ayer had been aimed at finding an importer. Broman—never easily impressed by sheer size—always thought that the Monopoly shouldn't be looking for one of the big-time liquor companies. It wasn't just any importer the Monopoly wanted, it was a partner.

Broman and Ekelund had drawn up a long list of characteristics of the ideal importer. The list looked like a description of Al Singer's Carillon.

Unfortunately, laid-back Al Singer came complete with his own advertising agency—Martin Landey, Arlow, on Third Avenue.

Broman asked Singer if they could continue to work with N. W. Ayer. The French bottle that Ayer had—if not liked—at least suffered, was in place. And there were five ad campaign proposals ready to go with it.

But his pleading fell on deaf ears. Singer blurted out that he hated big agencies. Just hated them.

No matter how hard Broman cajoled, Al Singer would never call Siano.

Broman calmed down a little when Martin Landey explained that Al Singer himself had asked for the Swedes to be involved in the creative work. Singer liked Broman, and Broman liked Al Singer, and Landey said that personally, he was impressed by the work that the Swedes had done on the bottle. In fact, one of his greatest desires was to put it on the market in true partnership with Broman.

After that, Martin Landey promised offhandedly that the Swede would get a third of all future commissions from the Absolut Vodka account.

Maybe it was the offer of that ultimate American argument—cash—that made Broman realize that they would never go back to Siano, and he would have to let go of the Ayer connection.

One day, one of Broman's employees had glued a one-crown coin onto a bottle, more or less as a joke. Björn Asp, of the design firm Asp & Jönsson, replaced it with a marksmanship medal he had won in the military. They liked it, but since Asp wanted to keep his medal, he put on a five-crown coin instead.

It turned out that the American admen loved this piece of foreign coinage. So Kotte Jönsson and Björn Asp were immediately given the assignment of producing seals by the dozen.

Kotte and Bjorn bought a hobby kit for molding tin soldiers and started to melt metal up in the studio. Using a paper matrix, they made piles of seals: shields, crests, swords, rifles, and cannons. They did a sheaf of corn, a human head, the three-crown national crest, a goddess standing in the entrance to a temple, a man rolling a barrel, a ship sailing to the horizon, a knight's helmet, a flower.

Finally they did a full Egyptian crowd scene with pharaohs and slaves.

Then someone recalled that the old Coca-Cola bottles had the name in relief. Björn Asp found a printing plate, made a reversed form in clay, poured "Absolut Vodka" in rubber into it, and started gluing the letters onto the bottles. They spent a week making new bottles. A solid plastic Absolut Coca-Cola soon stood waiting in the studio.

Cheered on by Martin Landey, Arlow, the Swedish designers rapidly created a seal that seemed to solve all of the problems. The name again was "Absolut Vodka"—they skipped the springtime "Country of Sweden" bit—written with a pink edging. The name was guarded by two golden lions with waving tails, each with a long, fire-engine-red tongue and wild, bulging eyes. Between the lions rested two boudoir-green wreaths, tied together with a light-blue and pink rosebud, all of which surrounded a baby-blue picture of L. O. Smith's Reimersholm factory.

It was a very dejected Gunnar Broman who returned to the forty-first floor of Burlington House and sat down with Jerry Siano to explain that N. W. Ayer was out of the picture. Broman related the story of the Monopoly's difficulties in finding an importer, how they had come to the end of the road, and were just barely able to convince small Carillon Importers to take it on.

When Siano heard the deal Carillon would get from the Swedes, his admiration for Martin Landey's business acumen rose. A fifty-fifty deal, without having to put up any money? The Swedes had been taken to the cleaners.

The two admen reminisced for a while about the good old days out at Jerry's garage, with Brindfors and all that Italian food. Broman told Siano he had a vague feeling that he, too, would soon be out of the loop. Then he came to one last sad matter: he had to ask the American to have all the vodka material—the research, the bottle designs and the ad campaigns—packed up and sent over to Martin Landey, Arlow.

Once more Gunnar Broman started making the trip across the Atlantic with a suitcase full of bottles. He came over with pink bottles, with silver-and-gold ones, ones that looked like Coca-Cola bottles from the fifties, and bottles with waving banners and L. O. Smith's factory painted in baby blue on the glass. Every two weeks Broman appeared with a new batch of bottles, presented them, and promoted the virtues of the new solutions. And every new model he pulled out of his case disgusted him even more than the last one.

No longer the happy magician, Broman had stopped laughing.

• • •

Most people at the Carlsson & Broman ad agency wondered who Carlsson was. Lars Börje Carlsson would arrive in the morning in a big, black chauffeur-driven Mercedes Benz, sneak into his office without a word, and stay out of sight for the rest of the day.

Broman was short and rotund, and he laughed easily. Lars Börje Carlsson was tall and thin, and he kept quiet, like a pious monk living a life of austerity. People said about Broman that if you asked him for an idea, ten came back, whether you wanted them or not. Seven would be fantastic and the rest borderline crazy.

From Carlsson you usually got one idea, and it would be brilliant.

When Hans Brindfors quit, everything—bottles, sketches, and plastic prototypes—was sent up to Carlsson.

Lars Börje Carlsson found the bottle out in his own garage. He was looking for something clean and clinical, and one day there it was, among all the boxes and cans he collected—the Bottle.

On the bottle it said *Liljeholmen's Vinegar Factory tel. South 235*. Carlsson especially liked that last part, *South 235*. Broman and Brindfors had each found a bottle of their own, and now Carlsson had taken over the project, and he had found one too.

Lars Börje Carlsson had started the agency in the mid-sixties with Per Blomstrand, an adman of legendary standing. The idea was that Carlsson would be in artistic control at the new agency and Blomstrand would serve as executive director. Blomstrand had invented a system that he felt would revolutionize the art of management. He had put up a red mailbox by the front door. When the art directors and copywriters left for the day, they had to put notes in the box saying how many hours they had worked on each project. A girl emptied the box every night, did the math, added a hundred percent, and billed the clients.

Later, Gunnar Broman, who had been writing ads alone in his basement outside Stockholm, joined them. The agency became Blomstrand, Carlsson & Broman.

•

Broman and Blomstrand discovered that Lars Börje Carlsson had an almost uncanny feel for what was "in" at any given moment. Lars Börje Carlsson believed that a sensitive adman could find the eye of the trend. It really didn't require big money; it just required sensitivity. One winter, on Carlsson's advice, they had sold ryecrisp by flying twenty farmers, complete with pitchforks, plaid shirts, neckerchiefs, the whole nine yards, down to the island of Mallorca. Everyone had the unsettling feeling that the hick factor was too high this time, but the campaign started a ryecrisp epidemic. It turned out that two million Swedish ryecrisp eaters wanted nothing better than to get back to their roots. They longed for the simple life on the farm. Within a year young people started moving out of the cities in droves.

Per Blomstrand eventually decided that he needed a break from the stress of management-by-mailbox, and he left Sweden. The agency changed names to Carlsson & Broman. They continued to win prizes and earn good money, but they refused to let the agency grow. Neither of them wanted to manage a big agency. Broman's belief was firm: Creative work is inversely proportional to the number of employees. When the number of people hired grows past thirty, creativity siphons off.

While Gunnar Broman could, with a roar of laughter, say to a customer whom he had just billed for a hundred thousand, "You know, I've got such incredibly bad taste," Lars Börje Carlsson was a perfectionist down to his toes. Carlsson was disgusted by the mediocre. The mere thought of spending time on something that he had not fully mastered gave him the chills. When he realized that he would never become the world's greatest driver, he quit driving and rented a limo.

He never accompanied the vodka delegations to the United States. Carlsson was equipped with halting high-school English, and he saw no reason to practice it on the Americans, who most likely had mastered the language to near perfection.

The sixties had been a time of suffering for Carlsson. People who had slopped a little paint around once or twice went around calling themselves "artists" and insisting that ugly was beautiful.

For a whole decade, his need to see beautiful things grew stronger. The seventies had been a slight improvement, but it seemed to Carlsson as though both advertising and fashion were striking a series of poses. But now it was 1978, and Lars Börje Carlsson had a distinct feeling that something was happening with taste.

• • •

Lars Börje Carlsson spent two weeks going through all the various components that had been tried earlier. He pulled out Royal Court Vodka, with the story about the fantastic Cadillac Seville on the bottle and asked Kotte Jönsson, from Asp and Jönsson, to create a text with the car ad's font as a model. Jönsson used a fine marker on one of his hardest papers to write out Broman's text:

This superb vodka was distilled
from grain grown in the rich fields
of southern Sweden.
It has been produced at the famous
old distilleries near Åhus
in accordance with more than
400 years of Swedish tradition,
and sold under this brand, Absolut Vodka
since 1869.

When Kotte Jönsson was finished, he enlarged it on the photocopier, made a few minor corrections, then used the copier to reduce it again. Then he worked over the text a second time, enlarged it, changed it, and reduced it once more. By repeating this process several times, the text lost some of its exacting, machine-made elegance and began to look hand drawn. When they transferred it onto acetate in order to place it on the bottle, the ultra-fine lines cracked, and Jönsson had to build them up a little more.

Carlsson knew that he could give Kotte Jönsson a simple sketch, or an ad torn out of a magazine, or a headline, and when he came back it would be technically impossible to improve on his work within the parameters of the assignment. Carlsson thought of Kotte Jönsson and his colleague Björn Asp as two extremely experienced auto mechanics who kept their heads down under the hood, rooting around with wrenches. They might not have known where the car was heading, but without their efforts, it wasn't going anywhere.

Broman and Carlsson set about creating a background for the vodka. The goal was to associate the vodka that was now being produced with the spirits sold by L. O. Smith a hundred years earlier.

For a while, they had tried to structure the front of the bottle around the year 1869. They had put 1869 on the seal, they had placed it directly over the name and created "1869 Absolut Country of Sweden Vodka." They had even gone so far as to change the name to "1869 Absolut Vodka," making the year the central element in big, fat numbers at the top of the bottle, with Absolut Vodka in thin handwriting.

But the real strength in the name lay in the fact that it was actually a value judgment—"absolut." At the same time, the connection to the past could not be too weak, as Jerry Siano had often pointed out.

Broman tried to go the whole way. He claimed that the liquor had been"sold under the *trademark* Absolut Vodka" back then, even if it wasn't exactly true. There was no trademark, and it wasn't vodka. It wasn't even *Brännvin,* Renat.

It turned out that what Smith had hot-filtered through his German and French columns and sold in 1869 was technical spirits. The *Brännvin* couldn't actually be traced farther back than March 1878. So they agreed on 1879, which meant that the newborn vodka was an even hundred years old.

Even "the name Absolut" could lead to a few awkward questions. In the 1800s, Absolut had been an indication of quality, not a name. But the whole idea of saying, *It has been produced at the famous old distilleries near Åhus in accordance with more than 400 years of Swedish tradition, and sold under the name Absolut Vodka since 1879,* was to give the impression that there actually existed a unique product at that time, and this was it. Sweden had been awash with Absolute pure vodkas. But then fraud had been part of the advertising business from the very beginning, as Ayer's Neal O'Connor had cheerfully pointed out to Broman.

Early on, the lawyers had made it clear that Absolut Vodka was a generic classification and that it would not qualify for trademark registration, either in Sweden or in the United States, not even if they removed the *e* from the English "absolute." The admen needed to squeeze in something more—"1869" or "Country of Sweden" or a seal—in order to register a trademark for the product.

Lars Börje Carlsson started all over again. He kept the thick, block letters that Arnie Arlow wanted, but used the ordinary Futura Extra Bold font that could be found in any basic type catalog. He reduced the space between the letters so that "Absolut" and "Vodka" each formed their own solid block. Between the two words, Kotte wrote "Country of Sweden" in the same style as the text on the bottle, but in a larger size. Carlsson had to change "Country of Sweden" several times before he discovered that he had to raise the *C* in Country and the *S* in Sweden, so that the letters came up to "Absolut" and connected the whole name together in a unified word image. Carlsson placed a small glass rim around the foot of the neck. With the help of the domed bottom, they could make the bottle a little taller, and the neck could be made longer.

They had experimented earlier on with a real cork in the bottle, but the corks had cracked. Then they had tried a cap that went down over the neck. Now they went over to a flat screw cap, with a matte metallic color.

Lars Börje Carlsson then shaped a slight buckle on the rear of the bottle, which gave the impression that the bottle was handblown and also refracted light through the glass, making it less invisible. Over everything else he placed a seal with an image of the liquor king, L. O. Smith. The bearded chin, the bald head, the rotund body. He couldn't help but grin when he saw Smith's profile.

Lars Börje Carlsson continued to make minutely small adjustments to the bottle's appearance. The secret was in the details. Each and every day, Kotte Jönsson and his colleague, Björn Asp, arrived with new solutions that Carlsson studied and sent back again. After a time, he felt there was a kind of musicality to the design. Except in the colors of the lettering. That was still much too noisy. He had tried to get away from the seventies feel of the Americans' bottles; he didn't like the mixed colors, the pink and light blue, or the gold and platinum, which were too expensive anyway; it was all too "flower power" and rummaging in the attic. But he didn't want to end up with Brindfors' chilly simplicity. He was looking for something else.

•

Carlsson sometimes went down to the beach by the small village of Ljugarn on Gotland, an island in the middle of the Baltic Sea, where he had a house. It was here at the shore, away from it all, that he received the message in the bottle.

Carlsson had uncovered a problem with Brindfors' silver design, a problem that Broman didn't want to know about. The lettering was clean and simple all right, but it needed some contrast to emphasize its simplicity. Jerry Siano and Martin Landey had been right: something had to be done with the bottle. Brindfors' design was too severe. Unfortunately, so were their improvements.

He wished he could find a balance between sensualism and purity. This should not be any ordinary bottle. And then, when he imagined that the bottle should be able to be painted in oils on canvas, it all came together.

In the end, Lars Börje Carlsson incorporated everything, both the Americans' and the Swedes' ideas, into his own feeling for the pure, exact tone.

The text, Broman's long piece of advertising poetry, in black.

The name, "Absolut Vodka," true blue.

"There," said Carlsson.

• • •

Appelbaum & Curtis, the design firm that Arnie Arlow had hired to fix the bottle, had come up with six different designs. When Lars Börje Carlsson's bottles arrived from Sweden, Martin Landey decided that focus groups were called for, to get a grip on the bottles' *ghestaaalt.*

Al Singer, Gunnar Broman, and Martin Landey sat down behind the one-way mirrors and listened to their guinea pigs discuss the various bottles, while the interviewer attempted to expose their hidden and complex motives for reacting the way they did.

People kind of liked Arnie Arlow's bottles. They looked really nice.

Carlsson's bottle got a quick reaction. They hated it. Each focus group contained a large and not particularly silent majority of bottle haters. They still thought that Carlsson's bottle, like its French predecessor, looked like a blood-plasma bag, a medicine bottle, or a receptacle for industrial alcohol. And then they patiently tried to explain to the interviewer why this bottle did not look like a liquor bottle was *supposed* to look.

But every time, it turned out that one or two respondents with differing opinions had sneaked into the group. Their reaction was just as firm as the majority's and, strangely enough, for exactly the same reasons. They pointed at Lars Börje Carlsson's bottle. There it was. Clear as a bell. That was their bottle. They were ready to buy it immediately. They wanted it—now.

When Broman and Al Singer went out to have lunch afterwards, Al commented sourly that he knew one thing for sure, and that was that he had godawful bad taste. It occurred to Broman that he too had godawful bad taste, but maybe not quite as bad as Al Singer's.

When Arnie Arlow wasn't allowed to redo the bottle, he started working on a creative outer packaging.

Arnie's idea was that since the bottle wasn't visible, it should be sold in a box. Broman got a look at Arlow's box and was seized by a major tantrum. What the hell was going on here, he asked. When they had finally found a bottle that most of them could agree on and some of the test subjects even liked, Arnie Arlow comes along with some goddamned phony baloney sheet-metal box that he wants to put the bottle in. Broman was having trouble speaking. He pointed at Arnie Arlow's box: "That's the kind of box you would put . . . a corpse in."

Martin Landey's impatience with Broman's behavior was growing. Landey had a clear idea about the bottle, which he put forward. Arlow also had an opinion. Al Singer had an opinion. Even Abe Rosenberg had an opinion. The whole world apparently had an opinion about the Swedish bottle, but the bottle was Broman's baby and Broman couldn't stand it when they messed around with his baby. The Swede wasn't acting like a professional adman.

The worst of it was that Broman struck back with coarse innuendoes about the American's being tasteless. Tasteless? Martin Landey was the embodiment of good taste on Madison Avenue. Landey had started the agency with clients from the fashion industry, and his ads were published in *Vogue*. It wasn't exactly a bunch of vagrant longshoremen that he had assembled at Martin Landey, Arlow. This was no J. Walter fucking Thompson, with its mass advertising, if that's what the hick thought. Martin Landey, Arlow were artists who produced elegant, high-class, sophisticated advertising. On Advertising Avenue they were *the arbiters of taste.*

And by the way, Martin Landey asked himself, what had Broman come up with? A urine sample.

At the next meeting, Landey suddenly declared that now that everyone seemed to agree on the bottle, he realized that it would be for the best if Gunnar Broman was taken off the project. Martin Landey said it coldly. No hard words. No daggers in the dark. It was a quiet little thing.

The reason, Landey explained, was that Broman had tried to manipulate Al Singer, since the Swede apparently hoped that

Martin Landey would lose the assignment. Maybe he wanted to give it back to Ayer or to someone else, maybe he wanted to keep it for himself. Whatever. That was the sort of thing that Martin Landey quite simply could not accept. He would not accept the fact that someone was going directly to the client behind his back, since his relationship with the client was sacred.

Gunnar Broman gazed across the table at Curt Nycander. Curt was a blank face with a moustache. He turned toward Al Singer, who just stared down at the table.

"Why didn't you say anything?" Broman asked, when they were riding down in the elevator. Nycander shrugged.

"But Gunnar, you know how the Americans are," he said. "Don't take it personally."

"You asked me to take care of it," Broman said. "You and Lindmark. Why didn't you tell them what you said in Stockholm?"

They came out onto Third Avenue and stood outside Smith & Wollensky's Steakhouse. It said *Since 1977* on the sign and Broman, who had always thought he had a particularly good relationship to dates, liked that sign. It should have read *1877*, of course. Then there would have been some meaning in it. But it said *Since 1977*.

"Things are starting to go down the toilet, Curt," Broman shouted. "It's starting to get fucking boring working on this thing."

"You know what, Gunnar," Curt Nycander said pensively. "They might be right, after all. I wonder if we shouldn't have a label. So that the bottle would be visible. "

The man from the Monopoly suddenly lit up.

"Or, you know what? Maybe a label on the back side."

CHAPTER 11
ABSOLUT VODKA

Monopoly Master Blender Börje Karlsson creates Absolut Vodka. And Peter Ekelund introduces it to the United States with a drunken song.

One sunny day in fall, another Börje Karlsson—Börje Karlsson with a *K*, the master blender and laboratory chief at the Liquor Monopoly, was called into a board meeting at headquarters on Saint Erik's Street.

The Monopoly had asked Börje Karlsson to specify the technical requirements for the export vodka. Karlsson had explained that a vodka made from potatoes was out of the question if the company really wanted to move into the international market. Such a venture would demand the finest grain that they could possibly find in Sweden, which the goddamned farmers would probably not agree to, since they were so well paid for their industrial-quality potatoes. But that's the way it would have to be. If he could use the new distilling plant that they were currently adjusting, and if he was given enough time, then yeah, Börje Karlsson reckoned there was a chance he could produce the best vodka in the world.

The technical director of the Monopoly had snorted and said that it all sounded very expensive, but Lindmark cut him off, saying that it could cost whatever it needed to cost.

•

The Russians used potatoes for their vodka, even if they certified that they used nothing but wheat, and the Poles used molasses, and Börje Karlsson could never figure out what the Americans were using. He had been in Hartford, Connecticut, and seen the gigantic plant with ten production lines, where empty bottles went in one end, and full ones came out the other. But Börje Karlsson didn't trust Smirnoff. Smirnoff was produced in Europe, too, and Börje Karlsson had personally seen to it that the only thing that was admitted into Sweden was American Smirnoff, from Hartford, Connecticut. They weren't going to have any goddamned European American Russian vodka as long as Börje Karlsson was making the decisions.

It was the Finns and the Americans that they needed to worry about, that much was completely clear to him. Koskenkorva and Smirnoff. Koskenkorva was pure, completely pure, but that was also the Finns' problem—it lacked character. Smirnoff had character, but it was far from pure. "That's where we have our borders," Börje Karlsson explained. "Somewhere between Kosken and Smirnoff is where we should place the world's best Swedish vodka."

The first thing Karlsson did was to put his associate Brita Grunditz to work running every vodka in the known world through a gas chromatograph. She would then compare the results with their own products, in various stages of filtration, and establish purity criteria. The question was how to distinguish among the various kinds of impurities. On the one hand, they wanted to remove the impurities, but on the other, they needed to identify the impurities that contributed to the aroma.

The strange thing was that with existing methods of chemical analysis—and the Monopoly's technology was as modern as anyone else's, as far as Börje Karlsson knew—it was completely impossible to determine exactly which elements gave the stuff its smell and flavor. He knew that it was those damned pyridines, the same pyridines that appeared in green bell peppers, fresh-baked bread, beer, and Renat, but no one knew exactly what it was that they did. They smelled. Okay, but then what? The chromatograph could put them on the right spoor, but after that they had to sniff their way along the trail. Suddenly everything seemed to hang on Börje Karlsson's nose.

There were those among the testing staff who thought that Karlsson sat with that nose stuck in alcohol all day long, and they found that funny. "What do you do when it tastes really good, Börje?" they sniggered."Take a quick shot?" Nobody ever joked about wine, of course, because wine was sacred, but it was fine to make jokes about liquor. To make things worse, he had started smoking again, but when he was working with the vodka, he couldn't smoke for a whole hour before the sniffing began. It was a pain in the ass. But that wasn't where the real problem lay. The problem was not to be able to taste with the tongue, but to be able to taste with the brain, to be able to think the taste.

Karlsson started with wheat. What is it, he wondered, that is unique about that smell? He sat at home at his kitchen table and concentrated on wheat. Wheat, wheat, goddamned wheat. Börje Karlsson imagined that he was breaking open a loaf of fresh French bread, and he thought about how some people only wanted the crust, and how they would dig out the middle with their fingers and gnaw on the crust as if they were rats.

Börje Karlsson had worked as a researcher for the pharmaceutical company Kabi, but research had been too insecure. Every other year he had been forced to apply for new funding, never knowing how much he would be granted. When he got married, he thought that maybe he ought to get a regular job. At that time, he had a cellar full of wine. Karlsson had liked wine since his student days at the Technical Academy, and now he had an offer of a job as a chemist at the Wine and Liquor Monopoly. Lindmark had recently taken over the Monopoly and had decided that the old tasters would be downsized right out of there. All the Monopoly's wine testing activities would be brought together in one department whose operation would be properly scientific. He turned to Börje Karlsson, a scientist who also happened to be a first-class wine connoisseur.

Karlsson had a couple of samples that they had used in a preliminary stage of Crown Vodka, one of the Monopoly's cheap, down-market products.

He used these samples to concoct a series of vodka cocktails. This was a little trick he had learned. Most people thought that fruit and vegetable flavors would mask a bad liquor, but the opposite was true. A Bloody Mary accentuated any bad tastes in the vodka. That was how he developed his method. First, he sorted by technical analysis, then by mixing drinks, and finally, he sorted with his nose.

Then the Americans came to Stockholm on a grand visit and Al Singer stated that the true test of a vodka was if it melted slowly over ice. If you put a bottle of Stolichnaya in the freezer, the liquid flowed slowly when you took it out again. This was a sign of quality. Before you tasted a drop, you should be able to see how the vodka sort of separated and slid like oil over the ice cubes. Since all vodka tasted basically the same, according to Singer, it was a matter of having those little characteristics that his salesmen could point out in their meetings with the retailers. It should be a creamy, oily liquor.

All vodkas the same?!

Börje Karlsson, the master blender, was discouraged. Here comes a bunch of Americans, who said they were so happy about being able to market the purest vodka in the world—it wasn't called Absolut for nothing!—and they ask him to add more fusel oil, the very thing that he had spent the past six months trying to get rid of, pyridine by pyridine. Now the vodka was supposed to be both the purest of the pure and yet packed full of fusel.

The Americans spent an entire morning in the lab demanding more fusel. The vodka should flow more and more slowly over the ice, they insisted. Finally, they were satisfied.

Up until the early seventies, the raw spirits had been produced by a chain of small, rural distillers under the chairmanship of Pontus De la Gardie, Count of Borrestad. But then, in typical fashion, a decision was taken to shut everything down. The Count of Borrestad had passed away, and the Distillers' Association was no longer what it had been. The distilleries were run down and the distillers themselves stood idle in the courtyards, old and tired and just waiting for the end. A single, mammoth national distillery was created.

That's when a bureaucrat somewhere made a mistake. One of the rural distilleries that had been closed down had produced the raw spirits for a domestic Swedish aquavit named Östgöta Sädesbrännvin (*Östgöta* from the province from which it originated, and *Sädesbrännvin* because it was made from wheat). No one bothered what might happen to Östgöta Sädesbrännvin when the old distillery closed. Someone must have assumed that things would just work out somehow. The plant had been one of the smallest. It didn't sell more than forty thousand liters a year. It was tended by a single old man and was situated in a corner of the country that even God had forgotten. Afterwards, it turned out that no one knew just what the old guy had been up to. And then one day they realized that the raw spirits for Östgöta Sädesbrännvin had simply evaporated.

First they tried to scrape something together on their own. That didn't work out. Then they were forced to go to Börje Karlsson and admit that they had run into a slight problem. In the great process of restructuring, they had unfortunately lost Östgöta Sädes, one of Sweden's finest products. All they had left was a single barrel with a few drops in the bottom. And they wondered if Karlsson might possibly be able to do something about this unfortunate situation, and preferably before Lindmark found out about it, since the Monopoly's boss had such a terrible temper.

They wanted him to recreate Östgöta Sädesbrännvin, bring that noble drink back to life without the fields of grain, the old farmer, and the exhausted old burners that had added that special aroma. Östgöta was pure "country" spirits. Börje Karlsson stuck his pipette into the oak barrel. It had the scent of buns, of coarse, country bread. In the old days, the spirits were always sweetened to hide the mash smell, and in Östgöta Sädes he could sense a little honey and plum. Then Börje Karlsson came down to the huge new distillery and quite simply recreated Östgöta Sädesbrännvin from scratch.

It was not until after Brita Grunditz had screened all the world's vodkas on the chromatograph. And it was not until after the visiting Americans had expressed their views about vodka being some kind of frigid lava running over the ice cubes. And it was not until he had once again returned to his mental wheat exercises at the kitchen table, that Börje Karlsson was suddenly struck by the memory of those "old country" spirits. It was the aroma of bread! And suddenly he had Östgöta Sädes in his nose. He had conjured it up in his mind: the old farmer peering out over the courtyard, the fields of corn waving in that damned country wind, the arthritic dog barking, the farmer's grouchy wife, and the beat-up boilers bubbling away in the distillery that they wanted to shut down. And over the whole scene, there was the scent of wheat rolls.

"There," said Karlsson.

• • •

By fall of 1978, everyone was mad at everyone else. Martin Landey wanted to get rid of Gunnar Broman. Gunnar Broman felt that Martin Landey had tricked him. Peter Ekelund thought that Martin Landey was a psychopath. Curt Nycander felt that Ekelund hadn't given the Americans enough support. Gunnar Broman considered Nycander's caution, now that they were creeping closer to a final decision, to be perverse. Martin Landey suspected that the Monopoly was backing out. The Monopoly was afraid Martin Landey and Al Singer were backing out.

Everyone just wished that the damn thing could finally be settled. But the people who could make the decisions, wouldn't, and those who would, couldn't.

The bottle went on a focus-group tour through New York, Chicago, Detroit, and Los Angeles. All around the country test subjects revealed their hidden and complicated motives, and all around the country the majority said no and the minority pointed to Lars Börje Carlsson's bottle.

And then one day Peter Ekelund had had enough. He called Lars Lindmark and said: "It's settled. Blue and red. Everybody agrees."

Then Ekelund explained radiantly to the others that Lars Lindmark himself had reached a decision. It would be Lars Börje Carlsson's bottle, with blue lettering for the 40 percent alcohol content and red lettering for the 50 percent.

Al Singer and Martin Landey were overjoyed. At the end of October they flew over to Sweden and had dinner at the Opera restaurant with Lars Lindmark, Curt Nycander, Peter Ekelund, and the Monopoly's lawyer. The next day, the bottles were displayed in the wood-paneled conference room in the liquor castle and the contract was signed.

The Monopoly and Carillon would not only be manufacturers and importers, they would be partners. The marketing costs would be split down the middle and the eventual profits divided in the same way. Their goal was to sell a hundred thousand cases with twelve bottles of prime Swedish vodka per case, within five years. It would mean a little money and a lot of prestige for the Monopoly.

Lars Lindmark prayed to God that it wouldn't be the end of his career.

Absolut Vodka's debut took place at the liquor trade convention in the Fairmont Hotel, New Orleans, in the spring of 1979.

Peter Ekelund had flown over with three cases of vodka as hand baggage, but he left them in his hotel room and had to rush back for them. When he arrived at the Fairmont, breathless, with the vodka in his arms, the distributors were already standing in Carillon's suite with drinks in their hands, waiting.

Martin Landey and Al Singer had decided that only those distributors who placed a large enough order would get the rights to sell Absolut Vodka, and they would also get exclusive rights in their region. But not everyone who placed big orders would be in on it. Carillon would concentrate on New York, San Francisco, Los Angeles, and Boston, where trends were created, where there was media and a bar culture. If you succeeded in Philadelphia, it didn't mean a thing in New York, but if it was a hit in New York, it would be echoed across the country. Several distributors from the Midwest were interested, but Martin Landey and Al Singer explained that their strategy was very clear: they couldn't back up a nationwide launch, so the Midwest would have to wait

Al Singer wanted to visit the retailers personally, to present his new product. He could meet his good friend Jack Papas up in Boston and address the whole sales force. Martin Landey thought it was strange that the Frenchman who was Carillon's sales manager did not get to come along, but Al Singer explained that nobody in Boston would understand what the Frenchman was saying. On the other hand, Al Singer was keen for Peter Ekelund to participate. He would give the vodka a face, Singer argued, suggesting that the event should be inaugurated by Peter singing that hell, guts, and gore song that Swedes usually belted out whenever they came near alcohol.

When Peter Ekelund stepped up to the podium before the salesmen in Boston, he had a mug in one hand and a bottle in the other. He talked about the new Swedish vodka, while he held up one of the first bottles that had made the long trip over the Atlantic. It was certified in writing on the bottle that the liquor had been produced according to centuries-old traditions at the ancient distillery town of Åhus.

In reality, it was all distilled at the newly built plant in Årstadal, just outside Stockholm, and each bottle had then been carefully wrapped in tissue paper. Börje Karlsson had produced the vodka in two stages. The main ingredient was completely pure spirits made from grain, to which he had added a small amount of scented spirits to capture that essence of wheat roll, that soft edge of honey. It was no more than a few parts per thousand, but according to Karlsson, it was enough to give the drink character. Up to the last minute Karlsson had experimented with two variations of Absolut Vodka, a stronger and a milder version. The stronger one was actually clearer and more direct, but he found that he got tired of it after a while. For two months he went down to the lab and smelled it a couple of times a day, and in the end it was too much. They would go with the milder one. And just as Karlsson had predicted, he landed right between Koskenkorva and Smirnoff.

Börje Karlsson planned for the scented spirits to be aged for three years in special wooden barrels down in Åhus. The "country" spirits would be restored to the soil of the motherland and Absolut Vodka would be the only vodka in the world stored in oak barrels.

At first, the farmers' cooperative refused to sell the grain to the Monopoly. They wanted to sell them more potatoes. According to the kind of reverse logic that dominated the agricultural industry, the farmers got their best prices for their worst potatoes, so they felt strongly that the new export vodka should be made from industrial potatoes. But Nycander had taken over negotiations and had been immovable. Absolut Vodka would be made from grain, and it would be the best grain in the country.

Peter Ekelund filled the mug with Absolut Vodka. He bellowed out a verse of a Viking drinking song and then knocked back the whole mug in one long, deep draft. As the liquor started to take effect, he stepped down between the rows of slack-jawed salesmen and wavered toward the back of the auditorium. Jack Papas and his liquor salesmen sat completely still, transfixed by this six foot seven Viking moving down the aisle with increasingly unsteady steps. Al Singer and Martin Landey grinned with satisfaction. Then the entire room exploded in a roar of primal glee. Jesus Christ, this was fun! *That Viking guy had made his entire presentation in Swedish and nobody had understood a single word! And then—the mug!*

Peter Ekelund set out on the road with a suitcase full of cash. He showed up like a menacing shadow in the door of every bar worth mentioning in New York, Boston, and San Francisco, always ready to hold a bottle up to the light and press a couple of twenties into the palm of a distributor or a bartender. At every sales meeting he stepped up to the podium, made his opening address in that strange foreign tongue, sang his hell-and-gore song, downed a mug of prime Swedish vodka, and tottered towards the back wall followed by Al Singer's delighted cackling. *"Peter Ekelund—a real Viking, give him a big hand!"*

Strictly speaking, Peter Ekelund didn't give a shit whether the bottle was short, tall, round, or square. Gold, silver, red, or blue, he just didn't give a damn. While all the others were playing with their toys, somebody had to guard the project, push it over the thousands of obstructions and around all the roadblocks. Someone had to guide the bottle through the Monopoly's hesitation, past the Americans' "minor" alterations, past Brindfors's unwillingness to abandon silver, Curt's caution, and Broman's demand for artistic control. The bottle had to get out. In the end, the whole project rested with a twenty-four-year-old fresh out of business school, who really only had one quality that was truly his own: he had nothing to lose.

He methodically drank his way through upper Manhattan. He would grab a stool at the bar, scan the crowd of stockbrokers, small-time gangsters, and admen, and then loudly order a whole bottle of Absolut Vodka and start drinking. He drank his way down Forty-second Street toward the East River, drank down Wall Street, drank his way up Broadway and downtown. He drank himself senseless in the name of duty more times than any liquor salesman had ever done before. One night he ran into two street bankers in the bathroom of a bar who felt that he should be immediately separated from his money. Ekelund contemplated the two jokers and tried to convince himself that the whole thing was a hoax. Then he found himself gazing into the end of something that looked very like a gun.

And then he thought about—Daddy.

Peter Ekelund's father was one of the few independent business executives in the Swedish clan system of loyalties and meat hooks, the latest in a long line of role models driving Peter on. His grandfather had taken a bronze medal in the high jump at the 1920 Olympic Games and then gone to Shanghai to work as an engineer. Ekelund senior-senior could still be seen every Saturday, strolling around the market in posh Östermalm with his cane, enjoying the plate of oysters and the glass of sherry waiting for him at a specially reserved table. Peter's grandfather used to show him a cigarette case with an engraving that said, "for contributions as a doctor during the cholera epidemic of 1846." He had gotten it from *his* grandfather.

And it had all come to this. One in the morning, half bombed, with his back against the wall of a toilet in a New York bar, facing two people who were removing his cash reserve while they pointed a big black revolver at his chest. They had a convincing argument. But what did he have?

Who was actually going to buy this thing he was pushing?

It seemed like the only place on the entire American continent that actually sold Absolut Country of Sweden Vodka was a bar down by the docks in Boston. An order for a couple of cases was coming in every week. Peter had checked out what was happening in Boston, and it turned out that the orders came from a place near the foot of Beacon Hill, a popular meeting place for gay men. That was just what he needed. The only people who drank his vodka were a bunch of queers down by Boston harbor.

Peter Ekelund had chosen to go somewhere where he could have something of his own, not the family's, not his daddy's. And what he had finally gotten was this. Something odorless, tasteless, and colorless. Almost nothing, but it was his.

But the two guys in the bathroom were not about to settle for nothing. Fortunately, Ekelund always carried a hundred and fifty dollars in cash.

Everything in life was business. Seventeen bucks to fill up on Absolut. A hundred and fifty to piss it out.

• • •

The last big fight between Broman and the admen at Martin Landey, Arlow concerned the first real ad. Broman claimed the copy was already there for everyone to see and read—there on the bottle. And who had written that? The Swede himself. By now they had had enough of Gunnar Broman at Martin Landey, Arlow.

The Ayer boxes contained, among many other things, the Ayer campaigns—the "Russians make better tanks," the "Absolut Welcom," the "Absolut Everything." They weren't deemed stylish enough. Just like the original bottle, the ideas were interesting, sure, but they were too punny and too obvious.

Not creative.

Neither Carillon nor the Swedish Liquor Monopoly were prepared to put up a great amount of money for a campaign, so there would have to be a single ad that could run for about a year.

Arnie Arlow felt he needed to explain the bottle. It looked so strange. You had to make it accessible. The "Perfection" or "The Absolut Perfection" theme from the Ayer ads was good, because it explained Absolut. Absolut in effect meant *perfection*. He could build on that. But you would have to work it up a bit.

Arnie gave the assignment to art director Mel Platt and copywriter Jennifer Berne. Mel quickly came up with the header: "The Absolute Truth." He just picked it up and penned it down with his magic marker. Then Jennifer wrote the copy. And Arnie liked it.

One idea Arnie had was to encourage people to actually taste the product. Like, it looked a bit strange, but you could drink it. It was still vodka, right? So the artwork would be a picture of someone about to taste it. The drinker's face, the small glass of vodka, it looked so stylish. But if the face and the glass took up most of the space, there was hardly any room for the bottle.

So much the better.

The copy read:

THE ABSOLUT TRUTH

Compare Absolut to any other vodka in the world. One magnificent crystal clear, icy cold sip will tell you the Absolut truth . . . Absolut Vodka is truly vodka perfected.

And then, under the copy, the kiss off:

FROM THE COUNTRY OF SWEDEN
VODKA PERFECTED

• • •

What plagued Arnie most about his partner was Landey's constant nagging about how other people, not least Arnie himself, were holding him back. When it was the exact opposite.

Marty constantly repeated that he wanted to play in the major leagues, if only they would let him. But while Marty said they should sell, or buy, or merge, Arnie thought, why not just do good advertising?

In fact, Arnie was so happy that he'd finally made Absolut perfect, that he submitted the Swedish bottle for the New York Art Directors Club packaging award. In his own name.

Arnie's father had come to the United States from Kobrin in the Ukraine. His real name was Orloffsky, Louis Orloffsky, and the last two letters in his surname, *ky*, marked him out as a kyke, a Jew. He'd settled in Brooklyn, which had evolved into a bubbling broth of poor Jews and Italians. Orloffsky's people were not German Jews, like those who'd come during the great wave of immigration in the 1850s.

The Russian Jews, Louis's people, arrived at the turn of the century. They were poor, hungry, and persecuted, ordinary Jewish farmers on the run from the pogroms that were sweeping the Russian subcontinent. Long afterwards, Arnie's father told him about the Cossacks, how they'd ridden down the village streets, swinging their sabers above their heads, mowing people down for fun. Louis Orloffsky had arrived on Ellis Island as a poor man but a free one.

The whole time Arnie was growing up, his father never had time to speak to him. Six days a week he went to his little sewing factory on Grand Street at six in the morning and came home at eleven at night, when Arnie and his sister had already gone to bed. On Sundays he was so tired that he slept all day with the curtains drawn, and they had to play outside so as not to disturb him. Arnie always felt bad that his father had to work so hard. He had a guilty conscience, as though it was his fault, and somewhere inside he knew very well just why his father worked as much as he did, why all Jewish parents did. The first generation of Jews who arrived denied themselves everything, and the reason was—education.

Their children were going to college.

With his friends Bobby Brandwein and Jordy Berkowitz, Arnie, who was the artist of his class at Public School 101 in Bensonhurst, always got to design the holiday decorations. One December Miss Klages took out a box of colored chalks, big fat chalks with crisp colors, and explained to the three boys that it was time to draw something nice for Christmas. "I want you to do a Christmas scene on the blackboards," she said, "a real Christmas scene."

Neither Arnie nor the other boys knew much about Christmas. They knew Hanukkah, but that was something else. Arnie had seen how his Italian classmates celebrated Christmas. He felt a bit jealous when he saw the Italian families and their Christmas trees, the children and the parents who got to be together all Christmas, with the wonderful lights and presents and the tree. The Jews had nothing like that.

They went to work on the blackboard at the back of the room. They drew a big open fire in a fireplace, and on the mantle above the fire they placed a long row of cards from friends and relatives. The children's stockings were beside the fire, waiting for Santa Claus. Mother stood on a ladder in the middle of the room, decorating an enormous tree with candles and streamers of tinsel and ornaments in red and blue and gold. A boy and a girl were taking more ornaments from a box. The head of this Christian family relaxed in his armchair with a pipe in his mouth, a newspaper open in his lap, and a pair of slippers on his feet. The Star of Bethlehem shone outside, the moon lit up the night sky, and the ground was covered in snow. It took the boys several days to finish the scene, and after every shift they covered the blackboard with a sheet so it would be a surprise for the others. Eventually they were ready to show it to Miss Klages. She clapped her hands in delight.

"Oh boys," she cried, "Oh boys, it's wonderful!"

There was just one thing missing. Miss Klages wanted them to add some holly. The three Jewish boys looked at each other, puzzled. What on earth did she want them to do that for?

None of the boys knew of the Christian tradition of hanging up holly at Christmas. But "holly" sounds a lot like "chally," the everyday slang for the Yiddish word *Chalah*, the Sabbath bread. Since the kids wanted to sound more American, they would soften some of the gutteral sounds of Yiddish and pronounce the *ch* as *h*, as in "halah," or "hally," and it sounded exactly like "holly."

Arnie Arlow and Bobby Brandwein looked blankly at each other and wondered what Miss Klages could want with chally in the middle of a Christmas scene. That was when Arnie had an inspiration: Miss Klages naturally thought it was unfair that the lovely drawing was only for the Italians, for the Catholics, and she wanted the Jewish bread so there would be something for the Jews, too.

Arnie took the eraser and wiped away five or six of the Christmas cards on the mantle. Up among the cards, he drew a nice big brown Jewish challah with a twist. After a while, Miss Klages came and looked at the drawing and asked: "Where's the holly?"

And the boys pointed to it.

"There it is. There!"

Miss Klages, who lived right there among the Jews and the Italians, said "Holly? Chally?" and then she started laughing. Miss Klages was a large round woman, and when she laughed her whole body shook. She wobbled like a jelly in the middle of the classroom, right in front of the Christmas scene. The boys had no idea what all the fuss was about until someone told them what holly was, and that it was holly, not chally, that Miss Klages had asked for. "Yeah, yeah, we knew that." And they were laughing too now. "We knew that all along," Arnie said.

Arnie always wanted everything to be perfect.

Later he won a Fullbright Scholarship to travel to Europe and learn to paint. He was twenty-one-years old and a fully fledged artist. Arnie spent the entire summer painting in Spain, but it was difficult to survive on the money from back home and he didn't want to live as his father had done. He knew his father had worn himself out on his behalf and the only place it had gotten Arnie was here, living on cheap red wine and white bread in order to afford oil paint. When he got back he took a job as an assistant art director at the *New York Times* to scrape some money together. Then he got a real salary and was offered a full-time job at an advertising agency that specialized in fashion. It wasn't that he was desperate for the cash, but he grew accustomed to having it. He wanted to have decent clothes and a nice home and enough money to have a good life. Eventually he wound up on Madison Avenue.

• • •

On a warm day in the fall, Dr. Stanley Noval, the Monopoly's American researcher, walked into Carlsson & Broman's advertising agency in Stockholm. He found Gunnar Broman wrapped in a forest-green sweater, flipping through an American magazine. Much to his surprise, Broman had just discovered a large picture of the Absolut bottle in an issue of *Packaging Digest*. Apparently, Dr. Stanley noticed, they had had some difficulty taking a photograph. Not so strange, considering the fact that the bottle was essentially invisible.

"Dr. Stanley," said Broman, "I don't know whether I should laugh or cry. Absolut Vodka has won a New York Art Directors Club award for best packaging of 1979.

"But, Gunnar! That's terrific news!"

"Well, that is the good news. The bad news is that the creator of the bottle and the winner of the award is a certain Mr. Arnold Arlow."

CHAPTER 12

ALMOST PERFECT

TBWA takes over the account and, thanks to the advertising revolution, the result is Absolut Perfection.

One morning Martin Landey and Gunnar Broman met, man-to-man, over a business breakfast. Broman reminded Landey that he'd been promised a third of the profits from the vodka account. Martin Landey had no recollection of that at all. Broman recited every insult he knew in the English language, plus a few more. Martin Landey pushed an envelope across the table. The envelope contained ten thousand dollars. Landey would later deny that this had ever happened.

They never met again.

In 1980, Martin Landey merged his agency with the British agency Geers, Gross. He had realized that in order to maintain his position as a force riding the European wave flooding America, the agency had to grow. A few months later, Geers, Gross declared that a conflict of interest had arisen between their Brown–Forman account and Landey's Carillon account. Brown–Forman had a cognac, a couple of cheap wines, and Bols liqueur, and they were unhappy about the agency's new entanglement with Grand Marnier and the Swedish vodka. Landey thought it was insane. Absolut was a vodka, for Chrissakes, and Grand Marnier was, well, it was Grand Marnier. And anyway, shouldn't Geers, Gross have said something about this *before* the merger? But Geers, Gross wouldn't budge. They billed Brown–Forman for fifteen million dollars a year; Carillon was worth only two million. After two years of hard work, the Swedish vodka was selling less than 25,000 cases, and Martin Landey had earned no more than thirty grand from Absolut vodka. He explained to Al Singer, head of Carillon Importers, how it had to be, that they had to let the account go.

Singer was inconsolable. After all they'd been through, all those years, it couldn't end like this. There had to be a way. But Martin Landey said there was nothing he could do about it.

Al Singer looked like a very old man. He cried.

Claude Fromm had recently left his position as Media Director at Martin Landey, Arlow to join TBWA, a small agency with American and European owners. When he heard that Landey had released the Carillon account, he called Al Singer. He took care of the press contacts for a French wine account, he said. Would Al be interested in promoting some exclusive wines?

"Can the bullshit," said Al. "You wanna talk business, come over, we'll talk business."

Claude Fromm and the boss of TBWA, Bill Tragos, went over to Carillon's tiny office on Fifth Avenue above Rockefeller Plaza. Al Singer asked them to do a presentation for the Grand Marnier and Absolut accounts.

Carole Anne Fine, creative director at TBWA, entrusted the Swedish vodka to two of the agency's finest wackos, Graham Turner and Geoff Hayes.

Graham and Geoff told Carole Anne it was impossible to do a professional job without a deep and comprehensive knowledge of the product. They started drinking. Hard. They discovered that the more they drank the Swedish vodka, the more they liked it. They just grew more and more motivated. As they put the product to the test, they studied the liquor ads of the past ten years. What they found was pretension and pomposity. Ad after ad depicted ladies in fur coats, gentlemen in tuxedos, and Rolls-Royces being driven up to the door, with a tiny little liquor bottle tucked in the corner. They did not find a single ad aimed at anyone under forty. They had to go all the way back to the sixties before they came across anything that didn't follow the pattern.

It was a campaign for Chivas Regal by Bill Bernbach, and it was fun.

• • •

Bill Bernbach ran a "Help Wanted" ad in the *Times* in the early sixties and Carole Anne Fine answered it. Bernbach interviewed her in person. He was pretty dubious. All she'd done was some promotional work. Actually, she'd been hired as a secretary to the promotional editor of a magazine called *Flying*. She'd told them she could take shorthand, which of course she couldn't. What she actually did was scribble a few squiggles that looked like shorthand, while her boss dictated a couple of letters, which she memorized and typed out later. And he thought they were wonderful. Then one day he dictated twenty letters in a row. She couldn't remember everything he'd said, so she wrote the letters herself, and he caught her at it.

"You can't take shorthand, can you?" he asked, and she said, "No."

"You're writing these letters yourself, aren't you?" he said, and she admitted that she was.

"Okay," he said, "you're fired. But you can certainly write. How'd you like to be promotional copywriter?"

"Thanks," she said.

Carole Anne was rehired.

So when Bill Bernbach said, "Miss Fine, you've done nothing but promotion, and we are looking for someone who can *really* write," he had a point.

She had brought samples of her work in a big shopping basket. The samples made little impression on Bernbach, but the basket was another matter. Bernbach loved it. Right in the middle of the interview he said, "Miss Fine, I really admire your basket."

He was so taken with Carole Anne's shopping basket, he hired it, and he got Carole Anne into the bargain.

And that's how she got started in advertising.

For the first few years she said nothing. She just went about her business, carefully listening to what Bill had to say and observing what Bill did. Eventually, she mustered up the courage to open her mouth, and everyone thought she was just hilarious. Every time Carole Anne said something, her coworkers just fell about laughing. She had such a kooky way of looking at things, they said. She was nuts. "When other people zig," she'd say, "I zag. When they zag, I zig."

One day, after she'd been there a few years, she and Bill were having a discussion about fashion. They were not in agreement. She was telling him what fashion advertising was really about, when he interrupted her in mid-harangue.

"Are *you,* Carole Anne, trying to tell *me* that *you* know more about fashion than *I* do?" And she said, "Well, yes, Bill. As a matter of fact, that's exactly what I'm trying to tell you."

"Get out, Carole Anne Fine! Get *out!*"

She never stopped being scared of Bill Bernbach. For many years she was a temp to him, with a temp's salary, for no other reason than that she never dared tell him that she wasn't a temp any longer. She was in charge of her own accounts. Big accounts. But Bill was scary. He had the iciest blue eyes you ever saw, and he could freeze you with them. He had a favorite little speech about touching people, reaching for their souls. "Feelings," he'd say. "Feelings. We're not here to rattle off a list of facts and figures about miles per hour or the dimensions of propeller shafts. Touch people's souls, goddammit. Do it different. Make them fall in love with the product. Charm their socks off."

And all the while those freezing blue eyes rested on Carole Anne Fine.

Bill had started out as head of research at the World Expo the year World War II broke out in Europe. In 1943 he became head of public relations at Weintraub, and in 1945 he was hired as a project leader at Grey. Two years later, Grey made him creative director. Then, in 1949, he founded Doyle Dane Bernbach with Max Dane and Ned Doyle. He seemed to know what it was all about even then. He said exactly the same things then as he did years later, and in exactly the same way. It was just that no one understood him back then. Other people reached life's great truths through experience. Bill Bernbach seemed to be born with his message.

David Ogilvy, who had founded his agency the year before Bill, had written his message down in his own handbook, *The 38 Rules*. It described in great detail the ideal construction of an advertisement. Ogilvy seemed less interested in the actual work his agency produced than in fine-tuning the rules for the Perfect Ad. He put one in mind of an eccentric scientist, repeating the same experiment over and over again, tweaking the variables, observing the results.

He seemed to be gunning for the Nobel Prize in Advertising.

Ogilvy was determined to uncover the secret formula: Say

this at that time in that way and they'll buy whatever it is you're selling. He was looking for the elusive DNA of advertising, the essence of the hard sell. David's ads, consequently, all looked almost exactly the same. It made no difference if it was Hathaway shirts, or Schweppes soda, or Rolls-Royce automobiles. David always used a large illustration, two-thirds the size of the page, a long slogan, an even longer subslogan, a really long text on the bottom third of the page, and a tiny picture in the bottom corner. The more text you had, the more sales arguments you could squeeze in. The more arguments you had, the better your pitch. Stood to reason. One of his Rolls-Royce ads had a seventeen-word slogan. The subslogan contained twenty-eight words, and the accompanying text was a five-hundred-word essay.

It was one of the best advertisements ever created, at least according to the author of *The 38 Rules.*

Ogilvy had his predecessors. Stanley Resor, who had bought a controlling share of the J. Walter Thompson agency in 1916 and made it into the most successful ad agency in the world, had planned a series of thirty-four guides to the different methods of persuasion known to the advertising industry. By the age of seventy-eight he had completed nine. Claude C. Hopkins, a legendary adman, had published a book entitled *Scientific Advertising* in 1923. The opening paragraph read, "We have entered an age when advertising, in the hands of some, has been elevated to the status of a science." Rosser Reeves, enthusiastic Madison Avenue dive-bomber, inventor of the unique sales proposition, claimed that his work, too, was based on logic coupled with scientific observation.

There were, in short, things you could do with ads, and then there were things you should most certainly avoid doing. The well-educated Ivy League graduates flocking down Madison Avenue were fired up on visions of a glorious future in a business that was growing at a rate of 9 percent per year, a business that guaranteed them money and fame. And they knew how it worked.

You had to trust the researchers, you had to lay out a strategy and above all, you had to learn The Rules—the rules for how an ad should look in order to sell the stuff you were charging a fortune to hawk.

If Bill Bernbach had merely protested against this state of affairs, he'd never have amounted to more than a rebel. But Bill was bigger than that. When a couple of Germans marched into Doyle Dane Bernbach and asked for Bill's help, everyone warned him off. "C'mon, Bill, you know it's just a bitch trying to sell those small cars in the States, and this is not just any small car, it's a *German* small car. Can't be done." Worse still, it was an ugly German small car.

It was probably the ugliest car in the world. In fact it didn't look like a car at all, at least not like a real American car. Plus, there was the inescapable fact that it was German, manufactured in Germany not yet fifteen years after the end of the war. If that wasn't enough to sign its death warrant, it had been Adolf Hitler himself who had given the order to develop a car cheap enough so that every Fritz, Heidi, and Gretchen could afford to cruise around the Fatherland.

All that the apostles of impossibility managed to do was inspire Bill Bernbach to try harder. He roamed the corridors reciting his mantra—Do It Different, Do It Different. What the hell was he talking about, Do It Different? Everybody knew that the whole point was to do it the same. Hadn't the formula for the ultimate automobile ad already been discovered? It was two-thirds illustration, slogan, subslogan flowing round small illustration to the left, and then as much text as possible in the remaining space about Super Enamel Finish that Never Needs Waxing, and

Aluminized Mufflers and Extra Long Life, and Stays Showroom Bright. A third illustration right at the bottom, just a small one. And everything retouched so that even the smallest of runabouts looked like a thirty-foot monster. And in chrome, so shiny that the happily laughing family in the ad could see their perfect teeth reflected in it.

In short, you had to squeeze in as much technical detail as possible if you were going to sell scientifically.

Helmut Krone was assigned the position of art director on the Volkswagen project. Carole Anne Fine thought that if Bill was a genius, then Helmut could be comfortably placed in the category supertalented. Bill and Helmut decided to pour the formula down the drain. They chose a black-and-white picture of the singularly repulsive German car, a picture that made it look even uglier, blacker, smaller, and more German than it was. Then they scaled it down to the size of a postage stamp and stuck it away in a corner of the page. There were no illustrations of axle shafts, engine blocks, shiny hoods—even the happy family was absent. Just the tiny black lump in the corner. At the bottom they wrote: Think Small. That was the slogan. Then there was a text, a mere fifteen sentences, most of which was grammatically incorrect, about how nice it was to have a small car that was affordable and easy to park. The text had evidently not been written by an experienced seventy-five-year-old Master of The Rules. On the contrary, it had more likely been penned by a twenty-three-year-old dyslexic who had daydreamed his way through more than a couple of classes.

Bill Bernbach had made a revolutionary decision: he was going to write his copy the same way ordinary people spoke. It was a weird language they used in that ad. There were like periods. Everywhere. Every word had its own. Period. Or so it seemed. It was a whole new. Language.

Billbernbachian.

Just thinking the thought that this ad had broken the rules was enough to attract the icy stare of Bill Bernbach, quickly followed by the hiss of his mantra: There are No Rules. And according to Bill, advertising, in case anyone was wondering, was not an exact science. It was not a science at all. It was an art form. It was art.

No rules? Art? The entire industry was going through a tremendous boom precisely because they had convinced their clients that they weren't just sitting in their fancy Madison Avenue offices billing insane amounts of money. Oh, no! Their work was based on market research and market planning—it was scientific. That was how they knew it worked. There were rules, rules that could guarantee a steadily rising sales curve. Whaddaya mean, *No rules?*

Bernbach and Krone kept right on churning out ads for the Hitlermobile. One after the other, each more wacky than the one before. They used a picture of tire tracks disappearing into a snowstorm, and underneath it they wrote: "We finally came up with a beautiful picture of a Volkswagen." They found a couple of hicks from the Ozarks and stood them beside the car, pitchforks at the ready. "It was the only thing to do after the mule died," they wrote.

It was the kind of thing people at other agencies did at 3:00 A.M. when they were tired and trying to cheer each other up. It was the sort of thing you would toy with when you were sick of explaining why your client's coffee was better than other brands even though it tasted exactly the same. It was understood that these ideas would never be seen by anyone, not by the account manager, and certainly not by the client. The client might think he wasn't being taken seriously. He might even assume the product was being ridiculed.

It was incredible that the Germans condoned it. Their car was a joke, true, but people got the joke.

In 1960 the sales of Volkswagen cars increased by 25 percent. The establishment took a standing eight-count. Bill Bernbach was a freak, no one could dispute that, but somehow he was selling that ugly little German monstrosity. But what would happen if everyone started doing these crazy ads, if they all broke the rules? The structure would break down. The clients wouldn't stand for it. The clients would abandon them.

Those who knew what was going on in Bill Bernbach's agency had even more horrible tales to tell. At other agencies it was the account managers who held the reins. He was the one who took the client for three-drink lunches at Voisin, 21, or Maud Chez Elle. He was the one who decided—together with the client, of course—which campaign they'd run with. This was all unsurprising and unremarkable, since both the accounts manager and the client's marketing director were generally clean-cut, strong-jawed WASPs with the same impressive business degrees. They knew how to plan a marketing strategy in an effective, scientific fashion. After that, the accounts manager would instruct the project leader, who would set about developing ideas for different ads and radio spots and posters, which the copywriters and art directors would then be charged with producing.

But not any more. Bill Bernbach had decreed that the accounts manager's collaboration with the marketing director was no more than a prelude to the real work, mere foreplay to the Creative Act. At Doyle Dane Bernbach they'd turned the world on its head.

The copywriters and the art directors came first. At Bernbach they had something they called creative teams. There were no project leaders telling people what to do. They just got on with it. Some people even whispered that at Bernbach the guys on the creative team got to talk to the client in person. And if Bernbach's clients didn't like what Bernbach's boys and girls had come up with, then they were unceremoniously dumped.

The client got the boot.

Without anyone really noticing how or when it started, a whole debate began on Madison Avenue on the subject of creativity. If the copywriters and illustrators saw something they liked, they said it was creative. If there was a manager they didn't like, they blamed it on his lack of creativity. At management level, Doyle Dane Bernbach was considered a freak of nature. The ones who actually came up with the slogans and designed the ads, however, considered Bernbach to be a *very creative firm.* And the reason for this was very simple. At Doyle Dane Bernbach, it was the creators who ruled.

• • •

There wasn't another agency on Madison Avenue where Carole Anne Fine could have worked anywhere else than in reception. Who would've hired her? She knew nothing about advertising. She was a woman. She was always saying crazy stuff. She *looked* crazy. And she wrote her ads in the same way, crazy crackers wrapped in shameless, charming razzle-dazzle, and people just loved them. Her puns, her hard-selling little absurdities, all of it written in pure Billbernbachian.

She was a basket case, and she was there because Bernbach had hired her basket. Then the people at DDB started to realize that ad makers all along Madison Avenue were imitating Carole Anne Fine. They were trying to make sense of her weird sense of humor, trying to figure out what it was that made her stuff so fantastic. And fantastic it was. She won awards. She was given the biggest accounts. At first she couldn't believe it herself. In another age—before the Sixties—she might have been an unknown poet, patching together nonsense poems for a wildly enthusiastic circle of perhaps five hundred fans around the country. Now, her words reached the nation. People down Madison Avenue studied her little commercial sonnets with a magnifying glass trying to find out what the big secret was.

And of course, the secret was—her. It was Carole Anne Fine.

Then Mary Wells turned up. Mary Wells was everything that Carole Anne was not. She knew exactly what she wanted, she could manipulate people without them even noticing it, and she could charm the socks off of her clients. She even married one of them. When Mary Wells came to work at Bernbach, she was thirty-two or thirty-three, and she was physically very beautiful. This was an issue. It couldn't be ignored, because it affected everyone who had to deal with her. Mary Wells was a classic beauty with green eyes and blond hair. Actually, with gray hair. She didn't become a blond until she turned forty, but she was always a beauty.

Mary Wells got to handpick the people she wanted in her group and she handpicked Carole Anne. Carole Anne immediately got a six-thousand-dollar raise she hadn't even asked for. She couldn't fathom why she was going to be paid six thousand dollars more. But she took it. Bill never asked her how much money she made, or how much she needed; he never cared about anything but her work. When she was pregnant, he didn't even notice. When she practically gave birth right there under the desk, he just got pissed. "Don't you think you'd better stay home for a while with that—thing?" he asked her.

There had never been anybody at DDB like Mary. She could deal with anything and anybody. She never failed. She was superhuman. And then she left. It sent shock waves through the entire agency.

Carole Anne discussed it with Max Dane. In the late sixties she had started ice skating, which incidentally became one of the great lasting passions of her life, and Max Dane loved ice skating too, so they used to go skating together. And one day as they were skating around the rink at the Rockefeller Center, to the sound of inane Christmas carols, she asked him about Mary.

Max explained that Mary had to go, or they had to let her go, because Mary was a power monger. Ned Doyle never got it, because Mary bewitched him, but that was the truth. Ned worshipped Mary and then she had to leave, and she broke his heart.

There were always smart power mongers and dumb power mongers. Mary Wells was smart. Carole Anne was one of the dumb power mongers, she never understood what was going on. She had this one big problem. Carole Anne was a good creative director, she knew a good ad from a bad ad, she knew what sold, she knew how to entertain and intrigue people, she understood the business side very well, positioning and all that. But she never understood the businessman.

One day Mary's right-hand man at her new agency, Charlie Moss, called Carole Anne and said, "*Mary wants you.*" He made it sound like a silly little tune, like a children's rhyme: "La-di-da-da. Mary wants you." And all she could say was: "All right." She packed all her things in her basket and left Bill.

Bill Bernbach had started a revolution. In the beginning of the sixties they had called him a freak. Now, ten years later, he wasn't just a prophet. He was God.

Billing for Doyle Dane Bernbach had gone from $25 million to $270 million. Billing for the ten largest agencies—and now Bill's agency was one of them—had gone from one-and-a-half billion dollars to four and a half. If the old men who still didn't get it had thought that Bill's philosophy would ruin the industry, they had made a big mistake.

At the end of the sixties the industry was swimming in money.

Nobody was surprised when Mary flew in a planeload of rustic furniture from Provence and had her new office at Wells Rich Greene redecorated in French Provincial style. That's what creative spirits were supposed to do. And if their offices didn't have the twenty-fifth-floor view overlooking Central Park, how could they be expected to create? They deserved the view and the French furniture because they were artists who had generously put their creativity at the disposal of some dull and grasping capitalist, and he should pay big time. And—strictly speaking—what was it that made the cars, the bars of soap, the instant coffee, and the cigarettes—the junk these misers sold—anything at all? Advertising. Advertising turned their boring pieces of crap into thrills, into fantasy, into art.

Carole Anne at last understood her own worth to the agency. She made a fortune for the clients, she made a fortune for Mary Wells, and for Wells Rich Greene. It was time she was making a fortune for herself, too.

She bought a house in the Hamptons. She had her very own roller-skating rink installed. If she went up from 119 pounds to 120, she jumped on a plane to the Caribbean and spent Saturday, Sunday, and five thousand dollars burning off that extra pound. Her boy came home from school and said he wanted to go skiing in the Alps. Sure. She bought a load of ski equipment and sent him on his way. She loved earning two hundred grand a year, and she needed no help whatsoever in spending the lot.

Mary Wells never gave up trying to make Carole Anne sophisticated. She wanted her to look proper. It was okay to be odd, but Carole Anne *looked* odd. Not oddly sophisticated, just odd.

In all honesty, she just didn't look as though she worked at Wells Rich Greene. Diamonds and ripped jeans, it just wasn't right. She was too off-the-wall. Mary sent her to a stylist, bought her new clothes, made an appointment for her at the right salon. None of it worked. Carole Anne refused to be made over. Mary Wells could deal with Carole Anne's image no longer. She had a copywriter she couldn't introduce to her clients.

Carole Anne was having her hair cut when a call came through from the agency and Mary's secretary told her Mary wanted to talk to her. Carole Anne asked if she meant now, or when she was through at the salon. She meant now. They had to take out all the curlers, and she went back to the agency with her hair in a towel and marched straight into Mary Wells' office, and Mary told her she was fired. Then Mary started crying, and Carole Anne comforted her, told her it wasn't the end of the world, everything would work out fine. She gathered her stuff together and left the office for the last time. She had been fired, and the only thing she'd done about it was comfort Mary Wells.

For a couple of years, Mary Wells had enslaved her. Mary Wells wasn't a mean person. But was she nice? The more Carole Anne thought about it, the more she felt sure that Mary Wells hadn't been nice to her at all. Then it struck her that it had been a long time since she'd met anyone in advertising who was nice—including herself.

•

The sixties passed. Ten years . . . . It was as though a hurricane had blown right through the city, right up Madison Avenue. The creative souls were all making money fast, most of them were losing it all again just as fast, and a select few, like Mary Wells and Bill Bernbach, had become rich. With hindsight, Carole Anne knew she'd been there at the zenith. She looked back at everyone who, just like herself, had been to the gala dinners, who had stood up and strutted triumphantly to the podium to give their acceptance speeches. So many of them were gone.

Some died of alcoholism. She had drunk some, too, but that was never her real problem. Some died of drug abuse, some of too much money, some of not enough. Some of them had heart attacks. An entire creative team had gone white-water rafting and drowned. God knows what the rest of them died of, but they were dead. And the ones who were left didn't learn any lessons. They kept right on doing what they had done all along.

A few years after Mary Wells floated her company on the stock market, the share price started falling. Everyone at the agency was still babbling on about how advertising had to continue to be top quality, how they'd never go back to doing the kind of boring drivel they did in the old days, before Bill's revolution. The boring drivel that did nothing but sell. That was the talk at the agency, and that was the talk in the industry papers when Mary went to meet the market. We won't do this. We're just too goddamned creative.

The men from Wall Street wanted to know what Mary's strategy was. "I'll tell you," said Mary. "We'll do *anything*. We'll do exactly what the client wants us to do." And that was the end of that debate. Everyone knew she was right. We'll do whatever you want. We're the same old three-dollar hookers we always were.

•

Carole Anne went back to Bill Bernbach, and then she was hired by Ron Rosenfeld from Rosenfeld, Sirowitz and Lawson, where she met Dick Costello and Harvey Baron, and they all just fell in love with one another. Eventually they stole some accounts, just like everyone had done at the start of the sixties, and opened Baron, Costello & Fine in May 1973. They were creators, no doubt about it, every bit as creative as they'd been ten years ago.

But it was the seventies, and people were getting sick of creativity. Did it really sell products, or did it just sell the creators themselves?

In the early seventies, Alka-Seltzer had commissioned one of the most original campaigns the world had ever seen, and it had bombed. Suddenly, everyone was talking about research again. Advertising had to be grounded on scientific analysis. Countless surveys of the American people were conducted. America was being mapped out, city by city and block by block. It was the kind of thing that, if it had been happening in Russia, would have had Richard Nixon screaming that it proved that the red menace must be destroyed once and for all. True, it wasn't the political persuasions of the citizens the researchers were registering. It was something far more important.

They wanted to know their favorite toothpaste.

Baron, Costello and Fine took home the awards, but it didn't seem to impress any prospective clients. Their billings peaked at five million. It was a joke. They were below the breadline.

And then the Greek came calling.

He wasn't really Greek, of course, but that was how he presented himself: "I'm a Greek, from St. Louis." His name was Bill. Bill Tragos. He'd lived in Europe for sixteen years and worked for Young & Rubicam in London, Paris, and Frankfurt. Bill Tragos had started what he immodestly referred to as "the world's first international agency" with three European ad guys who sounded as though they'd walked out of the plot of a Jackie Collins novel: Claude Bonnange, originally a musician; Paolo Ajroldi, an eccentric Italian duke; and Uli Wiesendanger, a Swiss who lived in Paris with a Chinese–American.

TBWA. Fascinating people.

And then Bill Tragos himself, the Greek from St. Louis, with his big brown eyes and enough charisma to power a small town. They realized pretty quickly that he hadn't come back to the States to fool around.

Bill Tragos made them an offer. He'd merge his international agency with their little sweatshop, and the three lovebirds would get twenty percent. His own TBWA would get eighty percent, and the name would be changed to Baron, Costello and Fine TBWA. To sweeten the deal, he'd take some clients with him from Europe, and he'd be a hands-on chief exec.

Bill Tragos explained that New Yorkers were a bunch of insular boneheads who had no idea what, for example, the capital of Denmark was. He was married to a Danish girl, so he should know. He'd come back to his homeland to teach his compatriots the European dogma: Less is more, and more is more expensive. All you had to do was spread a little of that European sense of quality and sophistication.

The European wave suddenly had another advocate on Madison Avenue. It was ironic, because Baron, Costello and Fine had also received an offer to sell out to European Disciple Numero Uno, Martin Landey himself. Landey turned up at the office singing the praises of the sophisticated European upper class in true American go-getting style. No one got to squeeze in so much as a syllable when Landey preached on the future of the agency's Europified psychodynamic ghestaaalt. His partner Arnie Arlow had tried to calm him down, but no. Landey had seen the light, and it rose in the east. He would pay whatever it cost, if only Baron, Costello and Fine would listen to his counsel.

When he'd gone, Dick Costello let out a sigh of exasperation and said that there was no question of selling to anyone, no matter how hard it was to find clients.

But it was a question of survival. They sold to Bill Tragos, and Bill was smart enough to let them have their way—at first.

Bill Tragos had a vision of how European advertising in America would look. First of all, it would not consist of puns and wordplay as it had in the sixties. Nor would it be based on reams of pointless data. It should be visual, but not weird, not Bernbachesque. It should be sophisticated, understated, tasteful. In short, it should be European.

Sadly, the sophisticated clients Bill Tragos had spoken of so warmly turned out to be as real as his Greek citizenship. His frustration over his lack of European credentials led him to take it out on Carole Anne, who was so obstinate, so odd, so, so—*American.*

One day when he got to the office, she'd had all her hair cut off. She looked even more like a feminist radical than before. He almost had a stroke. Didn't the woman understand she couldn't waltz around his office looking like that?

"Fine!" he screamed. "FINE!!! What the hell have you done with your goddamn hair?!"

"What about my hair?"

Well, she certainly hadn't cut it to be informed that she looked like shit, and she wondered if he meant that she should consult him next time she went to the salon?

Outside the office, however, he was gracious to the edge of unctuousness. In the first year, the agency's billing went from five million dollars to twenty. He took in Evian spring water and Le Coq Sportif, two modest accounts, and Ovaltine, a plump English drink account. Through his father, who had been a boxing promoter in St. Louis where the money came from brewing beer, he had secured a deal with August Busch, or "His Beerness" as Carole Anne called him, president of Anheuser-Busch, the brewery that owned half of St. Louis.

Bill Tragos was inexhaustible in the courting of prospective clients. He knew instinctively when to say yes, when to say no, when to smile, when to roar with laughter. He knew exactly when to shake his head in despair. If he had to talk golf with an executive, he made sure he knew how to talk golf. If the executive thought golf was a load of baloney, so did Bill Tragos. He was a true genius at winning people over. He did it harder and faster, longer and better than anyone else on Madison Avenue.

Bill interviewed young Bob Needleman from Scali McCabe Sloves over lunch at Jackson's Hole on Sixty-seventh Street. He tossed out Carole Anne's name and Bob lit up. Bob admired her; she was one of the sixties legends. Then Bill sugared the deal by saying that he was going to turn TBWA into New York's hottest agency. Yet, despite his detailed lectures on sophistication and visualization, neither Carole Anne nor later Bob could work out what Bill was really aiming at. He'd told Carole Anne a thousand times—or rather, he'd screamed at her a thousand times—"No more puns, Fine! That's it!"

But she went right on punning the bejesus out of their prospective clients, Italians and Frenchmen who didn't speak a word of English. And things weren't working out with Needleman either. If Bill happened to mention that he had to be more succinct—"Cut down on the words, Bob, okay?" Needleman screamed right back. He was TBWA's very own John McEnroe, and there were a few blinding center-court rallies between him and Bill, the hard-hitting wordsmiths.

Bill Tragos was sick of Americans. He wanted dyed-in-the-wool Europeans, with real European accents.

• • •

Graham Turner and Geoff Hayes had bumped into one another in the corridor at the London branch of Young & Rubicam at the tail end of the seventies. Graham couldn't have been more than twenty-one or twenty-two at the time, and his face was full of huge, weeping pustules that made people divert their gaze when they spoke to him. When Geoff saw him in the corridor, though, he didn't see the cartoon spots. He couldn't see past the big white plastic balls dangling from springs on his head. It was so incredibly childish that Geoff took an instant liking to him.

Graham Turner had come to the agency straight from art school. He could never get along with his copywriters. They had no time for his attitude to language. He wanted them to experiment with intonation and jargon. Usually he rewrote the slogans and texts himself to find the right tone.

Geoff Hayes was an art director. He'd left South Africa at the age of twenty-four after his National Service. When they started sending reservists to the war in Angola, he'd had enough. He moved to London. Graham and Geoff decided to work together. Graham would write and Geoff would design. Six months later they left Young & Rubicam and joined Euro, London's trendiest agency. They were there for two-and-a-half years, and toward the end they were doing most of the work and pulling in most of the profits at the agency. For this, they were rewarded with a poor salary, so they asked a headhunter to sniff around on their behalf. Their headhunter mentioned that there were a couple of

Americans doing interviews for an agency called TBWA, but it was for a placement in New York. Geoff and Graham knew nothing about the New York office of TBWA, but the London branch was widely regarded as one of the best. They thought it couldn't do any harm to go and check it out.

When they arrived at TBWA, the directors were late for the interview and Geoff and Graham said, "Screw this," and left. They received a call from the agency. "You can at least show us your stuff," they said. So they sent their portfolios up. Carole Anne and Bob, who'd been through at least a hundred portfolios, went through yet another. When they saw the stuff Geoff and Graham had come up with, among others a White Horse whiskey campaign, Carole Anne couldn't contain herself. "Jesus! Oh, wow! I *love* these guys!"

Bill Tragos was very pleased when Carole Anne came back to New York and told him that they'd found a couple of real Europeans in Savile Row suits. Three months later they turned up: a greasy, long-haired youth barely twenty years old and a guy who looked like the King of the Road, dressed in rags. Carole Anne thought they were great. The first week they were there, she took them downtown to the roller-skating rink at Twentieth Street. They waited in line for half an hour before the guard sent them away.

"No bums," he told them.

• • •

The TBWA people were wary of Absolut Vodka. Graham and Geoff had tried to make a list of the product's qualities, and most of them were negative. One big minus was the country of origin. No one associated Sweden with vodka. No one associated Sweden with, well, anything at all. The idea that anyone would switch from Stolichnaya to Absolut of their own free will was ridiculous.

The product had no history, there was simply nothing there. But what really made them uncomfortable was that the damn bottle was invisible.

Bill Tragos liked to have three alternatives at every presentation. It was his little trick, the Three Comp Pitch. He would toe the conservative line in the first option, the second option would be the one he personally preferred, and the third one would be way out there, so the client had something to turn down.

The first campaign in the Three Comp Pitch was a direct attack on Stolichnaya. The premise was to let the Swedish challenger take on the undisputed Russian heavyweight champion of the world in a no-holds-barred fight. One of the sketches showed a Russian border guard in a fur hat, ice on his moustache, peering through a pair of binoculars. In each lens was a reflection of a bottle of Absolut. The slogan read: Here's something the Russians would really love to put behind bars. *Behind bars!* Ha, ha. Carole Anne was delighted. They'd come up with a charming little pun.

The second alternative was firmly entrenched in Swedish tradition. Geoff and Graham had done their research and come up with a list of weird Swedish phenomena to try and imbue the country with a personality. Apparently, once a year, a quarter of a million Swedes put on cross-country skis and took part in a race that lasted from dawn till dusk. Another favorite pastime, presumably of the same quarter million maniacs, was to bore holes in the ice and swim back and forth between them. "There's nothing the Swedes enjoy more when it's cold," the caption read. And then the bottle in the right hand corner.

The third option was a spur-of-the-moment creation. One night, after he'd had his bath, Geoff Hayes sat in front of the TV and worked on yet another sketch for Absolut Vodka. While he was drawing the bottle, he went through all the superlatives they'd had in mind to describe the contents. The clearest vodka, the perfect vodka, the absolute vodka. He was trying to come up with a way of symbolizing purity. He drew a halo over the bottle. It was pretty funny. It reminded him of the little rascal in the cartoon strip just after he'd been up to no good. Innocence personified. Within fifteen minutes, Geoff Hayes was surrounded in sketches of the bottle, each one based on a visual pun.

The next morning he showed the sketches to Graham, who was rapturous. He thought it was a great way of portraying the vodka as pure and natural, but with a twist of humor, not so goddamned pretentious. All they had to do was find a slogan. Geoff had his own idea, or rather, he had recruited the slogan from Martin Landey, Arlow about Absolut being "vodka perfected," and wrote: "Absolut. It's the perfect vodka."

Graham thought it was too long. He wanted to say something like just The Perfect Vodka. Or something about purity—Absolut Purity. They knocked it about a bit but realized that "purity" was unusable, as it suggested that alcohol was somehow wholesome. Suddenly Graham said:

"Absolut Perfection."

It had to be a client's wet dream. The product was the only thing in the picture. It had a description of the product on the bottle. The copy was only two words long. And the name was one of them.

One of Geoff's sketches had the bottle with a pair of angel's wings. Absolut Heaven. Within five minutes they were up to a dozen different two-word slogans. Absolut This. Absolut That. Absolut Anything. *Absolut Everything.*

When Carole Anne Fine saw the sketches she hooted in delight. "I love it! Love it! Looove it!" People came in from the other rooms to see what all the excitement was about, and when Claude Fromm saw the bottle with the wings, he broke into spontaneous applause.

"It's so simple," cooed Carole Anne. "So simple."

She shook her head in admiration as she leafed through the sketches.

"There's nothing to remember, nothing to think about. Just Absolut Absolut Absolut. It's so . . . so . . . American."

It was unbelievable. They'd pulled off the old sixties trick. It was rock solid hard sell with a side order of charm.

Two words. Period. Fluent Billbernbachian.

A couple of days later, Bill Tragos presented the ideas to Carillon. When they were through, the liquor men said they might just as well give TBWA the account on the spot.

But Al Singer got a grip and declared that he couldn't put it on the line there and then. There were a few loose ends to tidy up. Actually, ninety-four agencies had shown an interest in the Carillon account, all two brands, and Al hadn't had the heart to say no to any of them.

Graham and Geoff wanted the bottle painted. Pop art was once more in the ascendancy, and they thought the bottle was pop. They wanted it to look as though Andy Warhol had painted it. Geoff's sketches looked a bit like the famous Warhol painting of the Campbell's soup can from the early sixties. It was packaging in close-up. It was packaging as art.

Carole Anne approached Bill Tragos with the boys' idea and Bill said, "Forget it. Not a goddamn chance in hell we do it like that." And he proceeded to lecture Carole Anne on the finer points of the nature of vodka. Vodka was pure and clean and exclusive. People had to see this with their own eyes, the clarity, the simplicity, the perfection. They had to be seduced into drinking it. No way were they painting the bottle in thick greasy oils. It had to be photographed.

For more than a month they argued about the ads. Geoff and Graham refused to back down. It would be pop art, and it would be painted, or it would be nothing.

Carole Anne never doubted for a moment that they could talk Bill round. How naïve she was.

Graham was probably the only one who had accepted the way things were at TBWA. When Carole Anne griped about Bill Tragos, he agreed that the money, the share price, it was all meaningless. All that mattered was the art. He wanted the bottle painted, too. But in the end—he knew.

He knew the decision wasn't theirs.

Carole Anne and Bill used to run into each other on the stairs between the eleventh and twelfth floors, and that's where they would let off steam. It all came to a head one day when Carole Anne screamed, "Who's the creative director at this goddamn firm anyway?"

And Bill Tragos just looked at her and replied, "I am."

She had nothing to say. He wasn't pretending anymore.

"We do what I say. Got it?"

• • •

Carole Anne used to tell her students at the School of Visual Arts that 95 percent of all advertising was boring crap. No, hang on, make that 97 per cent. And then came Bill Bernbach, and he saw the 3 percent, and the 3 percent was good. Three percent isn't that bad when you think about where we're coming from. We can make that 3 percent wonderful. It *is* art and it *has* charm and it *is* fun. She understood the 3 percent intuitively, the rest of it she never got.

In a way, Carole Anne admired Bill Tragos. He wasn't just a hard-boiled businessman, he was creative too. He had moments of sensibility, even femininity. Sometimes they put their heads together, halfway across the Atlantic, and she forgot that he was Bill Tragos, the Greek from St. Louis who had come to New York to be rich and famous. But when they got back, he was just as mean as he'd always been. He scored points off her. He put her down in public. He was a put-down artist. He was just too smart for her, always one step ahead. He always had the answer. He drove her crazy. She lost it. They were on the stairwell between the eleventh and twelfth floors going at it, and he told her who was boss, and that's when she smacked him right between his big brown eyes.

Soon after that crisis, Bill Tragos informed her, "Hey, Fine! I've just decided to appoint you International Creative Director. Congratulations! Pack your bags. You're off to Europe!"

It was the most ridiculous thing she'd ever heard. They went to Europe every other month. What was the difference? What the hell was she supposed to do over there anyway? She got hold of a headhunter and mentioned she was sick to death of Bill Tragos, and somehow Ed McCabe got wind of it. He offered her an incredible sum of money to jump ship. That cheered her up a bit. They threw a big party for her at TBWA when she left. Bill smiled. Carole Anne smiled. They all affected an air of joviality, his troops, her last, loyal, desperate supporters. They all smiled, and it was all about putting on a brave face.

Before she left, Tragos asked her to have a look at a few résumés and suggest a successor. She knew exactly what he wanted. She interviewed a handsome guy with wavy hair and an

Armani suit who would be perfect with the clients. He was Bill Tragos's dream.

She told him to hire Arnie Arlow.

Arlow never breathed a word about his past experience with Absolut Vodka. He never told her he'd worked with the invisible bottle before. He certainly didn't tell her he'd created it.

CHAPTER 13

STUDIO 54

Absolut Vodka enters the world of Andy Warhol, finds a place in the eye of the trend, and becomes a drink fit for a king.

The Frenchman had asked Titi to lunch with the people from TBWA. Over her chilled white wine, her thoughts strayed to that ice-cool warrior of the tennis court, Björn Borg, who was playing in the U.S. Open. Her mother was holding a reception at the Swedish embassy in Washington after the championship.

"Why don't we have an Absolut Champion party?" Titi Wachtmeister suggested.

The advertising boys printed mountains of Absolut Champion T-shirts. In one corner of the embassy residence Ulla Wachtmeister arranged an Absolut Bar. They'd always served Stolichnaya before. But Titi told the Frenchman to send over a busload of Absolut, and soon the embassy was bursting with bottles of Absolut.

Ulla was such a fantastic hostess. And not just the distinguished and attractive wife of the ambassador, either—she was an artist in her own right. Her Absolut Event put many in mind of the eventful evening when she'd invited Henry Kissinger and Liv Ullman over and served the guests in the kitchen. She'd redecorated it as an aquarium where Henry and Liv swam around like two shiny celebrity guppies.

But this was even better. In the middle of the smorgasbord, Ulla had created a tennis court. First she'd planted some quick-growing grass on a carpet of topsoil, watered it, and trimmed it with scissors, and then the staff had set up a net and the lines, just like the real thing, and all the way around was the buffet itself. Then she'd put the Absolut bottles in empty milk cartons and filled them with water, dropped in some flowers and stuck the lot in the freezer. When the water was frozen, she cut away the milk carton and was left with an ice block with the bottle and the frozen flowers, and—

"Ooh," Ulla cried out, "Ted Kennedy just walked off with three Absolut Champion T-shirts."

In short, it was a fantastic success. Everyone wanted an Absolut T-shirt.

Some of them even tried the vodka.

Afterwards Titi said to the Frenchman,

"Michel, you'd better watch yourself this time. If you take Absolut Champion away from me without paying, I'll sue."

It was just a joke, or—really it wasn't a joke at all, since he had actually stolen something from her. But, on the other hand, she never got paid, since everyone, not just Michel Roux (who was a pathological cheapskate) but *everyone* assumed that she wasn't in it for the money. They thought she did it for King and Country. Probably because she'd been granted a few royal favors in the past.

No one had such noble intentions these days. The king's own sister had driven a ruthless bargain to get more cash for promoting Swedish quality booze in Texas. They'd turned her down. Not even a real live princess was worth the kind of money she was after.

Also, Titi had helped Frusen Glädje, which didn't have anything to do with Sweden, but was produced by a couple of guys in New Jersey. At least it was a Swedish name. Frusen Glädje, Frozen Joy. The only thing they wanted to give her in return was a load of ice cream. What could she do with all that ice cream? She shipped the lot off to Diana Ross.

No doubt Diana could keep all that ice cream chilled.

The real fun started when Britt Monti introduced her to Olof Tranvik. She and Britt went back a long way. Olof, Britt, and Titi became the three amigos who started Scandinavian Specialties. Titi liked Olof right away.

Olof was so fantastically normal.

Every month some gossip journalist or other showed up from Sweden to write about Countess Christina "Titi" Wachtmeister, the king's childhood sweetheart, the world-famous ex-model, and tried to match her up, like an old broodmare from the stables, with Olof Tranvik and a crowd of other guys she'd never even have given the time of day. But there was never anything between Titi and Olof. Naturally.

Olof Tranvik was without a doubt the most normal person in New York during the Golden Age. That was probably why he got along so well with all the celebrities and crazy characters Titi hung out with. She brought him up to Andy Warhol's Factory, and Andy took an instant liking to Olof. Olof was sooo pretty.

"I'll sell Olof to you," Titi said, "for a couple of paintings."

In Andy's world, you were either rich, famous, or gorgeous. Even his dachshunds were rich and famous, *Archie and Amos,* Rich and Famous. Olof was category gorgeous. Titi was category all three.

"Titi, you're so famous," he'd sighed when they met, as though her fame was almost too much for him to bear. When the papers wrote that she'd had a relationship with Peter Sellers, Andy nearly lost it. She had to tell him *everything*. Good Lord, she'd lived with the man for years, what was she supposed to say? But on and on it went. You're so famous, Titi, so famous.

And Andy just couldn't tear himself away from Olof.

"Well then, let's go out for dinner," said Titi.

They all went, Andy, Titi, Bianca Jagger, and the fashion designer Halston. Olof tagged along. Then they all went to Calvin Klein's place. Diana Ross was there, too. And Olof handled it all really well, not the slightest bit breathless, just tall and cute and absolutely, unshakably normal. Olof kept right on being normal even when Bianca Jagger began flirting shamelessly. There was not a soul in the city as normal as Olof.

Olof Tranvik had come to the Chamber of Commerce in New York on a stipend. When the money ran out, he'd stayed on selling Swedish deli food.

There had been Scandinavian restaurants earlier, started by personnel from the famous America Line. But by then they'd all had plenty of time to go out of business, and they had. Then the Hilton hotel chain asked the celebrated Swedish restaurateur Tore Wretman to organize a *smorgasbord* at Windows on the World, on the 107th floor of the World Trade Center, right at the top. The idea was that the buffet would go on to cover the fifty states.

Olof Tranvik hooked up with Wretman and presented the Swedish smorgasbord notion at luxury restaurants across the U.S. This gave him the idea of importing Swedish gravlax and selling it to New York restaurants. A couple of mornings a week he got up at dawn and went out to Kennedy Airport to meet the flight from Stockholm and pick up the raw marinated salmon.

At that time, Peter Ekelund was renting space at the Chamber of Commerce in New York while he was on the road selling the new vodka, and Olof, sitting in the same office, couldn't help but notice him. It seemed as though Ekelund was mounting a one-man assault on the American liquor market. Olof tried to help Peter get Absolut Vodka into select restaurants along with his smorgasbord. No one wanted to know. The Americans asked for the old Swedish classics, O. P. Anderson, Mansion aquavit, and black currant aquavit—yes, they wanted Broman's old obsession, Black Vodka.

Neither Peter Ekelund, nor Tore Wretman, nor any of the others at the Chamber of Commerce knew of Olof's secret life.

When Olof finished up at the office at six, he would go home to his apartment and get on the phone to make the transformation to his other identity. Sometimes he would take a woman to a reception at eight, kiss her goodnight at eleven, and eat dinner with someone else at midnight. Not because he was a world-class Casanova, but because he was so friendly he simply couldn't say no. He wanted to be part of everything.

After midnight, he'd be on Fifty-fourth Street.

After midnight, it was Studio 54 time.

Steve Rubell, one of the owners of Studio 54, had told his doormen that he wanted a well-blended cocktail and word had gone out all over the city.

The first time Olof went there he came wandering up Fifty-fourth Street wearing his grey suit and a broad smile. The whole street was full of people: body-builders in leather and chains, fake Indians with mohawks, nearly naked girls with bodypaint, people with hair colored like a fire hydrant on acid, transvestites, punks, artists, gays, a group enjoying an impromptu cocktail party on the sidewalk, theatergoers in evening dress. And the whole congregation parted for Olof, like the Red Sea for Moses. This unbelievable weirdo—so, so . . . normal.

•

Andy had once said—and had already been quoted about three million times for saying it—that in the future everyone would be famous for fifteen minutes.

That evening he was saying that everyone would be famous *in* fifteen minutes. In fifteen minutes Mark Benecke, the doorman at Studio 54, would let them in. Presiding from his little platform in front of the door, Mark marshalled his troops.

Mark Benecke knew the face of every celebrity in the Western Hemisphere. But the trick was to recognize them halfway up the block. They shouldn't be kept waiting. (There was, incidentally, a back door on Fifty-third Street, but no one ever took advantage of it. Getting into Studio 54 without anyone seeing you was the ultimate exercise in pointlessness.)

The Studio wouldn't pander to any special category—except, that is, the superfamous.

Everyone came to Studio 54. Movie stars, producers, billionaires, football players, tennis players, politicians, admen, models, bodybuilders, mobsters, everyone. Everyone. It was the center of the world. The right freaks were let in, and the right jocks, and the right bankers, so that the cocktail was always an exciting one.

One night they let in a boy who had hitchhiked in that same day from Boondocks, U.S.A., in jeans and sneakers. He had the right blond fringe, and the next morning he was on the Concorde, on his way to Paris, to do a shoot for *Vogue*.

Anybody at all who looked right just there and then could be let in to mingle with the the celebrities. "You," said Benecke and pointed at someone across the street. "You!"

And the whole crowd went "Aaaaahhhhh." Some even burst into spontaneous applause for the hero of the hour who, grinning foolishly, was trying to squeeze through to the entrance.

It was dictatorship outside and democracy inside. Or so Andy said.

That sort of thing was not for Olof. Oh, no. Mark gave Olof the nod, and the blond Swede just strolled on in.

The first thing that struck you as you entered Studio 54 was the high percentage of men dancing with other men. On the far side of the gyrating boys, right across the Titanic dance floor, up to the right, were the stairs to Steve's office, where the VIP rooms were.

The private parties were held in the VIP rooms on the second floor, and there was a separate VIP bar that served everything you could dream of. Waiters in glossy shorts cutting into their cracks circulated with trays of white powder and appropriate silverware—a silver straw and spoon. The powder was consumed on the spot. It was considered a sign of unusually bad taste to sneak off somewhere. Only junkies did that.

The Studio wasn't a democracy, of course. That was just another of Andy's myths. The celebs wanted nothing less than to mix with the hoi polloi. They didn't want a flock of groupies and fans ogling them. Earlier, the superfamous had stuck to the basement, hanging around like tramps among the garbage bags and beercans, with the sound of six thousand stomping feet hammering above their heads. But then, apparently, it had gotten a little too much like the Last Days of Rome down there, and the basement was moved two floors upstairs.

Steve Rubell's office was the center. But except for the TV screen showing the scene at the entrance, Steve's room was no more remarkable than the supervisor's office at any number of factories in America. A desk, a couple of chairs, a sofa and a coffee table.

Olof went up the stairs. He had brought something. Tonight he had a package for Steve.

• • •

Olof Tranvik's climb up the social ladder gained momentum when Titi took him to a reception for the rock promoter Milan. That's where he was introduced to Carmen D'Alessio. Carmen and Olof became instant buddies. Olof was a Libra, which didn't surprise Carmen at all, since she was also a Libra. She explained to Olof that Libras were open, sensual, emotional, and—faithful.

A few hours later Olof and Carmen took a cab to her apartment on Fifty-eighth Street, after which they became even more infatuated with each other.

All of this happened as the disco era dissolved into the punk era and the gays came bursting out of their closets creating an era all of their own. People had money. It was the money era. The celebrities wanted to be seen. It all melted together. It all melted together into the Golden Age.

But none of it would have been possible unless there was someone taking care of the lists.

Carmen D'Alessio had a Rolodex with ten thousand names, all spelled correctly and every one with the latest address—both city and country—of politicians, rock stars, artists, celebrities, athletes, and people who just plain made money. And Carmen had another list, with the personal details of five thousand correctly spelled gays, a little treasure the FBI would have loved to seize.

A private reception demanded between one and two thousand invitations, including a lavish dollop to the gay community. A large affair could easily call for eight thousand invitations.

Carmen had the lists.

Carmen D'Alessio was part of the international jetset who moved among the three points of the Golden Triangle: Rio—Paris—New York. In the early days of the Golden Age, Peter

Martin asked her to take care of Tuesdays and Fridays at a place called the Tropicana. His idea was that since Carmen D'Alessio knew everyone, she didn't really have to do anything more than show up with some of her famous friends and the place would get its name in the papers. She did a lot more than that.

It turned out that Carmen had a talent for organizing parties. She transformed Tuesday and Friday at Tropicana into a New York tradition. People flew in just to go to her nights.

Infinity was run by Morris Brahms, and Morris desperately wanted to persuade Carmen to do his parties, too. He offered her so much money that in the end she couldn't say no, and Infinity became a success.

Morris Brahms's cousin worked with a guy out in Queens by the name of Steve Rubell. Steve and his buddy Ian Schrager ran a place called the Enchanted Garden at a golf club there. They courted Carmen with various ridiculous offers to come out and work at the Enchanted Garden. Carmen was shocked. Her friends were international celebrities. Her friends moved among Rio, Paris, and New York. Her friends would never, ever go out to Queens, not for so much as an afternoon, not even for a guided tour. The very thought was preposterous.

One afternoon, when Carmen was eating a pizza lunch at Gino's on Lexington Avenue, Steve and Ian came in and—of all the nerve—sat right down. After chatting for a while, they invited Carmen and her current husband—she was on number three at that point—to dine with them at a nearby Chinese restaurant.

That evening they managed to get Carmen so utterly drunk and stoned beyond the limits of consciousness that she would have agreed to go anywhere on earth, up to and including Queens. And that's how Carmen D'Alessio ended up organizing the parties at the Enchanted Garden.

She opened with A Thousand and One Nights. Live camels and elephants were brought in, along with Pat Cleveland, the most prominent black model of the day, as a sort of exotic jungle princess. Carmen did a series of wondrous, unbelievable, fantastic parties. There was one taboo, though. She just couldn't bring herself to tell her friends of her little treks out to Queens. Eventually people started to wonder why she hadn't said anything. The Enchanted Garden, way out there at the golf club in ridiculous Queens, was the talk of the town. Jesus, everyone was on their way to Queens! Grace Jones and her so-called entourage turned up. Fashion shows were staged. Artists wanted their exhibits to be hung in the club house. They had to arrange bus tours. In the end it was such a circus out there in Queens, that the neighbors demanded to have the place closed down.

One of Carmen's friends, Owe Harden, was the manager of an out-of-business TV studio on Fifty-fourth Street in Manhattan. Ed Sullivan had broadcast his famous show from the studio, but now it was only used for parties and exhibits.

The owner of the studio, art dealer Frank Lloyd, had introduced the world to Mark Rothko, one of America's most famous abstract expressionists. When the artist died, it emerged that in spite of his fame, he was poor. Frank Lloyd, though, was obviously swimming in cash. It turned out that the gallery and its favored clients, wisely enough, had decided to take care of the abstract expressionist's money in case he pissed it all up against the wall. Surprisingly, Rothko's children begged to differ. They thought it was time to call in the lawyers, and strangely enough, they won.

Poor Frank Lloyd. He was forced to leave his gallery, the studio, the isle of Manhattan, and flee to the Caribbean, never to be heard from again.

Now Owe Harden encouraged Carmen to arrange some financial backing as fast as she could, buy the TV studio, and open her own place there. Carmen couldn't be bothered thinking about money. It all seemed so terribly shallow and complicated. She had just started on her latest husband, she went out with her friends, she even got paid to do it. She didn't want to mess up the energies.

Carmen D'Alessio led Steve Rubell and Ian Schrager into Manhattan like a pair of schoolkids. She explained that it was time to play with the big boys. That same day they signed the contract.

On the opening night they had to lift Carmen's mother in over the heads of the crowd. The whole of Fifty-fourth Street was packed with people. Lester Persky, one-time producer of *Hair,* arrived with Warren Beatty and Michael Douglas, and they didn't get in. Frank Sinatra didn't get in. A huge party started outside for all the international celebrities who didn't get in.

Meanwhile, inside, a huge papier-mâché moon was lowered from the ceiling and the Man in the Moon hoovered up a long, beautiful line of powder that rained down on the triumphant revellers like a glittering meteor shower.

The whole evening was like a wonderful film by Fellini, with all the celebrities waiting on the street outside, while the fashion victims, the gays, the drag queens, were performing for one another in the spotlight inside. Everyone knew at once that from that moment on, this was the center.

After that, everyone seemed to be on their way to Studio 54. Mick Jagger came. Cher came. John Lennon came. Bianca Jagger was a fixture. Liza Minelli was an institution. Paloma Picasso, Halston, Calvin Klein, Michael and Tina Chow, Margaret Trudeau, Diana Vreeland, Truman Capote, Henry Kissinger, Olivia Newton-John, Andy and the gang.

Everybody came.

Sometimes one of Carmen's friends would ask her who that little grinning guy was who followed her around everywhere. It turned out to be Steve Rubell, the guy who owned the place.

Those idiots. Steve Rubell and Ian Schrager, they couldn't help screaming all over town how much money they were making. They were totally lacking in anything resembling class. It was so pathetic. Carmen even had to teach them how to dress. Steve still went around in tennis shorts and a weird padded jacket, saying it was so great because you could sleep in it.

But then it was time to pay the taxes. And suddenly it turned out that they were making even less than Carmen. They apparently imagined that the authorities had no time to read the tabloids. Maybe they thought that the IRS, which had once incarcerated Al Capone for not filling out his returns properly, knew less than people on the other side of the planet about the goings-on on Fifty-fourth Street.

Steve and Ian asked Carmen if she'd be interested in a piece of the action. Her accountant advised her to take her money and run and not to do any more business with those little wiseasses, which, when it all came to a head, turned out to be quite an exquisite piece of advice.

• • •

One night, at the height of Studio 54's glory, Titi said to Olof: "Andy should paint the bottle."

Titi and Olof had a finder's fee of twenty percent on everyone they found for Andy to paint. Andy took black-and-whites with his little Minolta. His assistants colored them after Andy had finished scalpelling off the double chins and bags and wrinkles under the eyes. Andy didn't like ugly people. For $50,000 he made sure everyone was in category gorgeous.

The trick was to make people believe Titi and Olof could persuade the famous Andy Warhol to make a portrait of them. Usually they would say that "Andy's in the mood today." The truth was that for fifty grand Andy was in the mood any day of the week. He'd paint a tin can if it paid him.

They sketched out how an Andy Warhol of the Swedish vodka would look.

"Wow," said Andy when they showed him the drawings: "Greeeaaat."

Andy often thought that things were great. He had a special way of saying it, slow and drawling and utterly without expression, as though he meant nothing at all by it. Or as though he really did mean it, but that, on the other hand, more or less everything was great.

The great thing about Andy was that he wasn't prestige-minded at all when it came to who actually did his work. He had absolutely nothing against Countess Wachtmeister doing an Andy Warhol. Quite the opposite. He thought it was a relief not to have to paint, so he could concentrate on the important part, namely to invoice.

"Andy, you have to think about if you really want to commercialize yourself like this," Titi said. "Think about Campbell's Soup."

But if there was something Andy wanted to do, it was to commercialize himself up the wazoo.

A lot of people had falsely and inaccurately accused Andy Warhol of turning art into commerce, when in fact his concept had always been to turn commerce into art.

•

Andy never could tell the difference between his signature and a trademark. He'd started out as an advertising illustrator with an ambition to break through into the serious art world. He discovered that the more effort he expended on artistic painting, the more the established artists and influential critics despised him. It was the very effort that made them dislike him. Here he was, a little illustrator walking up and down Madison Avenue with his sketches in a paper bag, thinking he'd wake up one morning like the ugly duckling and find himself transformed into a real artist.

His first portfolio at the Art Academy consisted of ordinary advertising art, designed in a slightly more artistic style, as though that's where the art was, in the style. It was as though he seriously believed that if a designer just became artistic enough then—Abracadabra!" he changed into an artist.

You didn't all of a sudden become an artist because you could paint pretty shoes or flashy flowers like little Andy had. You became an artist because you placed yourself outside the bourgeoisie. You turned your back on the money. You followed your calling, no matter what, like the celebrated abstract expressionist Mark Rothko, for example. Warhol lacked the inner strength to forego a safe, well-salaried job, and that's why he was on Madison Avenue and not in SoHo.

In the early sixties, Warhol had retaliated by giving the art establishment, the prosperous gallery-owners of midtown Manhattan, the curators at MoMA, and the whole colony of abstract expressionists down in SoHo a broadside from which they'd never recover.

After ten years of trying to distance himself from advertising, he pulled a U-turn and embraced it with a howl of joy.

He simply stopped trying to paint artistically. Instead, he began producing completely soulless paintings of the garbage his mother had been squirreling away in her basement for years. Soup cans and Pepsi bottle caps and boxes of Brillo. All those things cried out to little Andy, demanding to have their portraits painted. After all, Andy loved celebrities, and things were celebrities, too, weren't they? Well, at least that's what the admen said.

So Andy started painting Things, as though Things were celebrities. (Fifteen years later he would paint pictures of real celebrities. He would then, of course, portray them as Things.)

Things were kings. These were the kind of images Bill Bernbach would have loved—except they didn't have charm. They were exactly the opposite of what you'd expect from an artist. They weren't at all stylish, not clever in the slightest, not beautiful, not insightful. Dull, dead paintings of dull, dead Things. And they expressed absolutely nothing. They put you in mind of the German car stuck up there in the top corner of the page, a black lump of steel.

And that was the whole point.

One day Andy painted a can of Campbell's beef soup. No more, no less. And he ensured that no one had missed the point, that the very fact that it didn't look like art was what made it art, real art, and not some collection of illustrations that had got lost on its way to a packaging convention in Chicago. He devised an ingenious trick. He painted lots of cans. He copied the pictures. Andy didn't paint one can, he painted thirty-two. And that was just the beginning. He didn't paint one dollar bill, he painted hundreds. He had whole tapestries printed with soulless cows, flowers, and (the only human beings) *dead* movie stars. It was as though he wanted to ensure that he'd insulted the art establishment so outrageously that he'd never be ignored again.

If art worshipped the original and the unique, Warhol's battle cry was, "Imitate and Repeat!"

•

When Titi tried to warn Andy that perhaps the whole vodka idea, when you thought about it, might be just a shade *too* unashamedly commercial, it was a powerful signal to him that here was ART in its most potent form. He stared at her sketches and said, "Wooow," in his most unenthusiastically bored tone. Then, just to show her that this bottle was something he really cared about, he added: "Greeeeaat."

He never touched liquor himself, he claimed. He used it as deodorant. But one night he'd embarked on a five-minute conversation with her answering machine and Titi was pretty sure he'd used the Swedish quality product on something other than his armpits.

Titi's idea was that the painting could be used as an ad. In that way the deal would be a sweet one for Michel Roux and Carillon, too. Andy had tried for more than a year to convince Absolut Vodka to advertise in his magazine *Interview* without luck. Now he saw the opening. He'd paint the bottle, Carillon would buy the painting, and they would buy space in *Interview* to publish it, thereby securing a double payout for a true piece of serious art.

Titi spoke to the Frenchman. She suggested sixty thousand. Roux thought it was an insane joke. Sixty thousand dollars for a painting of a bottle? No way! They could talk to Bill Tragos at TBWA about that.

The curious thing about the Frenchman was that he was so incredibly tightfisted, yet at the same time so outrageously flashy. He could invite Titi and Olof to lunch at a gourmet restaurant and order one of the most expensive wines, turning a three-person lunch into a bill for a thousand dollars. Throughout the meal he would assure them in his hysterical French accent that he was paying, they didn't have to be shy. Oh, non.

•

In the middle of all this, the king of Sweden was coming to town. Dear old Carl Gustaf, there would always be a place for him in Titi's heart.

She called him up and said that if he and the queen were free one evening, she would love to arrange a party for them in New York, something a bit different. There wasn't really any ulterior motive. Well, perhaps just a tiny one. That German woman had made a wonderful queen of Sweden, and she and Titi were such great friends, but she couldn't help wanting to show that here in New York, capital of the world, far away from Stockholm, and a long way off from their teen days at Sigtuna Boarding School, it was she who was queen.

Titi invited everyone she knew, and everyone said yes, of course. More than everyone. Wild panic erupted when the invitations were sent out. There were only sixty places at Regine's Café Reginette. People were ready to commit murder if it would secure an invitation to Titi's dinner party. Some of them would even have committed suicide if it had helped.

The Americans were shaking like leaves in the breeze. They just couldn't believe a real live king was about to show up.

"But Titi," said Andy, "Do you reeeeaally think the king is coming?"

"Of course he's coming," she said.

Andy had been a pest all week. He'd called her three times a day demanding that some pretty boy be allowed to come and threatening to deprive them of his presence if this did not come to pass. But naturally, he came.

Then, when the king finally showed, late as usual and looking about as bored as he normally did, she tried to present Aileen Mehle to him. The king asked who she was, and when Titi explained that she was one of those people who wrote in the newspapers, he gave a look as though he had just bitten through a lemon. Titi tried to explain that she wasn't a normal journalist. Aileen Mehle was a friend of the Reagans, she knew the Kennedys, she knew everyone, she was, in short, extremely famous in her own right, but under a completely different name—you see, she was Suzy. A kind of stage name.

Titi neglected to tell the king that Suzy had a society column in the *Daily News*, or that Titi herself used to write the column when it was about her own parties. It wasn't easy to explain to the king that a gossip columnist could be an established figure and that one might actually say hello to such a hyena, help her with her column or—God Forbid!—invite her to dinner. It was the Cultural Divide.

In any case, two days later, under Suzy's byline, and a photograph showing how she had looked at some point in the early fifties, the world could read that they had served *magnificent* Swedish gravlax (Olof's dead fish), *flown in just as fresh as could be for Their Majesties' pleasure.* For Their Majesties' further pleasure, they had quaffed Château de Beaulieu and emptied the last bottles of a specially made Grand Marnier Royal Celebration, before washing it all down with Absolut Vodka, which was *Fit for a King.*

Titi and Britt had frozen the vodka in blocks of ice with Swedish wildflowers, just as Ulla had taught them, and placed the vodka on the tables.

The Frenchman's comment on all of this was: "I have the largest liquor store in town and everyone just takes what they want."

He tried to claim that he had in some mystical fashion been taken to the cleaners. All the free advertising, Suzy's column, Fit for a King, all the rest of it, and it was just a ruse to part him from his beloved booze.

"Michel," she said, "relax, I don't even drink the stuff."

Which was true. She couldn't understand how anyone could touch that crap. And no one in her circles did, for that matter, not in Sweden at least. ("Absolut Vodka, it was just Renat reinvented.") It still smelled like that stuff you poured into the car in the winter.

Afterwards, a select elite of the select few were supposed to wander over to Regine's for an after-dinner drink. The king refused to go if there were photographers around. Titi was forced to plan a secret route for him so he could slip in through the kitchen. When she went down to fetch him, Carl Gustaf was standing outside with his nose pressed against the glass. The staff had refused to let him in, and when Titi arrived they asked her if she knew the guy glowering at them out there. Then she and the king ran up and down the stairs, between pots of spaghetti and small swarthy men shouting at one another. And naturally the king was grumpy as hell, par for the course when there was fun to be had.

Titi could see that the Frenchman was impressed. The "Fit for a King" thing finally did the trick. So much publicity for so little outlay. Just by giving away a little booze. It worked. And it worked much better than ordinary publicity. Because everyone knew that ordinary plugs had been bought and paid for.

It was after the royal dinner that they formalized the system. Titi would send out the invitations to a private reception or a private dinner, Michel Roux would cough up the drinks, pay for the overheads, and pick up the $10,000 invoice they sent him afterwards. The penny had finally dropped.

Even when the event was held at Studio 54, it always said on the invitation that Countess Christina Wachtmeister was hosting a party in honor of this or that or the other grand person. The idea was that one grand person would invite another grand person. And there was nothing as grand in American eyes as royalty and nobility. It made no difference how many albums they'd sold, or how big a movie they'd starred in, or if they bathed in cash—nothing beat a European title. A real live Swedish countess throwing a party—sweet Jesus, they fell to their knees.

Titi invited no more than three hundred guests, often less. Sometimes only twenty people would be invited to a private apartment in New York or a dinner at the embassy in Washington. It had to be exclusive, and everyone had to be on the same level, because the invitees always asked the same question: "Who'll be there? Who'll be there?"

And the Frenchman subsidized the lot. Now he got the picture. He was soo cunning. The other liquor labels had to bribe their way in through restaurant owners and bar managers. The Frenchman got his booze in thanks to Countess Wachtmeister. He got his vodka into celebrity parties, VIP bars, gossip columns, and through-the-keyhole documentaries.

When her good friend Roger Moore opened a mini-bar in the new Bond film, what was there on shelf, right in front of Her Majesty's Secret Agent 007, if not the invisible bottle?

A year after Olof had gone back to Sweden, Andy Warhol called and told him that Michel Roux had asked him to paint the bottle. Andy said that he had no option but to accept since the offer had come directly from Carillon.

The truth was that Warhol personally offered to do the painting for Michel Roux. He even claimed there was a version ready and wondered if Roux was interested in doing business.

Bill Tragos and Dick Costello at TBWA were less than convinced. At first they didn't realize that Roux wanted to use the painting as a regular ad. They thought it was about some kind of support for American modern art. They knew that Warhol had previously done a painting of a French liqueur that hung in Roux's office. Having Andy Warhol do a painted ad seemed like a departure from the campaign's central idea, which was—wasn't it?—to have the bottle photographed.

But Roux was determined. And these days he made all the important decisions himself, not just about sales, agents, and marketing; even individual ads passed through Roux. He took one of the Warhols with him to Stockholm to show Lars Lindmark. Lindmark thought it didn't even resemble the bottle.

The bottle Warhol had painted was black.

After all the carnage, here was Broman's clear bottle, but now it was black.

Black Vodka.

• • •

But that night—that night before he went back home—that night Olof had come to Studio 54 with the package for Steve.

Clutching it under his arm, he elbowed his way through the seething crowd. He climbed the stairs to Steve's office. It was like boarding the *Titanic.* Here it was. Center of the world. Rod Stewart sprawling over the sagging sofa. Steve slightly crazed out, nodding, nodding, as Olof unwrapped it.

"That's so cool. That's so cool."

Well, there it was. On Steve's table. Just as he had promised Peter Ekelund. He had placed the bottle in the eye of the trend.

CHAPTER 14

MICHEL'S REWARD

Andy's friends paint the bottle, too, and daring Michel Roux orchestrates Absolut's wildly successful campaign. He deserves a medal, he feels.

The first person they approached to photograph the bottle was Michael O'Neill. Michael took pictures for everyone at that time. He always had a shoot in the morning and another in the afternoon. But his pictures turned out funny. The backdrop was pitch black, and that made the bottle stick out like a ghost in the night. It looked like the bottle was filled with milk.

Geoff Hayes, the art director from TBWA, asked Michael to have another go at it, but he said he was too busy. Already the rumor had started that the bottle was unphotographable. It was neat, sure, but you just couldn't capture it on film. Geoff remembered a young guy from Syracuse, called Steve Bronstein, who'd done some nice work for a Swiss watch manufacturer. He asked Steve to give the bottle a day or two, to go into the studio and just play a bit.

Bronstein placed the bottle on a sheet of black card with a slight ripple. It looked almost as though the bottle was walking on water. The ripple gave the picture a horizontal line, something rarely seen in American ads. In the United States, products were supposed to just float in the air. He used a neutral sheet of blown Plexiglas as a backdrop, lit in such a way that it was given a soft luster, a mild sheen as of a divine apparition. The picture was dark at the edges, and became steadily lighter toward the center. The bottle itself had a burning white halo. In that way the contours on the bottle achieved a well-defined contrast. Bronstein used only two spots. He had the whole studio full of reflectors and a big eight-by-twelve-inch camera, really just a big box with a lens at one end.

The bottle in the picture was crystal clear. At last it was visible.

The budget for Absolut Vodka was so ridiculously small. All the other labels spent millions of dollars advertising in the prestige periodicals with national distribution. Absolut couldn't afford that. Two ads in *Newsweek* or *Time* would devour the entire budget. In order to achieve some semblance of penetration, Claude Fromm at TBWA was reduced to utilizing regional and special-interest magazines. He bought space in *New York* magazine, *Los Angeles* magazine, and the *The New Yorker*. Around '83 or '84 he started placing ads in Andy Warhol's publication *Interview*. Like other magazines, *Interview* used to send gifts to bookstores, hotels, and newsstands in order to be taken up in the selection or be given better display space. *Interview* got to buy in Absolut Vodka at cut price and give it away to customers. Fromm bought space in *GQ*, which at that time had a readership that was 50 percent gay and reached a lot of African-Americans. He collaborated with Peter Frisch, editor of *The Advocate*, an openly homosexual publication. And the gay community was setting the trends.

They had bought advertising space for Absolut in the eye of the trend.

To get into the *New York Times*, Fromm had to negotiate a special tariff. Normally, a full-page ad cost $36,000, but he bought it for $12,000. The disadvantage was that the guys on the *Times'* advertising desk got to choose where and when the ads would appear. The first ad TBWA sent over was Absolut Heaven. Geoff and Graham had decked the bottle out with angel wings. When Fromm leafed through the paper, he discovered Absolut Heaven opposite the obituaries.

Jerry Ciraulo sat in his tiny cubbyhole in Carillon's office above the Rockefeller Center trying to calculate the sales figures for the next quarter. He was way out. Whatever way he tackled it, he was way out. Eventually, Ciraulo started making prognoses that were totally insane. He was looking at sales increases that predicted that every single American citizen would soon be sitting with a huge grin on his face and a bottle of Absolut Vodka in his hand. And even those calculations were way out. No matter how he looked at it, Ciraulo came up short.

The year following Absolut's debut at the New Orleans convention, they sold 11,000 cases, each containing twelve bottles of prime Swedish vodka. The next year they sold 45,000 cases. That was 400,000 liters. The year after that they sold 70,000 cases. Then they doubled up and sold 135,000. Then they said to one another that that must be it. It wasn't possible to keep going at that rate. The next year they sold 250,000 cases. Two million two hundred and fifty thousand liters of vodka right down those thirsty American necks.

And the Swedes ran out of booze.

Warehouses stood empty on the East Coast of the United States. At the factory in Åhus, the foreman had to appeal to the public, and the good people of Åhus responded. Schoolchildren, housewives, and cripples were set to work at the distillery, and soon the liquor factory was in production twenty-four hours a day, churning out vodka for the thirsty States. They had to fly the stuff over at horrendous cost, just as Gunnar Broman had done when he booked a first-class seat for the first few cases.

After only four years, they overtook Finlandia as the second biggest imported vodka. In 1985 they passed Stolichnaya and became number one among the imports. This was something special.

After all, vodka was Russian. Wasn't it?

Afterwards, some attributed Absolut's success to the advertising, the incredible advertising—those two-word ads!—but in the early years no one even mentioned the ads. It took two or three years before Madison Avenue even noticed the ads. Sure, people came up to Geoff Hayes and Graham Turner at the bar and gave them a little pat on the back—"great job with that Swedish vodka"—but no one breathed a word about the fact that there might be something special about those ads.

First, the explanation was that the Russians had gone into Afghanistan; three years later it was that they'd shot down a DC-10 over Korea; but none of this showed up in the sales curve. The curve wasn't even a curve, it was a straight line. It went steadily upward, with not so much as an earthward glance. It was entirely independent of what the Russians did or did not do. Someone happened upon a picture of the north face of Mont Blanc, a cliff that went almost vertically all the way up to the blue blue sky, and that's the picture they used to illustrate their sales figures.

One day Al Singer proclaimed that he had just turned seventy, which came as a complete surprise to everyone, not least his wife. No one had had any idea how old Al Singer was before he invited all of his buddies out to the track at Green Meadows. Pacing the premises in his bathrobe, he explained that he was considering fucking retiring and stuffed hundred dollar bills into the hands of each and every guest so that they could celebrate his big day by playing the ponies with him.

When Al Singer went out to pasture, everyone thought that Tim Enos, second man at Carillon, would take over. Strangely enough, the job went to Michel Roux. What was even more surprising was that Roux immediately underwent a complete change of character.

Earlier, Roux had always walked one step behind Al Singer and always said the same things as his boss, even if he made it sound a bit different.

The day after Roux took over, he reinvented Michel Roux and became *Michel Roux*.

This new Michel Roux had a will of his own. He had opinions not just on the art of selling liquor, but on advertising, fashion, art, all aspects of American society. It turned out that Roux had been secretly studying the Americans for twenty years. Now he was ready to take control.

The real shocker came when Michel Roux suddenly revealed himself as Absolut Frenchman. No longer was he the Frenchman trying to pose as an American. He came out of the closet, wearing a beret. Suddenly he was devilishly charming. Suddenly he was perpetually flirtatious. When he caught sight of a beautiful woman, or of any woman for that matter, it was as though the entire male population of France demanded that he do something about it. Michel Roux reinvented himself as the ultimate American cliché of a Frenchman. In the coming five years, he would also reinvent the whole concept of marketing.

• • •

Michel Roux had worked in the hotel business before France's colonial war in Algeria, then he'd been a conscript for three years. When he returned to Paris in 1962, the only jobs were for night porters, so he applied for a U.S. visa.

At that time there was a special offer on tickets from Paris to Houston, so Roux ended up in Texas. He found a job as a dishwasher at the Rice Hotel in Houston and thought it better than walking up and down empty hotel corridors in Paris. After a couple of weeks he advanced to the position of receptionist, then he managed to land a job at a resort hotel in Corpus Christi, and he could finally afford to fly over his wife and son.

Roux was transferred to another hotel in Rockport, Texas, deep in the Bible Belt. At the end of the eighteenth century a band of Frenchmen had arrived in Rockport and made an eternal impression on the town's citizens by immediately succumbing to a mysterious plague. The good folks in Rockport had not seen a Frenchman in the flesh since, but they remembered them clearly as a gang of depraved, salacious rogues, whose sins explained their sudden and unpleasant demise.

When Michel Roux turned up, the people of Rockport took him to be a delayed relative of the earlier visitors, and no doubt an emissary of the Devil himself. They locked up their women and barred their doors.

Still, their attitude toward the Frenchman was not entirely uncomplicated. The male patrons of the country club assumed that since Roux was out to pervert their women with his beer and spirits, he could also arrange comprehensive female entertainment at any given hour of the day. But where were these high-spirited ladies to be found? Everyone in Rockport knew everyone else by name. Roux couldn't conjure up carnal sin from thin air, no matter how much he would have loved to.

After a couple of years in Texas, Roux was able to open a little restaurant in Dallas that he called La Petite France. The chef at the restaurant was a Belgian called Jean Bite. *Bite* was French slang for the male reproductive organ, and poor Jean had developed such a complex about his surname that he'd been forced to emigrate to America. He had hoped that in Texas he would be spared the sniping remarks he had endured in Belgium since childhood.

It turned out that the Americans pronounced Bite as in a "little bit." Jean Bite was a very big guy, a Belgian giant. Things were little better in the new country.

Jean Bite had sadly accepted his bitter fate and prepared the meals for Michel Roux's guests at La Petite France. While he produced one gastronomic marvel after another under extremely trying conditions, Jean consumed prodigious quantities of beer. Being a Belgian, he already had a predilection to beer, and he'd learned to appreciate Lone Star, the light golden beer of Texas. In the confined, stifling kitchen Jean Bite's enormous frame demanded lavish quantities of the liquid. Every evening the chef of La Petite France exhausted an entire case of Lone Star. Michel Roux watched him, hunched over the saucepans and casserole dishes in the oppressive heat, as all the beer the enormous Jean drank sweated out of him in droplets and rained down on the sauces and sizzled on the steaks, adding to the flavor.

Michel Roux had hoped that the only French restaurant in Dallas would soon be a must.

In the Land of the Free, however, it was not as easy to run a business as he'd imagined. Sometimes the dishwasher went AWOL, sometimes the bartender personally tested the quality of every liquor behind the bar before the customers arrived, sometimes the great Jean Bite would fall ill from the heat and the beer, and a replacement would be rushed in, and every time Michel Roux went to work the tables, his new dishwasher would rush out to the yard with a side of beef and hide it behind the garbage cans.

The big problem was that the guests who frequented La Petite France were not untutored cowhands, they were cattle millionaires, oil billionaires, people like Stanley Markus or members of the Hunt family, who had traveled the world and eaten at three-star restaurants in France, Lucas Carton and Le Tour d'Argent, establishments Roux had never been near.

On occasion they sulkily pointed out to Roux as he rushed out of the kitchen after another game of tag with a new chef, that the duck tasted better at some Seineside restaurant in Paris, and what did Roux have to say about that? Ah, Roux would answer, we've had problems with the suppliers, and then, it must be said, the ducks of Texas are not quite what they were.

And that was how Michel Roux discovered his talent. Something he did made people smile.

He had no idea what it was, he just had a feel for what to say to make the millionaires in the dining room and the cooks in the kitchen feel good. Whether they were more sophisticated than he was, or less sophisticated, it made no difference.

Roux had learned all about feeling inferior back home. If there was something his compatriots had drummed into him, it was how your nose gets rubbed in it, and it was the last thing he wanted anyone else to experience.

Salesmen were constantly passing through La Petite France, selling French wines. Roux, who worked from sunrise until the wee small hours without ever having any money over to pay himself, thought this was perhaps the business to be in. I am a Frenchman who came to Dallas by mistake, he thought. I should travel around and talk to the good people of Texas, make them smile, feel good, and buy French wines.

He got in touch with one of the bigger distributors in Dallas and asked for a job, but they explained that he was their best customer in the whole region, and the last thing they wanted was for him to close his restaurant.

It was at this point that Michel Roux bumped into Al Singer. Al had a little wine agency, and he was prepared to employ Roux as a wine salesman for six thousand dollars a year. True, Roux knew nothing about wine, but he had his French accent, the significance of which was not lost on shrewd Al. He took the job and hit the road for three months at a time.

Wherever he went, he talked to people, made them laugh, and sold them wine, along with another one of Al Singer's products, the famous French liqueur, Grand Marnier. An exquisite product, but unfortunately the Amercians had a tendency to keep it in the kitchen cupboard instead of in the bar.

The Frenchman turned up everywhere in his old Mercedes, and everywhere he turned up he touched something in people. He made them laugh. He made them feel liked. He had the gift.

He made them laugh in Texarkana, he made them smile in Hot Springs, in Little Rock, in Baton Rouge, and in Lafayette. Yes, sir. In the liquor store in Texarkana they had hung Roux's portrait right beside that of the president.

In the end, Roux sold La Petite France to Jean Bite. By that time another French restaurant had opened in Dallas, owned by one of Roux's countrymen, a man known only as Marcel, who a short time later died of cirrhosis of the liver. Marcel had had a fondness for alcohol all his life, and a year before it ended, the doctors had delivered their verdict. Marcel used the time left to him to travel home to France and choose a final resting place. His affinity for wine was so great that he had a gravestone fashioned in the shape of a bottle.

Marcel was a close friend of Francine, who was married to George, the chef at the restaurant. When Marcel died, Francine had him lie in state for three days right there in the middle of the restaurant. When the time came to screw on the lid and send Marcel home to rest under the stone bottle in France, Francine opened a magnum of Grand Marnier and poured it over the coffin.

Roux thought that if all Americans were sent off in the same splendid fashion as Marcel, he wouldn't have to teach them to drink the stuff with their coffee.

Roux liked to tell his customers that down by the coast, at the high-class yacht clubs, the rich Texans called the French drink not *Grand Marnier* but Grand Mariner. In Dallas they were more sophisticated, and there the drink went under the name of *Grand Manière.* But way out west, on the prairies, the cattle millionaires called the fine liqueur *Grand Manure.*

"Whatever you want to call it," said Roux to the happily chuckling customers, "is fine, so long as you buy it from me."

• • •

Roux had only meant to use the Warhol painting once. But then something peculiar happened. It became news. All the major newspapers printed the painting without so much as a dollar changing hands. This time he'd touched something special.

The buzz was a little strange. It wasn't the first time a company had hired an artist to do an ad. In the seventies, ITT had spent a fortune getting Salvador Dali, but there had been no fuss then. Perhaps all the attention had to do with the fact that Warhol, in true Warhol fashion, wasn't ashamed in the slightest of stooping to the level of advertising. He had no need to play the artist and do something intellectual and deep. He did a celebrity portrait. And in the end, wasn't the bottle a celebrity? It was right there with the other celebrities at Studio 54, night after night.

The bottle had never looked better than when Warhol was done with it. He'd done what he usually did with obese millionaires and grotesque rock stars. He took away the odd double chin or two and slapped on a little panache and glamour. Despite Titi's fears, it didn't have the dreary look of a Campbell's soup can at all. The bottle looked regal.

It was a terrific success. The ad won a Clio, and Roux was itching to repeat the trick.

People treated him differently after the Warhol ad. He was no longer just another liquor dealer, but a patron of the arts. Roux asked Warhol if he could recommend any young artists. That's how the Frenchman got in touch with Ed Ruscha, Keith Haring, and Kenny Scharf.

Scharf had been on the streets of New York with his buddies and a bag full of spray cans, covering buildings with graffiti just a year or so earlier. Haring drew funny little cartoon figures in the subway. Both were under thirty. Roux proclaimed to the world that this was Absolut Art.

The young artists demanded incredible amounts of money. Haring told Roux that he wanted the same amount as Warhol.

"But you're not Andy Warhol," said Roux.

"Nope, I'm better," said Haring.

"No, you're not," Roux replied. "If you'd been better, I would've asked you first."

These guys weren't like artists from the old school who liked drinking cheap red wine and eating pigeons they'd trapped in the park. They saw themselves as rock stars. It was a matter of honor for them to name a price that made Roux light in the head. Then they complained that he was cheap. Roux should be grateful he was allowed to buy their work.

But the first artist Warhol mentioned was a boy from the

Caribbean, Jean-Michel Basquiat, a primordial artistic force who, a year earlier, had been given the honor of a joint exhibit with Warhol at the Tony Shafrazi Gallery and who had, according to some of those in the know, wiped the floor with the father of pop art. But Warhol won out in the end anyway, like he always did.

Basquiat and Warhol had painted the canvases together. As was his wont, Warhol made Basquiat's art look like part of his own work. Basquiat created his own art, but Warhol created Basquiat.

Jean-Michel Basquiat refused point-blank to paint so much as a stroke for Absolut Vodka. Roux visited the artist in his studio. He'd never met a person so strongly under the influence of marijuana. Basquiat floated round under the roofbeams in big sweeping circles, paint dropping from his brush onto the Frenchman below. The artist explained that his father had abused alcohol and drunk all his money and been unable to support the family and had eventually died of cirrhosis of the liver. Basquiat had sworn never to touch liquor. He explained that after what had happened to his father, the very thought of doing an ad for liquor was offensive. He was purging his body of all synthetic substances.

But the very next day the artist called Roux up and said he was now ready to do an "Absolut Basquiat," to which the Frenchman replied: "Thank you, but *no*—in the name of your father!"

After the success of the paintings, Roux realized he could use the Absolut ads as a force in American culture. Earlier he'd thought that he'd just do everything bigger than everyone else. When the talk turned to big billboards, he thought of the biggest big billboard in the United States of America. The canvases would be 150 feet long. If there was a waterfall in the middle, he wanted a real waterfall. Now he realized that he didn't have to do it big. He just had to do it different. The market analysts could discuss whether or not he was doing it to sell vodka. Roux was going to do it with style and bravado and audacity. Something people would really remember.

And so he set out.

He did Absolut Fashion, an eight-page spread in *Vogue*.

He did Absolut Style, a ten-pager in *Elle*.

He did Absolut Fashion once again, surrealist-style this time, in *Harper's Bazaar*.

He did Absolut Menswear in *GQ*.

He did Absolut Design.

He did Absolut Artists of the Nineties.

He did Absolut Cartoons.

He did Absolut Symbols, with gay artists.

And that was just the beginning. Then came:

Absolut Statehood, one ad for every state in the union.

Absolut Cities, covering all major American cities.

Absolut Glasnost, with twenty-six young Soviet artists.

Absolut Jobim, a record.

Absolut Postcards.

Absolut Film & Literature.

Arnie Arlow and his cocreative director at TBWA, Peter Lubalin, managed the Absolut campaign very carefully. Arnie decided it had to follow a linear path, a gradual slope. The campaign had started with just the bottle, that was before Arnie, the bottle and the halo. Ten years later they were putting the final touches to Absolut Evidence. This was just a thumbprint, a little black smudge in the right-hand corner of the page, almost like that little black German automobile thirty years ago. Absolut Evidence—a sticky-fingered signature left by a thief, and within the thumbprint was a tiny, tiny, *tiny* Absolut bottle. You almost had to use a magnifying glass to see it.

Arnie loved it. Ten years ago, even five years ago, it would have been impossible. But they had taken the now famous photographic ads along the gradual path, carefully managing the campaign from the photographed bottle thru the artwork by Warhol and his friends, and eventually to this . . . a thumbprint.

Sometimes alternative newspapers and magazines would do their own Absolut ads, and sometimes they turned a blind eye at TBWA. Arnie loved the things they did. They were so young and experimental. They were doing just what he had wanted to do when he was twenty. They were rebels looking to break all the rules. After all, Andy Warhol himself had once been a maverick. People had laughed at his soup cans. Now they were as valuable as a Picasso. Keith Haring had started out as a rebel. Now Warhol and Haring were considered masters, even Absolut Masters after Michel Roux and Arnie had commissioned their work.

They started out by changing the bottle in the ads ever so slightly. They took "a few liberties," as they said, smiling knowingly, as if they had done something completely out of line. In a way, they had. They had put the bottle in an aquarium. Then they had thrown roses over it and made it in gold—still on the linear path—and then again in marble. They had made it BIG, swimming-pool-big, like in Absolut LA, and Central Park big—Absolut Manhattan, or ski-slope big—Absolut Peak. Then very, very big—they found someone who had planted a whole goddamn bona fide cornfield shaped like a bottle out in Lawrence, Kansas.

This was modern advertising at its best—very creative, but still following the gradual path. Two words (one of them being the name of the product) and the bottle. It certainly had legs.

Then they had made it incredibly small, like the entry in a dictionary. And then they took it away completely. Arnie had once taken the cork out of Grand Marnier, but now he *removed the whole bottle!* It was Absolut Larceny, just the wet ring of the bottle (actually, that was Graham Turner's idea from the very first pitch with Carillon. At the time it was deemed too experimental).

Arlow and his team followed the linear path very closely. By now they understood that what they were doing was much more than advertising for a liquor. This was an advertising phenomen. They received one big award after the other. An Effie. The Kelly Award (twice). Induction into the Marketing Hall of Fame—at the same time as Coca-Cola. Now people in the business were talking about the best print campaign *ever*. People all over the country collected the ads. They wrote asking for some missing ad they needed for their Absolut Collection.

Arnie didn't do many ads personally during these years. Just as he had done at Martin Landey, Arlow, he provided the creative environment of fun and laughter and style. But being not an artist but a master doodler, Arnie did one of the very small ones. He did Absolut Doodle.

There was no end to his creativity, not on the gradual slope.

When the vodka was launched, Al Singer and the Swedes had decided that a certain percentage of the profits were to be pumped back into marketing. Since the first few years were modest, they agreed to increase the amount substantially. As sales increased, so did the advertising budget at TBWA.

From day one Roux had declared that he would never price promote the brand. He would price the Swedish vodka at the highest level. And if people weren't prepared to pay the price? "Well," Roux defiantly declared: "let them drink Smirnoff!"

He kept piling money back into the campaign. The Swedes in their surreal political environment were mostly worried that one day they would have to publicly confess that they were making profits from the exports, so they thought it a very good idea to "build the brand." Roux encouraged them to reach further. The advertising budget grew from $750,000 in 1981 to $25,000,000 in 1990. Absolut, from the Country of Sweden, a country where they advertised liquor on the back of matchbox covers, was the most heavily advertised spirits brand in the world—ever.

Everyone was expecting the product to plateau. Roux shot back: "One day it *might* plateau, but not at three or four hundred thousand cases. I'm looking at five *million*."

The figures were so fanciful, they were just over the top. There was no way of disproving them. You either were a true believer, or you weren't.

It was much more fun to believe.

Apart from the new ads from TBWA every season—each and every one approved by Roux—he was constantly commissioning new Absolut paintings, Absolut quilts, Absolut pitchers, weather vanes, tapestries, sculptures, chairs, dolls, everything, everything he could think of.

Roux ordered the world's first talking ad, which proclaimed its support for endangered species. He commissioned an entire series of ads on the theme of American folklore, and every December he demanded that Arnie Arlow and his gang prepare a masterpiece—a seasonal ad that would knock the picky American public clean through Christmas.

Since Christmas decorations were one of Arnie's specialties, he had no trouble knocking out singing Christmas ads, talking

Christmas ads, Christmas ads with silk stockings for women and handkerchiefs for men, even ads with falling snow, all of which cost a good deal more to produce than the publications that printed them. And the wonderful thing was, it made news all around the world.

Some of the Christmas ads cost more than $1 million. The admen quickly calculated the value of the free publicity to be $5 million.

Roux was the smiling Sun King of advertising, floating over the landscape of American Culture, throwing money around.

It was good to be the king.

Countess Titi Wachtmeister had once called him up and said:

"Michel! Send me ten bottles—fast!"

The next day a truck pulled up outside with ten cases of Absolut Vodka, three cases of cognac, several cases of liqueur, and so on, until her Sixty-eighth Street apartment was transformed into a liquor warehouse. "This is his way of trying to impress me," she thought. "First it was expensive wines for lunch, and now it's a truckload of liquor. It always has to be too much."

Of course, "too much" was exactly what some of them demanded.

Kenny Scharf, the artist, said years later (*after* he had gotten his money from Roux): "Oh, but he's such a peasant!"

They all thought he was. Andy would've said that Michel Roux wasn't category anything, neither rich, famous nor gorgeous.

He couldn't even speak proper English.

At the end of the eighties, when Absolut's triumph was secured, Roux began wondering aloud just what one had to do to be considered for the famous Swedish Order of the Northern Star.

Titi knew then that her fears had been realized: success had really gone to his head. The only person outside Sweden, except kings and presidents, who had the Order of the Northern Star was Greta Garbo.

"We can't give the Northern Star to a liquor merchant from Texas," she told her father, the ambassador. Eventually he got hold of a little marksmanship badge for Roux to hang on his wall at home. But the Frenchman wouldn't let it lie. During one of his visits to Sweden he went to the theater and learned that the eighteenth-century building was threatened with demolition. Roux stood up, made a little speech about Culture and donated a quarter of a million bucks on the spot. He always did it with panache. When Titi's father, the longest-serving diplomat in Washington, left his post, he was replaced by a politician, and the first thing he did was to award Roux the Grand Cross of the Order of the Northern Star.

Then he was awarded a French Order. Titi and Andy were invited to the celebratory dinner at the Plaza Athenée. Roux was the guest of honor, and in the middle of dinner, the French ambassador pinned the medal to his chest.

"Michel loves medals!" whispered his wife.

EPILOGUE

Twenty Years After

In a wonderfully contradictory pronouncement, Absolut's advertising agency, TBWA once tried to explain the secret of its signature account:

". . . Absolut would also be unpretentious and not take itself—or the world—too seriously. Now, many years, and hundreds of awards later, the image of the Absolut bottle is embedded in our collective consciousness."

Absolut vodka landed on American soil in 1979. To mark its twentieth anniversary, TBWA presented a stunning booklet (a little late) in the summer of 2000, for which twenty American celebrities were invited to share their favorite Absolut ad with the world.

Here were Salman and Susan, Philip and Philippe, Gore and Spike.

Here was the Absolut Ad. Advertising advertising advertising.

Here was Absolut Vodka, all grown up and seemingly taking itself very seriously indeed.

Courting the world is a serious business.

JERRY

N. W. Ayer boss, Neal O'Connor, managed, within the space of a few months, to buy up a string of thirty agencies all over the world. The campaign the agency put together for Pan American

World Airlines"—"We fly the world the way the world wants to fly"—led to the announcement that the airline was moving all its international and domestic advertising accounts, with a combined turnover of $32 million, to Ayer.

In the spring of 1979, N. W. Ayer was voted Advertising Agency of the Year. Ayer CEO Lou Hagopian accredited the success to the firm's creative director, Jerry Siano. Ten years later, Siano himself was CEO at N. W. Ayer, the first in the agency's one-hundred-and-twenty-year history to come from the creative side.

When people in advertising mentioned Absolut, Jerry Siano used to tell them that Ayer had actually helped create the brand. In spite of his many years in the business, he only got snide remarks; he was trying to jump on the bandwagon of something that was by now a formidable success. As if he had something to prove. He stopped mentioning it.

MYRON

One day Myron Poloner was called in by his patron at N. W. Ayer, Lou Hagopian, and told, "You're not gonna go anywhere here."

Doing what he did for Hagopian, Poloner had attracted an enormous amount of resentment at Ayer. So some time after his work on the Swedish vodka ended, Myron Poloner left the agency. For a while he tried to get in on the vodka project again at Martin Landey, Arlow. The Salieri of Burlington House could recognize a perfect pitch when he heard one.

Myron Poloner went on to have a successful career in the advertising business.

ARNIE

He took to the podium, dwarfed by the enormous bottle on the screen behind him. Smiling coolly, Arnie Arlow accepted the diploma and made his way back through the tables, buoyed by the applause of his peers.

He had submitted the Absolut bottle to the New York Art Directors Club and won a Distinctive Merit award. But then those Swedes had started to make trouble. Curt Nycander had telegraphed long protest lists with the names of Swedes Arlow had never met or even heard of, and they had been forced to withdraw the submission. The Art Directors Club had recalled every copy of the yearbook and shelled out for reprinting the page where the damn bottle had been.

Winner number 614 no longer existed. Gone. There was just a white patch left on the page.

Two years later he left Martin Landey for good. He'd always said that Marty would've cut off his mother's legs for a quarter, and now he knew it was true. The entire reason behind the merger with Geers, Gross was money and power, power and money.

Leaving Marty was like escaping from a bad marriage. It had taken up fifteen years of his life and was in the process of finishing him off. The only mystery remaining after he left was why he'd stayed so long.

Arnie was made creative director of TBWA, and led the Absolut campaign to triumph after triumph throughout the eighties and nineties.

He was blessed with a grandchild. He remarried. Suddenly he felt at ease. At the wedding, his best friend got up and said he'd always known that if only Arnie could be *given* something, he could begin to give himself. And it was true. He'd *taken* that goddamned Swedish bottle, claimed it as his own work and won, but they'd taken it away from him. Then, as though by a miracle, he'd gotten the bottle back, and he'd repaid them by leading the world's most successful advertising campaign for ten years. He'd won every prize there was for them. And what had he really done to deserve it? He'd received and given back in kind. That was the whole story.

MARTIN

Martin Landey retired a rich man and devoted himself to deep-sea fishing off the coast of New Jersey, until he gave in a few years later and started a new agency.

BILL

Bill Tragos consolidated TBWA's position as the fastest growing agency in the States. Thirteen years after he took control of the Absolut account, TBWA was named Advertising Agency of the Year. In the mid-nineties the agency Bill had built billed for seven billion dollars. They bought up Chiat/Day and became TBWA Chiat/Day. Two years earlier they had sold to Omnicom and made out like bandits.

GRAHAM AND GEOFF

Graham Turner and Geoff Hayes returned to England briefly. When they came back to the U.S., Geoff started working at TBWA again.

Absolut Vodka won its first Magazine Publishers of America Kelly Award, and the hundred thousand-dollar prize money that went with it, in 1989. Graham waited for Bill Tragos to call and congratulate him. But Tragos never got in touch. Geoff Hayes took his share of the cash and bought Graham a video camera. He told him to film his newborn child.

MICHEL

Michel Roux transformed the modest import house of Carillon Importers, founded once upon a time by Al Singer, into a company whose profit-per-employee was said to be the highest in America.

Once a year, every publication in the United States that wanted Absolut Vodka to buy advertising space was obliged to make the trip out to Teaneck, New Jersey, to take part in a widely hated "media marathon." They were supposed to present their ideas for Absolut ads and Absolut campaigns and Absolut events. Each one was granted thirty minutes to bow and scrape before King Michel.

In the spring of 1994, the Monopoly suddenly terminated its cooperation with Michel Roux in favor of Seagram. It didn't take long before Stolichnaya called.

STUDIO 54

Carmen D'Alessio ran into one of the doormen from Studio 54, and he told her that at the end of every shift, they'd take all the money, stuff it in garbage bags and stick it behind the air conditioning up on the roof.

Steve Rubell was indicted and convicted for tax evasion. Before he went to prison, he threw one final party at Studio 54. Everyone was there. They played "My Way," and the bar was open all night. It was like the Golden Age again.

But it wasn't the Golden Age. In 1983, one of Titi Wachtmeister's friends was stricken by a mysterious illness. He developed large lesions on his face, he lost weight, and a couple of months later he died. Then people started dying in droves.

Britt Monti went home and took a job at IKEA.

Olof Tranvik became the boss of the Coca-Cola Company in Norway, and later in Thailand.

Titi Wachtmeister died suddently at the age of forty-two, when a blood vessel burst in her brain.

ANDY

Andy Warhol hated doctors and hospitals, and he refused to get help for a gall-bladder infection. He eventually went into the operating theater and died the next day. Warhol left 4,118 paintings and sculptures, 5,103 sketches, 19,086 lithographs and 66,512 photographs. They were valued in court at $491 million.

RUNE

Executives at The System Company, which oversaw liquor stores in Sweden, were irritated when the Monopoly started exporting to the United States without asking them first, and Rune Hermansson, general manager of The System, expressed his displeasure with Lars Lindmark's adventure in overseas sales. At first The System refused to sell Absolut in Sweden. The union protested that the bottle was improperly formed, *ergonomically* wrong. You couldn't lift it, they said. Of course they'd be happy to take on the export vodka in the stores, but the Monopoly would have to redesign the bottle first.

Today Absolut Country of Sweden Vodka is sold even in Sweden. It is, of course, a much smaller product than Absolut Rent Brännvin—Renat.

PETER

Peter Ekelund, who had sung and drunk an unsteady path across America in the cause of Absolut, was forced to leave the Monopoly following severe internal criticism. He had gone public with the revelation that Sweden was actually exporting liquor, and had even said that the goal of the state Monopoly was to sell as much Swedish vodka overseas as possible. He went over to the advertising business, became boss of a European cable television company, and reappeared at the end of the nineties as CEO of a broadband company and a prophet for the "new economy."

ROLF

When the Liquor Monopoly organized a day out for the old boys in the early nineties, the ex-administrative director, Rolf Arfwedson, turned to his former colleagues. He had read in the staff magazine that the general opinion was that in their time the company had been a Sleeping Beauty, "slumbering" under the spell of the state. This upset Arfwedson. Hadn't they closed factories, too, and built new ones to replace them? Didn't Kinna-Erik establish the special wine ships *Vinia, Vinlandia,* and *Vindemia?*

But of course all paled in comparison to Absolut Vodka. It was the only topic of conversation these days. Absolut. Absolut. Absolut.

Arfwedson wrote a letter to the staff magazine, but it was never published. The Monopoly was looking forward to its seventy-fifth anniversary, they said, so the past was a closed book.

TORSTEN

Torsten Bengtson, the teetotaler on the Liquor Monopoly board, once got involved in a debate with the new chairman of the board, Egon Jacobsson. Jacobsson was a politician and a renowned tippler. Every time parliament debated alcohol policy, he told anyone who'd listen that the Swedish people had learned how to handle their alcohol.

Bengtson had gone to hear Jacobsson speak at a teetotalers' meeting. He was immediately recognized and invited to take the stage. He declared that when the decision to launch Absolut Vodka had been taken, he had voiced his concerns in a memo, but the memo had disappeared.

"It's part of the record," Jacobsson muttered.

"Well then, send it," retorted Bengtson.

But they never sent the memo, and he knew damn well they

never would, because his reservations against this exercise in moral bankruptcy were to be ignored.

MAGNUS

Lars Lindmark's right-hand man, Magnus Lagerkvist, left the Monopoly when Lindmark's modernization program was complete. He became a well paid consultant and started his own consulting firm. He chose three words as the company motto: Modesty, Morality, Artistry. Even if modesty wasn't exactly Lagerkvist's strong suit, it sounded good.

As far as Lagerkvist could tell, he and Lindmark had been able to get the export project past the Monopoly's board because they had taken the key decision before the board heard the proposal and, when that wasn't enough, they had replaced a few members of the board. After a few years as a consultant, Lagerkvist had worked with most of the companies on the Swedish stock market. He had closely observed the actions of a string of CEO's. He thought Lindmark could be compared with the best of them.

LARS

Lars Lindmark was appointed chairman of the Monopoly but was forced to resign when K-O Feldt, the outgoing socialist minister of finance, wanted the post for himself. Right in the middle of his second term, with enough Absolut money pouring in from the States to finance all Sweden's liquor imports, they threw him out like a sack of industrial potatoes

Lindmark felt he'd lived his life in eternal dusk. First he'd been in the civil service and helped create the Great Welfare State, and he hadn't even been a socialist. When he'd switched to the private sector, everyone had assumed he *was* a socialist. He could sense them whispering behind his back. If he'd been a socialist, he'd have made it all the way to minister of finance, and then that little Feldt could never have stolen his seat at the head of the table.

One summer, the advertising boys had come to Lindmark with a label for an Italian country wine bottle. It didn't look particularly Italian to Lindmark—a wooden door slightly ajar, some weeds round about. It looked like a Swedish outhouse.

But the outhouse won prizes.

That's what you had to remember, he told himself. You had to trust people. And that was the little secret Lindmark had carried around with him for years, from the precarious beginnings of the export venture to its successful conclusion.

He always thought Broman's bottle was so ugly it looked like shit.

When Lindmark left the Monopoly, he decided to quit smoking, start training, and live a better life, to think of himself a little more for a change. Six months later he was dead. They found him lying on the running track. His dachshund was beside him, keeping guard.

CURT

When they sent the first shipment of Absolut to a cruise liner, every single bottle leaked. The duty-free store was stormed by angry vacationers who had alcohol all over their suitcases, where it did them no good whatsoever. The shipping line called in the middle of the weekend. They'd had enough. Absolut Vodka was out. The Monopoly dispatched a man who spent the next night going through the entire shipment bottle by bottle, screwing on caps. He swapped and screwed, swapped and screwed and checked, while the boat bobbed on.

The Monopoly's Curt Nycander couldn't understand why they couldn't get their act together with the caps. They'd produced the best vodka in the world and poured it into the most unusual bottle in the world, and now it was dripping out all over the place. Nycander was sitting there toying with an aluminum cigar tube. They ought to be able to knock out a cap like that. It worked. Plastic with an aluminum shell. Simple.

As soon as any other liquor producer copied the bottle or the marketing style—and they did frequently—Nycander dragged them before a judge in New York and sued them for such incredible sums that they never thought about trying it again. One company had the gall to publish an ad with the legend *Absolute Improvement.* Absolute Improvement? *Come on!* They'd come up with a stubby bottle with no label. The name was printed directly on the bottle. It was practically invisible. *And where have we seen that before, Your Honor?* The vodka was allegedly Icelandic. As it turned out, it was distilled in Arizona and shipped over to Iceland with bottles from Kentucky.

They got a court ruling right between the eyes.

The stream of vodka was flowing freely from Sweden to America. Production and logistics in Åhus were working to perfection: 200 bottles a minute with a line efficiency of 93.6 percent.

When Nycander was appointed vice president of the Monopoly, the justification given by the civil servants was that it was Nycander's stubborn perseverance that had forced the meeting between the Swedish and American admen. Broman and Brindfors had refused to put a label on the bottle. The Americans had demanded either a label or an abundance of colorful symbols. Nycander's thoroughness was the key to the elegant solution.

But there was no escaping the fact that the bottle was a bit difficult to see—even after that. For years after the launch Nycander would hack away at what would have been his final contribution, The Historic Compromise. His answer was simple but brilliant: he put the label on the back of the bottle. It looked awful, but perhaps they could persuade customers to *take the label off* when they got home. One idea was to have a lottery on the label, or a cartoon strip. They considered amusing slogans, like "Strip me before drinking" or "Get lost the Swedish way." True to his nature, Nycander investigated each possibility exhaustively, until it decomposed into its constituent parts and withered away. And vanished.

He did, however, make one small change to the bottle. He altered the copy so that Broman's claim to Absolut's one-hundred-year heritage became more vague. And thereby more correct.

When Curt Nycander showed guests around Stockholm, he told them proudly that everything they saw—buildings, people, factories, everything—would be gone in three hundred years. But people would still be drinking Absolut Vodka.

He was no longer the consultant who had written an eighteen-inch-thick report in less than six months and then been brought to the Monopoly by Lindmark to do a quick job.

He wasn't even Lindmark's hatchet man any more, taking care of all the nasty, unpleasant little jobs the CEO wouldn't touch. He was head of exports. He was the boss of the world's fastest-growing liquor brand.

All the others were gone. Lindmark, Lagerkvist, Roostal, Ekelund, Broman, Brindfors, Carlsson, Siano, Singer, even Roux, now that Curt had dumped him.

He was the only one left. He was the Keeper of the Bottle.

And Curt believed he was the only one who had never been conned by that bottle.

HANS

After quitting his job at Carlsson and Broman, Hans Brindfors started his own agency. The Brindfors Agency took all the credit for Absolut Vodka. The bottle was proudly presented as a Brindfors product.

A while later, the Monopoly gave Brindfors the Swedish Absolut account. By the end of the eighties, the entire Swedish advertising community was convinced that the bottle had been developed at Brindfors, at that time Scandinavia's most successful advertising agency.

But Hans Brindfors himself never liked the finished bottle, not really. Long after Absolut had become such a success that everyone—especially those who had hated the bottle—said that success had never been in doubt, and long after the bottle had made its way into every other résumé in the advertising industry, Hans Brindfors was adamant that it was wrong, wrong, wrong.

"The lettering should be in silver!"

STANLEY

Everyone agreed: The success of Absolut rested on positioning it as a superpremium in the upper price range, with sophisticated marketing aimed at well educated and well paid Americans who wanted to show that they were part of the great European wave sweeping the continent.

In his office in downtown Manhattan, Dr. Stanley Noval sat doing market research for the big American conglomerates. He was still faithful to the rules of statistics, which were now so complicated that Dr. Stanley himself could hardly account for them all. He was often charged with testing new names and labels, looking to see if there was a free segment in the market somewhere, some undiscovered bohemian or urbanite out there prepared to embrace a new product. He would usually throw Absolut Vodka into the questionnaire as a benchmark. Like everyone else, he assumed that Absolut was a characteristic premium label, maybe even a superpremium. That meant that a small percentage of the study group would like the vodka a lot, but for the most part it would be regarded as snobbish, a luxury item for the rich. This was the reaction to Mercedes-Benz and Armani, for example.

The strange thing was that Absolut Vodka didn't behave that way at all. Everyone liked Absolut. Rich and poor. Absolut was not perceived as a luxury item. It was a product for everyone.

That little, no-neck, socialist bottle had touched the soul of America.

SWEDEN

By and large the Twentieth Century was a period of ambitiously restrictive alcohol policy in Sweden, the upshot being that eventually there were fewer alcohol-related illnesses in Sweden than in any other country in Europe. The Swedes couldn't handle their booze, it was said, and that was true. What was not said was that the French, the Italians, and the Germans—who could handle their booze, insofar as they didn't drink themselves unconscious every time they cracked open a bottle—drank less. Because they didn't. They drank more. A lot more. One hospital bed in five in Sweden was occupied by a patient with alcohol-related problems. In southern Europe the figure was 65 percent. In the spring of 1999 the prestigious French daily *Le Monde* declared alcohol "Public Enemy Number One."

When Sweden applied for membership in the European Union at the end of the Eighties, the government demanded that, out of respect for the success of Sweden's alcohol policy, an exception be made to the Union's liberal rules and regulations. The

Swedes wanted to keep their Monopoly. They also wanted to hang on to their strict ban on the marketing and advertising of alcohol: a fine old Swedish tradition since the days of Ivan Bratt, explained one diplomatic delegation. Profits and alcohol don't mix, you see.

"So," said one of the Brussels bureaucrats in summary, "you, the Swedes, owners of a state-run monopoly that spends more money advertising a single liquor product than anyone else in the world, you want to *avoid* a commercialization of the alcohol industry?"

"Or," he concluded, allowing himself a faint smile, "have I misunderstood the Swedish point completely?"

On 1 January 1995, the Wine and Liquor Monopoly lost its unique and sole right to produce and import alcoholic beverages, more than eighty years after Bratt founded the company.

Absolut had destroyed the Monopoly.

The party was over. It was time for the Swedes to start drinking.

HELMUT

All this *"lagom"* business was really just a huge misunderstanding. If anyone had thought to ask old Helmut Hagar up there in his attic, he'd have put them straight on that issue.

Lagom, you see, was something quite different from what everyone thought. It had nothing to do with "just right" or "not too much, not too little." It had nothing to do with reason, common sense, temperance, or abstinence. Quite the opposite. Hagar would have told them to imagine a horde of Vikings, a thousand years ago, huddled round their campfire celebrating another bloody victory. The word *lag* meant company, a group of people, and *om* meant round. *Lagom—round the company.* In other words, something sent round the campfire, enough for every man. What could it be that they were partaking of? The gourd, of course. The chalice. *Liquor.*

Lagom didn't mean that no one should get drunk. It meant that *everyone* should get drunk.

Before Helmut Hagar passed away, he saw his daughter take over the Wine and Spirits museum in Stockholm and make it one of the most respected in the world.

CAROLE ANNE

It was just like reasoning with a seasoned alcoholic. You ask them what they've learned while they've been busy breaking up the family, dragging their name through the mud and pissing their bank account up against the wall. The truth is that they haven't learned shit, of course. Carole Anne Fine hadn't learned shit either. She hadn't learned anything from Mary Wells. She hadn't learned anything from Bill Tragos. That was no fault of Bill's; he'd been a first-class mentor in the put-down business. But she still stubbornly refused to learn. She learned nothing from Ed McCabe, and Ed kicked her out on the street. After that she stopped working. She sat at home in the dark for a year, staring at a stain on the wall, while her answering machine filled up with messages from people in advertising. Please, call me. Please, Carole Anne, call. She never called back, and eventually the machine went quiet. The only way to tease her out of the apartment was to ask her to go ice skating. About a year later, for some unknown reason, she decided to go for an interview for a new job, and the slip of a girl interviewing her said something very insulting. When she got home she took a good look at herself and realized that enough was enough. She wasn't going to help those people make another fortune.

Carole Anne Fine went back to school and became a nurse. She set about helping alcoholics get their lives back on track.

She never returned to Madison Avenue.

GUNNAR

No one remembered that it was Gunnar Broman who had built the platform for Absolut Vodka. The Monopoly forgot his involvement completely. In Sweden, the Brindfors Agency was considered the Creator. When Broman was introduced to Bill Tragos, the boss of TBWA, as the Man Behind the Bottle, the American burst out laughing.

"Yeah, right, another one of the ten thousand that made Absolut Vodka what it is today." He turned on his heel and left.

In the mid-eighties, when the campaign was fully up and running, and the vodka was such a huge success that no one, except maybe Curt Nycander, really understood the scope of it, Broman was invited to speak in New York.

Broman delivered a quirky little speech about the importance of making mistakes, not a message destined to appeal to an audience of American advertising people. When it was over, there was a long silence. Up on the stage, the audience saw the stocky, rotund man, bearded, bald, and beaming. Behind him on the screen was the bottle with its seal.

The picture Peter Ekelund had found, the one they wound up using on the seal at the top of the bottle, portrayed L. O. Smith, the Liquor King, with a beard and very little hair. The funny thing was, it looked just like Gunnar Broman. Broman had created the bottle in his office in Smith's old apartment, Peter had found the picture and Lars Börje Carlsson had stuck it on the neck of the bottle. Then it turned out that Smith and Broman could have been twins, separated by the blink of a century.

The applause started slowly. Then it mounted and grew. The Americans whooped and cheered, they stamped their feet and applauded wildly. Someone rushed up to Broman and hugged him, with tears streaming down his cheeks.

"Gunnar," he sobbed. "Gunnar . . . this has never ever been done before."

The rest of what the man said was lost in chokes of emotion.

Late that night Gunnar Broman had a revelation. The Americans somehow must have thought that here at last was an adman who had actually signed the product. They thought that he had put his own picture on the bottle. And Gunnar Broman laughed in his hotel bedroom.

But it *was* ugly. Lindmark was right. And that was the whole point. The ugliness of the bottle proved that all it claimed to be was true. Which it wasn't, of course.

To con the con men, you had to look like a plasma bag—or like a hick. The pushers were roaming up and down the street, pushing their stuff, praising, promising.

Still turning the minds. Still something out of nothing.

Acknowledgments

This account is based first and foremost on the recollections of the people involved, their experiences, and opinions. Individual memories are often impossible to reconcile; this is part and parcel of the retrospective conviction every researcher and reporter will recognize. My task here has not been to adapt the recollections of those involved into a lowest common denominator. Rather, it has been to set them against one another. Neither have I attempted to assuage exaggerations, antipathies, or personal prejudices and convictions, other than when ethics dictate. As I see it, these are important elements in the subjective world of those involved.

Is this account genuine? This is my reconstruction of the chain of events when Absolut Vodka was created and launched based upon interviews, documentation, and literature. *But* no one *single* account can ever be complete. It is always possible to present another side of the same story. Through interpretation and digression, I have chosen my theme, and thereby given my version. *The purpose has, of course, always been to come as close to the truth as possible.*

When I use direct quotation in the text, it is because someone has been able to give an account of what was said at the time. In a few cases I have attributed quotes based upon a general description of a conversation, written memos as preparation for a meeting, or remarks made at another time regarding the situation in question. On a few occasions, I have used knowledge of future events to illustrate someone's character, but only when it has had no effect on the logic of the account. In some cases I have given the credit for an advertisement or a campaign to the managing director of an agency without mentioning employees who may have been directly involved.

Most of the main participants have read drafts of the manuscript, in whole or part, and have had an opportunity to comment. I have attempted to contact all involved; unfortunately, in a very few cases, this proved to be impossible.

• • •

I would like to heartily thank all the people who generously and without reservation contributed their experiences and opinions.

Göran Aneer, Lasse Lillnor, Bernt Ehn, Kotte Jönsson, and Björn Asp who worked on Gunnar Broman´s team and gave me access to original sketches. Christophe Dolhem, who designed the original black-and-white cover for the Swedish version of this book.

Jena Pincott, my editor, who personifies TEXERE's ambition to put the author first. Jody Lanfrey who helped me rewrite an essential chapter for an English-speaking audience, making many creative suggestions in the process. Annie Maccoby Berglöf who read early drafts and gave invaluable advice. Scott Clarke who demonstrated sound judgment and helped make important decisions during editing. Rick Ball, who gave the text coherence and wryly recognized the parallell between his own work and the events described in the book.

I would also like to thank: Myles and Lee Thompson, Steven Leto, Beth Tondreau, Liz Paley, Loretta Nauth, Joan Nagy, Millicent Cho, Pavel Martin, Debbie Siemen, Svante Weyler, Agneta Markås and Gerd Rönnberg at Norstedts, Annika Planck, Erik Berglöf, Åsa Levin, Hans and Rosanna Levin, Bo Hultén and Rose Qvarfordt, Adolf af Jochnick, Alberto and Cathinka Wahlström Antonini, and, always, Suzanne Zackrisson.